CV

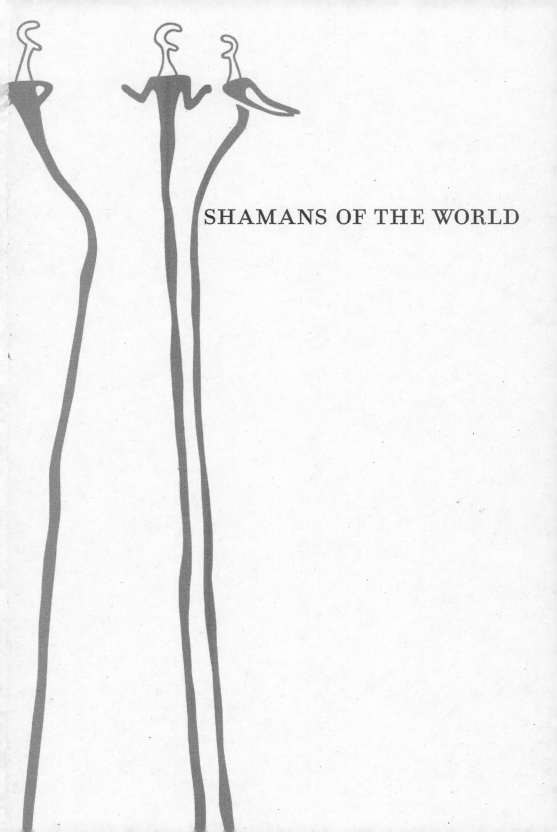

SHAMANS OF THE WORLD

SHAMANS OF THE WORLD

EXTRAORDINARY FIRST-PERSON ACCOUNTS
OF HEALINGS, MYSTERIES, AND MIRACLES

edited by Nancy Connor
with Bradford Keeney, Ph.D.

SOUNDS TRUE

Sounds True, Inc.
Boulder, CO 80306

Book design by Rachael Tomich

Printed in Canada

                    Library of Congress Cataloging-in-Publication Data
Connor, Nancy.
    Shamans of the world : extraordinary first person accounts of healings, mysteries, and miracles /
Nancy Connor and Bradford Keeney.
        p. cm.
    Includes index.
    "Excerpts from Ringing Rocks Foundation's Profiles of Healing book series as selected by Nancy
Connor, founder and chairwoman of Ringing Rocks Foundation."
    ISBN 978-1-59179-957-3 (hardcover)
    1. Shamanism—Cross-cultural studies. I. Keeney, Bradford P. II. Title.
    GN475.8.C66 2008
    201.44—dc22
                                            2008004787

10 9 8 7 6 5 4 3 2 1

Excerpts from Ringing Rocks Foundation's *Profiles of Healing* book series as selected by
Nancy Connor, founder and chairwoman of Ringing Rocks Foundation.

To the healers presented in these pages:
thank you for sharing your worldviews and yourselves.

To Bradford Keeney:
thank you for your wisdom, dedication, joy,
and struggle in bringing the healing wisdom
of these elders to the world.

— *Nancy Connor*

CONTENTS

FOREWORD

SHAMANS OF THE WORLD presents the transcribed words of respected healers from cultures around the globe. Though these elders represent the ancestral wisdom that preceded the world's great religions, few of them get a chance to present their own voices. It is time for the Original People to be heard and for us to learn from them. The forthcoming chapters contribute to this mission.

I am most grateful to have been a part of this historically important project. I took a sabbatical over a decade ago to conduct the fieldwork that created these interviews. This work would not have been possible without the support of Nancy Connor and the Ringing Rocks Foundation. I express my deepest appreciation for their enabling me to do this work: to Nancy for her long-term commitment to the work; to Carey Zimmerman for all her patience and cheerleading, including helping me keep accurate records of goats given to African villages; to John Myers, whose dialogical voice kept the work honest and whose passion for soulful living assured everyone of the importance of both continual levity and trusting relations; and to Ed Rosner and David Robkin for overseeing the integrity of the institutional aspects of the foundation.

The original book series from which these interviews were taken was a partnership with others. Karen Davidson was the brilliant designer of the original books. She successfully found the most appropriate and aesthetic ways to present diverse cultural traditions. Karen and I worked closely together to transform raw footage from the field into beautiful texts. Kern Nickerson did most of the photography and brought a kind presence to his interaction with other cultures. My wife, Mev Jenson, volunteered for the audio recording and project management in the field while our son, Scott, contributed audio engineering and technical support. This work would never have been possible without the sacrifices and contributions of my family. And because of the friends we made around the world, our lives will never be the same.

I want to acknowledge the many consultants, technical assistants, guides, drivers, and interpreters who also helped in this long-term ethnographic work. In particular I am grateful for the support of Paddy Hill, operator of Pride of Africa Safaris, for his help and collaboration in the African bush. There were many other people who contributed in special ways to make this work possible. Blessings to all of you!

It is the shamans and healers who are the main characters of this work. I have done my best to allow their voices to come through the text. As I did in the original works, I will again minimize the presence of my own voice and understanding: I have told my personal story elsewhere (*Bushman Shaman*, Destiny Books, 2005).

In this special compilation, Nancy Connor selected passages from the original books, doing so in a way that demonstrates how their contributions are both distinctive and connected in the greater fabric of collective wisdom.

Welcome to an archive of global wisdom, a conservatory of healing traditions, and a collection of remarkable stories. May this work inspire you to be good to others and relate to one another as you would hope others would treat you. Let us join our hearts together and celebrate this opportunity for learning from one another in a gentle and loving way.

—*Bradford Keeney, Ph.D.*
Santa Fe, New Mexico, July 2007

INTRODUCTION

Many years ago, I became ill and went to the local hospital, which misdiagnosed my appendicitis and sent me home. By the time I was admitted, I was very close to death from sepsis and required nearly a week of intravenous antibiotics to reduce the infection to the point where my burst appendix could be removed. A week after I was released, I found myself back in the operating room due to an abscess formed by infectious material that was left behind during the first operation.

A year or so after this event, I found myself very sick once again, suffering from terrible headaches, weight gain despite eating very little due to a lack of appetite, constant ringing in my ears, menstrual disorders, and many other problems. I went from internists to specialists, who all ran their own batteries of invasive and often painful tests. Each came up with a common diagnosis: "Our tests show that nothing is wrong with you; your problems are all in your head. See a psychologist for some stress-management techniques."

After several years of this, I began to think that they might be right and it all might be in my head. Then a friend of mine told me that she had been diagnosed with and treated for a systemic candida infection. She told me that my symptoms were similar to hers and suggested I look into it. Sure enough, all of my symptoms came down to a common cause, which was easily treatable. Within three months, I was back to normal and feeling great.

When I returned for a follow-up visit with my endocrinologist, who was treating what she considered the hormonal imbalances causing my menstrual difficulties, I was in for a shock. She told me that she had suspected I had a candida infection, but she believed that this had nothing to do with the symptoms she was treating, so hadn't bothered to mention it. When I explained that all of my symptoms had disappeared, she said that she'd have to run all of her tests again so that she could see where the problems now lay. Nothing I said about how each of my problems had disappeared would satisfy her. Needless to say, I left the office extremely disappointed and feeling very hurt by her attitude—never to return.

This series of incidents, as well as several other minor issues over the following years, led me to a deep feeling of mistrust of our modern medical system. Don't get me wrong; if I were seriously injured in a car accident, there would be no place in the world I'd rather be than in a modern hospital. However, it seemed to me that when a health crisis was involved, modern medicine did pretty well, while when it came to chronic disease or subtle problems that tests couldn't easily and accurately diagnose, the system was lacking. I began to see our system as one of disease management, not health care. Instead of looking deeper to understand the fundamental cause of a medical problem to resolve it, modern medicine simply treats the symptoms of the suspected disease with drugs and surgery until all of the symptoms disappear. I also began to see that doctors were disinclined to believe their patients, despite the fact that a patient is more familiar with his or her own body than a doctor looking into it with diagnostic tools could ever be.

I began to look into various aspects of alternative health care techniques and systems: where they originated, how other cultures looked at health and disease, what alternative diagnostic tools were available and how they worked, as well as how successful they were. At the same time, I began to explore my own beliefs about how healing worked and the power of the mind and spirit in achieving physical health. I became a certified Reiki practitioner and found that I seemed to have a natural talent for the work. I also attended quite a few meditation retreats to explore my spirituality—and often the lack thereof—along with its possible effect on my health.

It wasn't long after I began to get serious about these explorations that I had the good fortune to be able to retire. I had started a software company with a few friends around the time of my appendicitis. The growth of that company over the following few years had been fueled by the tremendous increase in the use of personal computers in all areas of business and by the success of the revolutionary new idea of computer networking. When the company was taken public, I decided to bow out as CEO, and I took some time off to continue exploring this new direction my life was taking.

Ringing Rocks Foundation

Although retirement gave me the opportunity to travel and continue my pursuits, I found that I wanted a better focus and a new outlet for my explorations. After speaking with a few friends about ways to create a context for my studies, I decided to establish Ringing Rocks Foundation (RRF). I created RRF with a mission to explore the world, documenting and conserving healing practices and spiritual traditions. Although the foundation's programs have evolved over the twelve years that it has been operating, its focus has always been on three main areas: collecting first-person information directly from other cultures, finding ways to help those cultures with whom we established relationships support their traditions, and disseminating the information we collected to the modern public.

Not long after we formed RRF, my friends introduced me to Dr. Bradford Keeney, whom they had met at a psychology conference. In addition to being impressed with his work in the field of psychology, they were also aware of, and impressed by, his work with indigenous healers. They recommended that I read his recently published book, *Shaking Out the Spirits*, to get an idea of what he could bring to the RRF table. He and I immediately hit it off, and he agreed to join us in exploring and documenting not only alternative, but also indigenous, ways of knowing and healing.

Since RRF uses the term "indigenous peoples" frequently, a definition may be in order here. The term has no universal, standard, or fixed definition, but it can refer to any ethnic group that continues to inhabit the geographic region with which it has the earliest historical connection; has maintained, at least in part, its distinct linguistic, cultural, social, and organizational characteristics; and in doing so remains differentiated, to some degree, from the dominant culture of surrounding populations.

Other often-used terms for indigenous peoples include aborigines, native peoples, first peoples, Fourth World peoples, and first nations. However, "indigenous peoples" is the preferred term, as it is a neutral replacement for other terms that may have taken on negative or pejorative connotations through their prior association and use. In addition, it is the preferred term in use by the United Nations. As such, it is the one that the staff at RRF uses.

Profiles of Healing

Brad Keeney told me about Alice Fletcher and Francis La Flesche, who studied many Plains Indian tribes during the early years of the field of anthropology at the end of the 1800s and who, in the process of their research, recorded hundreds of songs and ceremonies on wax cylinders. These cylinders made their way into the hands of the Library of Congress and the Smithsonian Institute's National Museum of the American Indian, and these recordings later served as reference materials for tribes that had lost these songs during their (often forced) integration into American society in the early to mid-1900s. Without the recordings, vital parts of these tribes' culture would have been lost. Thus Brad proposed the *Profiles of Healing* book series as one of our initial programs, with the aim of providing a similar record for other indigenous cultures around the world.

The *Profiles of Healing* books are first-person narratives from indigenous cultures around the world. Each volume is the voice of a different culture, telling the story through the healers' words, as well as visually through photographs, and acoustically through a CD attached to the book.

Traditional anthropological practice requires that the culture be explained by an "authority" in modern terms through lenses that often distort the meaning or importance of any given practice. Allowing the healers instead to speak directly about the aspects of their culture that are most important to them permits the reader to experience the culture as the healers do. While the *Profiles of Healing* books were transcribed and edited from interviews Brad conducted with the healers, each maintains the original voice of the healers as they describe their view of the world.

As Brad went into the field—not only in the United States, but also in Japan, Botswana, Paraguay, South Africa, St. Vincent, Namibia, Brazil, Bali, and many other remote locations—to sit with each healer and listen to the worldview each had to offer, he also recorded the sounds of the community and the healer him- or herself on audio tapes, which were then edited into the CDs included in each book. He also brought along an excellent photographer who was able to take pictures that not only expressed the healers' spirits, but also respected the culture and practices being recorded.

There was a dual idea behind the series. First, the raw material collected for the books could serve as a historical record of the many indigenous cultures that are in danger. Young people in these cultures are becoming more interested in playing video games and earning money to buy TVs than they are in learning their own language, culture, and traditional forms of healing. In most indigenous cultures, traditional healers have very hard lives where the demands of their calling do not allow them to take on a paying job. As these cultures become more modernized, the people tend to lose their traditional ways of supporting themselves and living off the land, leaving healers without a means of support. Modern material culture, which includes conveniences such as electricity for refrigerators and lights and better access to water, tools, and building materials than are commonly available in such remote areas, can therefore seem very attractive, and it becomes harder as time goes by to find members of the younger generation who are willing to give up a modern life for a traditional one.

Second, not everyone in the modern world can (or wants to) go and sit at the feet of these elders for weeks, months, or years in order to learn from them. In providing the text of the healers' stories, as well as context through beautiful photography and a CD that offers the sound of their voices and cultures, we felt that we could bring people living in the modern world a glimpse into the indigenous world's ideas on health and healing and their cultural and spiritual view of the world in general. As more and more visitors from outside an indigenous culture, who have little awareness of their impact, start to come into regular contact with people living traditionally, they become incredibly disruptive to the traditional ways of life within the community.

To write this series of books, Brad spent seven years in the field, starting with cultures where he already had ties, gathering stories in the healers' own words, and editing them into book form. He often risked his own health and sanity in order to collect the stories, photos, and sounds from each of these cultures. Many of them put him through rigorous tests to confirm that it was appropriate for them to share their knowledge with this outsider. He spent not only his waking hours on the project, but also many of his sleeping hours experiencing dreams that directed him where to go next. It took time, patience, vision, and persistence to gain the acceptance of the shamans and thus bring their wisdom to the world.

Along the way, I was privileged to be able to join Brad on his trips, meeting and participating in ceremony with these elders and healers. By traveling with him, I learned how rigorous the travel he endured could be, and I also experienced firsthand the rewards of making the effort. These people were a fountain of knowledge, willing to share as much of it as we could understand. They were playful at times, making sure that they, and we, didn't take all of this too seriously. At other times, they were serious, making sure that the proper respect was shown for their ceremonies and the knowledge being shared. They were outgoing, unconditionally accepting me as one of their own from the time I arrived and for the entire time that I was with them.

This book was created from the *Profiles of Healing* series as an introduction to several indigenous cultures and their healing practices and, as such, stands alone as a gateway to each of them. Every chapter contains carefully chosen excerpts and images from a volume of the series that will give you a taste of that culture and its healing practices. If the stories in these chapters touch you, you can find more of the information in the original full-length books, including suggestions for further reading.

Observations on Indigenous Healing

I am not an accredited anthropologist, nor do I profess a complete understanding of any of the cultures represented in this compilation. However, in spending time with many of the individuals described on these pages, I have come away with my own insights and threads that connect these cultures and healers with those of us living in the modern world.

Healing in an indigenous culture is inextricably tied to that culture and its worldview. Often, healers are the leaders of their communities. Their worldview is one in which body, spirit, and mind are not separate ideas or parts, nor are cultural practices separated from healing practices or language. This viewpoint is as important to these cultures as are the separate institutions we have in the modern world: hospitals with doctors and nurses for physical healing, churches and temples with priests for fostering spiritual practice, families with parents for emotional and social training, and educational institutions with teachers for training the mind.

In contrast to our separate institutions for healing and education, indigenous cultures' healing and educational practices revolve around the family and community. Although there are specialist healers, just as there are farmers, herders, fishermen, and others who make a functioning village, the entire community takes part in turning a child into a whole functioning member, with an intact body, spirit, and mind. Often, being a healer is a part-time job, undertaken only in times of need. Just as often, healing is regarded as a community-based event, occurring in a village-wide dance or ritual that heals all members and brings them back into correct relationship with one another.

This is not to say that individuals don't go to healers for one-on-one sessions. In the case of a severe or prolonged illness, they will go directly to the healer for a cure. Because of the worldview held by these indigenous cultures, the cure may be an herbal one, a psychological or social one, a ritual one, or a transmission of energy. There is no sense that it is wrong, silly, or strange to believe, for example, that making up with someone you've had a falling out with will relieve your physical symptoms. Nor is it considered weird to believe that sitting on a drawing will make your illness leave your body and settle into the drawing, which can then be destroyed, taking your illness with it.

Having personally experienced the relief resulting from indigenous cures that many in the modern world would say are impossible, I have to agree with the wise ones who say that on a very basic level, whatever works, works. In anthropology, the term "going native" refers to scientists who have adopted the ways of the culture they are studying and are no longer considered "objective observers." So you can say that I've gone native and my opinion isn't valid as an objective measure. You can also say that these cures are just placebos, or explain some of them away with the scientific basis for an herbal cure, or postulate that a particular psychological problem can lead to a particular physical illness. But the true bottom line is that it doesn't matter why it works, or even that an outsider would say that healing has actually occurred. If we feel healed of our illness, we are grateful. Or, at least, we should be.

One of the easiest objective measures of whether or not an indigenous healer is a good one is if he or she can tell you what is going on before you speak. In a modern doctor's office, you tell the doctor what your symptoms are, when they started, and what you've previously done to try to cure them. In indigenous practice, the healer tells you these things as a way to establish trust so that healing can take place. From a modern person's point of view, seeing this occur with great specificity was enough to help me get over my need for explanations of how, why, and what had just happened when I walked away healed.

In our modern culture, we are often "touch starved." In indigenous cultures, however, touch is a constant between both friends and family, from hugs to hand holding to massage. Healers "lay on hands" to diagnose, as well as treat, illness and it is not considered improper no matter where on the body they touch. Touch is often used just to create a connection between the healer and the patient, so that there is a feeling of trust as well as the possibility of obtaining information that would otherwise not be available to the healer.

Most indigenous cultures have an ongoing relationship with God based on love. Prayer is a constant part of life, and it is considered necessary, as it connects each individual to God. Prayers are expressions of gratitude, conversations about proper conduct, and requests for food, water, or healing. Prayer can be ceremonial or it can occur in temples or churches, but more often it is just a simple conversation between an individual and God. It is not considered crazy for a healer to claim to be speaking with or for God. Often, when an indigenous healer speaks for God, his or her voice and even facial features change to indicate which aspect of God he or she is connected to.

Information vital to the survival of the culture is obtained by speaking with God through prayer: making the connection between hunter and hunted, bringing rain to those who ask for it, and teaching healers about the cures necessary to heal the sick. Plants giving visions of how they can be used for healing and animals sacrificing themselves to provide food are normal occurrences in indigenous cultures. These cultures believe that God loves them enough to want to ensure their survival and, as a result, answers these prayers for the benefit of the community.

God is the purest love in most indigenous cultures, and God's love for us is expressed in ways that modern citizens would consider supernatural. God wants all of us to love each other, and gives us many ways to relate with God and with each other. Most indigenous cultures believe that we all share the same god, even if we use different names for the same entity. Most of the individuals within these cultures also believe that when they speak of many gods, each of them is simply an aspect of a much bigger God.

The healer in these cultures has a deeper relationship to God based on his or her ability to enter the state of consciousness where healing information is transmitted, but all people are healers in their own way. It is up to the individual to decide whether or not to develop the capacity to deepen that relationship to the point where he or she can be of specific aid in healing his or her fellows, and to accept the calling if and when it comes.

Those who are chosen to be healers are called to serve because they have a better aptitude and/or sensitivity for it, although everyone heals (or harms) others all the time. It's just the same as professional singers being better at singing through aptitude and training than others, although everyone can sing. Each of us has ways of healing others—through music, art, writing, or simply by giving another a smile or hug at just the right time. When a shaman speaks of "being chosen," he or she is referring to the specific calling he or she felt to allow healing to be the major path in life from that time forward. There are also cultures in which the individual is called to be a healer after his or her children are grown and there are fewer practical demands.

A shaman's power is believed to come from God and, if misused, can be taken away by God. This is especially true when the healer works by energy transmission. The shaman's power may manifest energetically through sucking out the illness, laying on hands, or blowing health into the sick part. In many cultures, the healers who are most prized are those who can heal by touch. They are considered to be the strongest healers and the ones most in danger of losing their power if it is used unwisely or they do not keep themselves pure.

The energy flow in a healer can be evident by a simple trembling of the hand to diagnose where an illness lies or an ecstatic dance that takes over the entire body such that the healer's body shakes with that of the patient. There are also healers who simply lay their hands on the patient while the energy flows invisibly and nearly undetected. Some patients may experience the energy transmission as a tingling sensation or a feeling of heat or cold. In most cases, the energy flow is completely involuntary once a connection is established between the healer and the patient, although in some cases it is consciously maintained and directed by the healer.

In order to make a connection with a patient, healers usually enter a state of mind that is different from the ordinary state of consciousness.

There are many means of entering such an altered state, including the use of sound, drugs, fasting, or simply inhaling smoke. While some cultures use drugs such as peyote and ayahuasca as a means of entering the healing trance, they are not used in every case — even in cultures where the practice is considered conventional. Depending on the severity of the illness and the cultural practices of the healer, different levels of trance state may be necessary for each treatment.

Sound is a common way for a healer to enter a trance state, and it may be brought on by singing, making random sounds, chanting prayers, banging hollow bamboo poles on the ground, clapping, or drumming. The healer, helpers or apprentices of the healer, or the community at large may make the sound. In some cultures, it is believed that the more people participate in the healing, the more power the healer will have at his or her disposal and, therefore, the more powerful the healing will be.

In short, any process that allows the healer to connect deeply with his or her patient, to understand what has caused the illness, and to provide an answer to allow healing to occur is completely valid. I invite you to expand your ideas of what a healer looks like, what processes may be used for diagnosis and treatment, and, in general, what health and healing mean to you.

Shamans of the World

The chapters in this book are arranged in ascending order of observable energy, from the healers who mainly use traditional or herbal medicines and barely observable trance states to the wildly ecstatic trance dances of the Bushmen. In this way, I hope that by the time you finish, you will be able to take the energy of all of the healers you've encountered with you into your everyday world. Although this arrangement is imperfect, since healing techniques can run through a wide range of styles in both the individual healers presented and the cultures as a group, it is as good an arrangement as any.

We start with Walking Thunder, a Diné medicine woman from New Mexico who uses herbal remedies as well as ceremonial sandpaintings and chanting to effect her cures. We then move on to João Fernandes de

Carvalho and Otavia Pimental, two healers from Brazil who use simple prayer, laying on of hands, and herbal remedies to help others. Next is Gary Holy Bull, a Lakota Sioux from South Dakota, who uses the traditional Yuwipi ceremony to treat patients. The next culture we visit is the Guarani, who use rattles and bamboo poles to induce altered states of consciousness during both individual and group rituals for healing. Then we shift to Africa, where we visit with Vusamazulu Credo Mutwa, who uses a variety of techniques, from throwing the bones to deep shamanic trance states, in a range of contexts to effect healing. The next stop is Bali, where we visit with several Balians who also use an assortment of techniques, from ceremonial drawings designed for protection to wild group trance dances, to achieve balance in life and therefore healing. Ikuko Osumi, a Japanese healer who uses the intense power of seiki to instill health and well-being, is next. The last three cultures we visit are all African in origin. First we hear from the Shakers of St. Vincent, who use the power of mourning and ecstatic prayer to create community-based healing. And we spend our remaining time with the Bushmen of Botswana and Namibia—represented by both Kalahari Bushmen Healers and Ropes to God—who use ecstatic community trance dances for both individual and community healing.

I hope that you enjoy your journey through these pages as much as I enjoyed my journeys with these wonderful people.

—*Nancy Connor*
Chairwoman, Ringing Rocks Foundation

WALKING THUNDER

DINÉ MEDICINE WOMAN

Introduction to *Walking Thunder*
by Nancy Connor

Walking Thunder is one of the most unique individuals I know. Her life has been one of commitment to the Diné traditional ways, but she is still willing to educate the outside world about her culture, even though speaking about it to outsiders goes against Diné tradition. In order to grant permission to publish traditional knowledge in a book, Walking Thunder's elders held a ceremony in which she and Brad Keeney were tested for a full day, a night, and part of a second day with no food or sleep. Obviously, they were successful in passing the test, since the book was indeed published. As a result, she became the first medicine woman authorized by the Diné to speak about their traditional medicine ways.

In addition to telling her story in the book, she has also spoken about her culture and demonstrated sandpainting for the public at museums and cultural centers throughout the Southwest. She spent three weeks in New York City doing sandpaintings and lectures at the National Museum of the American Indian. She is currently working with Ringing Rocks Foundation to take her traditions into classrooms throughout New Mexico and Arizona. And yet she still makes time to heal, teach, and support her own people and their traditions for hundreds of miles around her home.

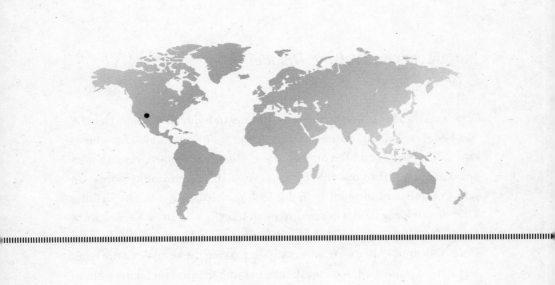

Early Memories of Traditional Medicine

My nation, the Navajo Nation, is located in the southwestern United States, with land stretching from the northeast corner of Arizona into Utah and New Mexico. It is the largest reservation in the United States. We call ourselves Diné, meaning "the People." I was born on May 8, 1951, in the old hospital at Shiprock, New Mexico. A black nurse looked at my black hair and called me Juanita. That name stuck with me ever since. On my mother's side, my clan name is Hashtl/'ishnii, referring to the Mud People, or "those who came back with muddy water during the time of origin." I have never known who my father was, so I cannot say anything about his side. I grew up in the Two Grey Hills area where a respected man in our community named me Walking Thunder because the name fit my personality and how the people see me. You can call me by my medicine name, Walking Thunder. Welcome to our sacred land.

Finding My Voice

After my first ceremony, I started asking a lot of questions about traditional medicine. Why this? Why that? I deeply wondered about what happened when certain practices took place. I even tested things myself. Sometimes I went into the fire to find out things. Sometimes you have to experience things firsthand in order to find out if it's true or not.

Figure 1.1

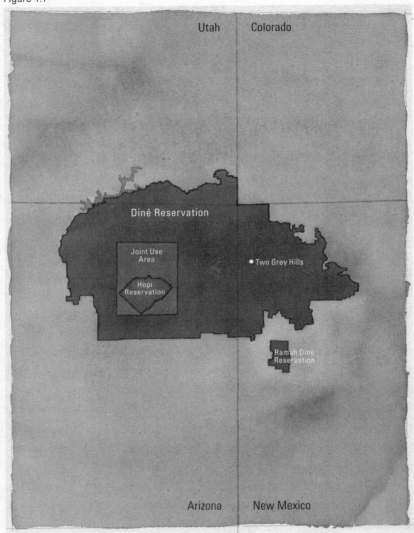

For example, when I was about twelve or thirteen, the community held a performance[1] on my aunt and I decided to test what was going on. I asked why the medicine men said and did certain things. For this performance, they were making all kinds of dolls. Without thinking, I automatically took one of the dolls and broke it in half. I thought that a doll was just a material thing that had no power. Although I had been told that the doll was supposed to be a holy person, I went ahead and broke the doll in half. I also broke a whistle and smashed the arrows that came with it. I didn't stop with that. I went on to examine the yucca soup and throw it out. The medicine man said to me, "Since you did these things, something is going to happen to you."

I didn't believe him. I shouted, "Nothing's going to happen to me!" But within two weeks, I became very sick. I couldn't move. When I tried to walk, I just keeled over. People thought I was crazy. During that time, I wanted to murder my stepfather, and I almost did it. I had discovered a mean streak in my body. I ached for worse things to happen, and my body felt like it wanted to hurt something. I was told that I was sick, handicapped, retarded, and crazy. Everyone rejected me. That's how I stepped into the fire.

My mom took me to a medicine man and asked what was going on because I was not myself. I drooled and twitched a lot. All the hurt around me made me angrier and angrier, and I wanted to do away with somebody. The medicine man did a performance to find out what was happening to me.

He conducted a Talking Back Ceremony where you examine your past and talk back to it. He dressed me up as a bear symbol and painted my face black. He placed many things around my waist and herbs around my body. While he did this, he told me things. He put a band around my head and blew a lot of whistles around me. When he blew those whistles, I felt a wound opening on the top of my head. I felt him take something out of my head with his mouth. He growled, pulled it out, and spit it into the fire. The flames immediately jumped in a frightening way.

---

[1] The Diné sometimes refer to their ceremonies as performances. As for why the ceremony was performed in the first place, that is not stated in the original text.

What he destroyed was a curse. I learned that my aunt got sick because people had witched her. Those little dolls they made for the ceremony were actually the images of sickness that they put in her. Although they said the doll was a holy person, it was actually a curse. The medicine man went on to tell me, "For some reason you didn't like the doll. You automatically destroyed it, and that's what got you. Now we know that you're not on the bad side." He explained that there are good medicine people as well as bad medicine people. "Because of this," he added, "you should never trust anybody. Trust only yourself. You have no friends, and you have no one you can truly rely on. You are your own friend. And your mind and your breath are yours."

He said many more things before he let me out of the hogan. Going home, I fought for my voice. If he hadn't done those things for me, I'd probably have died a long time ago. I had been cursed because I destroyed that doll and smashed those arrows. Instead, the medicine man helped me regain my life and gave me a Warrior's Shield.

At my ceremony the medicine man said, "Now you can start visioning the future. You'll be surprised, and you won't believe what's going to happen to you. Also, you're going to have two minds about these things, but in the end you'll get it." Everything he told me was true. He finished by saying, "I will never see you again."

I wondered why he had said that, but sure enough I never saw him again because he died soon after. While he was alive, my family had gifted him with sacred things. We had given him two Navajo baskets full of corn pollen. With those gifts, my mother had begged for my life.

Although we sometimes disagree, when I think back to what my mom did, when it comes to traditions, I know she's on my side. In the details of everyday life, she's often against me, but in our traditional ways, she would never say anything that would harm me.

All you can do is pray for a person who is very sick. Sometimes they get well, but sometimes you can't get them well. You always have to leave things to the Creator. When I destroyed that doll, it was inevitable that something was going to happen to me. The medicine man who helped me explained how I could overcome it, but he advised me to be careful if I decided to learn how to backfire (i.e., reverse) things. He explained that a medicine person had to choose whether they would backfire in a good or bad way. My husband, David, learned the positive way of backfiring.

Learning from the Elders

David's grandpa was the best medicine man around, and all his uncles were also medicine men. His side of the family was all medicine people, going way back. The person they learned it from was called Wind Singing Man. That's who my relatives learned medicine from, and they passed it from one generation to the next. I learned from many medicine people. Sometimes I saw a medicine person in my dreams, and then I went to find the person who appeared.

Also, when I was young, I would run up to any elder medicine person and start asking them questions. My sister was ashamed of me for doing that. She would say, "Why do you ask all those questions?" It seemed obvious to me—I wanted to know more. In these ways I learned our traditional Creation Story. I was also taught sandpainting[2] and what to do in traditional performances. I now do these things in the correct traditional way. Some people add their own stuff and do it their own way, but I do it the traditional way. Among the traditionals, we support others who do it the right way. If someone starts doing it their own way, we don't say anything; we just walk away. It's not wise to criticize another medicine person. They might be practicing witchery. You never know what you are up against. You never question; you just walk out. That's what I was taught.

One of the beliefs we, the Diné, have in our healing tradition is that you have to mean it when you help a person.

---

[2] Sandpaintings are temporary paintings made of sand that are used for teaching traditions and for healing purposes. A ceremonial sandpainting is made on a bed of riverbed sand that has been smoothed with a weaving batten. Then designs are drawn in a ceremonial way with colored sands according to the ceremony being performed.

If the sandpainting is used for public demonstrations or for sale, the rules for preparation are much less stringent and the drawing is changed so that it is imperfect and therefore does not draw in holy power.

When I was a young girl, there were many medicine men. (Also, many people did the trembling hands and there were many vision makers.) However, there weren't as many medicine women. I remember a few ladies around our area who were medicine women, but they did hand trembling or charcoal visioning. I remember one who was called White Shell Dawn Lady. She was very tiny and she used to give advice to the councilmen. She gave advice to other medicine men when they got into problems. She was there for them, and I used to envy her.

Then there was another lady, called Singing Woman from the South, who used to perform in the Native American Church. I admired her. I liked her teaching, her talks, and her jokes. She was my main aunt. Two weeks before she died, she realized how much I admired her and said, "You should have talked to me before. I would have taught you how to bring the eagle to the ground." She could call an eagle down from the sky and pluck out his feathers while the eagle sat on her. She had that kind of a gift. I admired her because she could call an eagle down.

In the last two weeks of her life, Singing Woman from the South was sick in the hospital at Gallup. We went to visit her. When we got there, I walked right up to her, looked at her, and said, "You're a medicine woman. Why are you just letting yourself die?" She looked at me and then told the other people to leave the room. She told me about eagle feathers—how to carry them, take care of them, their purpose—all in great detail. She kept asking me if I was remembering what she was telling me, and she kept questioning me to make sure that I was remembering. "Do you know which side of the feather to use? Do you know which area to place the feathers on?" We repeated this many times until she was satisfied. She taught me the four ways of the eagle feather. At the time, I thought all the ways were the same. During her last days, I asked Singing Woman from the South how she was able to call the eagle down from the sky. She said that even if she gave me one of her songs she uses to call the eagle, I wouldn't be able to do it on my own. "You have to learn to control animals and to control a lot of things. Prayer alone won't work. But if you want to learn I can teach you. However, you have to sacrifice somebody in order to receive this knowledge. You must sacrifice someone you really, truly love, not someone whom you hate. It must be a person who is close to your heart." But I wasn't willing to do that. That was bad. I chose to stick with the good ways.

Many years after Singing Woman from the South died, I thought about what she had said about the four ways of the eagle feather. That's when her teaching all started to make sense to me. That was one of the ways I became a medicine woman.

One of my gifts is that I ask too many questions; I do this because it brings me knowledge. On the other hand, the holy people sometimes say, "If she really wants to know, let's give it to her directly from the holy side." I'm grateful to have all the ways of receiving sacred knowledge. I have no intention of giving up my search for more knowledge. It's going to be with me for the rest of my life, for as long as I live. This is what I tell my kids, but I also tell them that I'm a living person. I will do something wrong, and I will not be perfect. Nevertheless, I will still be a medicine woman. That's the way I put it.

Sticks, Pollen, and Horny Toads
When I was a child, kids my size used to ask me, "Since you're always in the Navajo traditional way, do you think you can do something to help us get over this sickness?" I would say yes and then go break off a stem from one of Mother Earth's plants and start singing. I would sing away and say a prayer, pick up some rocks or another stick and hold them while praying. I would pray in this way for my childhood friends. At the end, I would make a big joke about it. I would shout, "Now you're better!" Then I would pull their ears or pull their nose. They'd start laughing. I would say, "If you're laughing, you're going to get well." That was one thing I used to say to the kids who came to me when they were sick. Or I would just tickle them and say, "You'll be okay."

Even then, as a child, I knew that a stick is a root of life. It can come out good or it can come out bad. I remember one dream that I had as a young girl. In the dream I was in a fog picking up sticks. After the dream I started picking up sticks for my childhood ceremonies. The dreams gave me an education. They told me things, made me wonder, and helped me understand.

Once, when I was in boarding school, our dorm attendant asked me, "What are you going to do with all those sticks and rocks?" I replied, "We're going to build something out of them." She said, "You can't build anything with those sticks and rocks." I responded by going to my friends and having them help me make things. Some sticks became an automobile, while others became tools, trees, and houses. So the sticks in my dreams were about educating, helping, and moving others.

Every time I see a stick I think about this education I was given. I believe that if you carelessly break a stick, you may be breaking your own dream. That's what I always say. That's why I tell my kids to not break sticks. The stick in my dream was a life-teaching root. The rocks in my dreams were the same. The heart of rock teaching is found in the designs of the rocks. If you look carefully at a rock and focus on it, it may tell you the life story of the world. This is because rocks hold the stories of the world. That's how they hold Earth's wisdom.

Growing up, I picked up rocks and sticks, learning from each one. If I ever needed help, I just picked up a rock or a stick and said a prayer. To me, they were sacred. Today, people sometimes ask me why I have so many rocks along the walls inside my house. I tell them that rocks are my education. Then they ask me why I have rocks inside my house since there are so many other rocks out in the world. They don't understand.

My little girl, Nicole, is the same way. She'll bring rocks home and she'll look at them. However, she doesn't keep them. She puts them back where she found them. She treats them like one must treat a horny toad. If you pick up a horny toad and play with it, you must put it back where it was found. If you don't put it back, you cut off his trail and you cut off your mind. That's what we say about horny toads.

POLLEN

My mom and my grandmother taught me that pollen is used to bless ourselves with beauty. All pollen on Mother Earth, along with the plants and flowers, is a medicine. If you put all the pollens together for a woman to drink, she will not have any problem having babies. She'll deliver quickly and have no difficulties. When a woman drinks the pollen of medicine earth, she will heal and become a virgin again. That's what we were taught. Pollen is pure and has been used as a medicine for women for a long time. When we perform a Walk in Beauty Ceremony, we use corn pollen. In traditional sandpaintings and singing, we use all of Mother Earth's pollens.

As a little girl, my mom taught me the sacred ways of pollen. She'd take pollen from its source and put it into a basket. Then we'd cover it with a cloth and say to the sunshine, "This is not yours. This is mine to heal." I was taught that if you didn't say something like that to the sun, it would eat up all your pollen. I tested it and it happened. To this day, I always say, "This is mine, this is going to be for our healer, that's why I'm taking it, leave it alone." We still cover the pollen with a cloth and let it sit there. My mother sang to the east, asking for the one who heals. She'd set the basket on the floor and sing her pollen song[3] that first talks about one's feet being blessed and then the whole body being blessed. Then she'd go back to the basket and see the corn pollen sitting there like sand. A few hours later we'd check the basket, and the pollen would still be there. Again she would say, "Don't eat my pollen, sun."

My pollen song is different from my mother's song. I usually have a gourd that I shake before I sing my song. Once in a while, I'll sing it around the house, but not all the time. The pollen song goes with the birds and the flowers. We get all our songs from our hearts. This is especially true for our healing songs. When you sing the healing way, you have to name all the body parts of a human and then state that each of the parts walk in beauty. This has to be done in all directions.

HORNY TOAD

When I was young, a medicine man from Shiprock used to ride a horse all the way to Two Grey Hills, where I lived. When he came, he'd bring a big black box of candy. They used to let us know when he was coming,

---

[3] In the traditional Diné way, there are songs that are sung to respect plants, animals, the sun, and all of creation. In this case, the pollen song refers to a song her mother was given to honor the spirit of the pollen. These songs are given directly to each person or healer by the respective spirit (or person, as the Diné would say).

and we ran over there just to get a piece of candy. When we knew he was on his way, we'd make something for him, like a corn pollen bag or jewelry to trade with him for candy. One time, a day before he came, I spent all day looking for a horny toad. I knew horny toads were sacred to him because he had told me a story about them—how they are made and what they stand for. I didn't let the other kids know about the horny toad. They were making pouches, bags, or beads while I sat in one place, meditating, and I said, "Where's the horny toad?" A certain place came to mind and sure enough, I found one there. I kept it in a glass jar with holes in the lid and gave it cornmeal and pollen.

First thing in the morning, I ran down to my uncle's house, and the medicine man from Shiprock was there talking away. I said, "I've got something for you." He wanted to see it, so he took out the horny toad and started praying and putting pollen on him. After that, he dipped it in some water and announced, "We're going to get rain now." Again, he dipped the horny toad in the water, took it out, and put corn pollen on him. He told the story about how a long time ago the lightning put a mark on the horny toad. The strike challenged him, but he survived. The sacred victory the lightning had was that it gave a song to the horny toad that would help heal sick people. The medicine man from Shiprock talked about the horny toad that way. He counted the spots on the toad and said, "This one is still young." After telling his stories about horny toads, he put the horny toad against his heart and said, "Whatever sickness I have, you take it away, grandpa." When he put it down, he blessed it and told me to put it back where I got it. He gave me my candy, and I ran back to return the horny toad.

Being Tested

When I was learning to be a medicine woman, various medicine men came around to test me. They asked me to make a certain sandpainting and to tell them the painting's purpose and what it meant. One night, two medicine men came and drew a big sandpainting and asked me about its symbols. It had arrowheads and lightning. One arrowhead was black and another was turquoise with different designs on it. Some designs didn't belong there in the traditional way. I guess they were testing me. I showed them the ones that weren't supposed to be there. They looked at me and asked how I knew. I answered that it was because in this ceremony lightning is never in the arrow; it's only on the person's body. The lightning represents the movement of the human body.

Then the medicine men put the rainbow down in the wrong way. In the healing ceremony, it's supposed to be put down straight, not curved, just straight down. They asked me about the rainbow symbol. I told them that the red one was for taking pain into the outside and the turquoise was for bringing back the inner beauty for healing. To heal a person, the red one is supposed to be inside. These were the kind of tests I went through.

They also asked me about herbs. They showed me different herbs, and I had to say the name of the herb and what it was good for. I failed on two. One was for whooping cough and the other for sinus headache. I thought the latter one was for some kind of a lung problem. They laughed when I made that mistake. At the time, I didn't know that there was a medicine for whooping cough. This medicine smells very strong and makes you sneeze a lot. You sneeze for a while but then that's when the cough stops. Your nose drains for about five minutes and then you forget that you had a cough.

They also tested me on how long I could sit. We started in the evening and sat still through the night. We sat with a medicine man, The Man Who Walks Away, who was doing a crystal vision. He had a big crystal, and after he started talking, I became dizzy. He tested me. We talked all day and then he talked all night. The next day, he began to lie down, saying he was going to rest his back. He was tempting me but I continued doing my work. At first I did my beadwork. Then I did my sandpainting while he kept on talking. Next I did my carving and then my spinning. I always made sure I had something to do while he was talking. I concentrated on what I was doing. That's how I passed the test. We stayed up for thirty-six hours. He was the one who went to sleep. I stayed awake. My husband was chewing and smoking tobacco and then whispered, "He's testing us." I whispered back, "Oh." We just kept doing all those things. After the medicine man left, my bed looked so good and I wanted to jump in, but I didn't. Sure enough, two hours later the medicine man came by the house again while I was cooking. If we had jumped back in bed we would have failed. He popped in and said, "Oh, you're still up?" I said, "Yes, we're still up. Do you want to eat with us?" He came in and ate with us, sat there for a while, and then said, "I'm going now, for sure." We didn't take the chance and waited until the sun went down before we got into bed.

I was also tested to see whether I could find a lost person and diagnose a sick person with my crystal.[4] A medicine man, who is like a clan brother to me, sent his son-in-law, who said his son was sick. The grandson of the medicine man said, "It hurts right there." I looked at him with the crystal and saw that he was not sick. I said, "You're not sick. But you can go outside and shovel my dirt." That brought a smile to the medicine man.

My mom tested me, too. She would say, "I lost my wallet and I don't know where it is. Can you find it with your crystal? I've been looking for it for two days. It has a hundred and fifty dollars in it, and I'm really anxious to get some of that money." She did this when I was about twenty-two. I did a crystal vision on her and saw her standing in the woods, laughing. That told me that she was faking. To my surprise, the crystal vision also showed me where she was keeping the wallet. I took her straight to the wallet and told her, "It's going to backfire on you if you continue to play jokes on me." When you play with the traditional ways of medicine, it will cause trouble for you. For example, if you play games with money, then you'll have problems with money. That's what my mother did with me. She played by saying she had money, but never that much. Ever since then, money has been awkward for her. Even though she did that to me, I still help her. That's never going to change.

David Peters

The first time I met my husband, David, I assumed that he lived far away from me. To my great surprise, he lived only two miles away. This was when I was in school. The day I met him, my teacher told me to

---

[4] Crystals are used by the Diné as a tool for having visions, diagnosing illness, and locating lost items. Using the crystal in this way is called a "crystal vision."

take a film projector to the next classroom. When I went into the class-room, I saw him there. I looked at him and he looked at me. It was love at first sight. In our minds it felt right. He told me later that he was thinking, "She's going to be my wife." At the same time, I was think-ing, "That's the man I'm going to see without pants." I stared at him for such a long time that the teacher shouted at me to wake up. I just looked at David, put the projector down, and smiled. All his classmates were laughing.

I never had a crush on anyone but him. He was my first love. However, on that day, we didn't talk. We just looked at each other and smiled. He later wrote me a letter in which he put my name with his last name. That's when I knew for sure that I had him. I was so happy.

He was a nice man, and our marriage was very good for thirty years. It was good until the last two years of his life. The doctor told him that he was going to die because of a heart problem. But David never told me. He just said he wanted to enjoy life. His life ended due to heart failure at the Comfort Inn motel. He said he was going to die in style—the room had a big TV and a big bed in it. He just lay down on one side of that bed and died there.

David was a good medicine man. I remember he once gave a perfor-mance for two young girls who were twins. He said he was going to do a Warrior Prayer for them. His father wanted to witness it, so David's dad and I went up there. When we arrived, we found people dressed in traditional full skirts. The people who lived there had sheep and lambs, which they were feeding with a bottle. They lived very traditionally. They had no running water or any other modern conveniences. David's job was to say a prayer for these twin girls. I wondered how he was going to do it, and before I knew it, he began to pray. I saw that he went deep inside himself, and I didn't hear anything around him. He just prayed for the little ones.

After a while, he began talking. At first, I thought he was talking to me, but he was talking to someone else. I didn't know who he saw, but when I asked him afterward, he said it was a holy person. The holy per-son blessed those two girls and said that something was going to happen to one of them. David's father knew he was talking to a holy person, so he poured water onto the floor. Then he put pollen on the spilled water for the Holy One present at the ceremony.

After we left, we went to a big yucca plant and David pulled it in four different directions. He stabbed himself with the plant. When I asked him about it, he said it was because he was worried about one of his patients, the little girl. He then started crying. He started bleeding from the yucca and he gave his blood to Mother Earth. His father did the same thing.

Every time a medicine person does a traditional Diné practice, they have to do something to their body if they believe something bad is going to happen to a patient. True medicine people do it. I asked David about it, and he just said it's one of the traditional ways. As a natural law, it's a way of communicating with Mother Earth and Father Sky. Because they spill their blood for us, we sometimes must do the same. There's a telephone line between the Creator and us. Everything we medicine people do helps communication take place with the Holy Ones.

I never knew my husband was a medicine man until we were married. We were married at the Bureau of Indian Affairs (BIA) up in Shiprock. It wasn't a big ceremony. The only witnesses were my sister, my mom, and David's father. The BIA bought us a small cake. That's how we got married. Afterward we went to the highest mountaintop, put our vows together, and said things to each other. Then we used the whistle to bless one another. We also cut ourselves. I still have the scar from that cut on my hand. That's our way of having a traditional marriage.

One night we both dreamt about a medicine pouch and how we were going to make it. I got out of bed and walked around looking for the buckskin to make the pouch. He was looking for the buckskin at the same time. We didn't know that our son had taken it to the hogan to make a drum out of it. Finally we met in the middle of the room and David asked me what I was looking for. We then realized that we were both looking for the same object to do the same thing with it—to make a medicine pouch from a dream. We knew then that we had experienced the same dream at the same time.

Another time, we had a dream about his mother. We both jumped out of bed together and said, "Mom is dead!" We said it at the same time. We ran to her house and sure enough she was dead. That's the way we dreamed.

On another occasion, we both had the same dream about buying a car. In the dream, after we left the car dealer, we had an accident. We had actually planned on buying a car that day, but we changed our minds because of the dream. We didn't buy a car until a whole month later. David said that we needed to have a moon change before buying a car.

My husband believed in the Moonways, the Storyways, the Windways, and the Rainways. He said those were his messengers. For example, after staring at a storm cloud, he announced that a war was coming on very soon. I said, "There's no war. Vietnam is over." He kept looking at the storm and said, "I feel there's going to be a war, and there's this one person getting all his feathers up." Sure enough, Desert Storm took place soon after his vision. The storms told him things like that.

The Medicine Way

I believe that we pray to one God. I know there's a holy person out there somewhere. I don't talk against the Bible or other ways of worshipping God. All ways to God are good.

I was taught that you should listen to the thunder when you have an important decision to make. Most of our older people look out the window and listen to the thunder when it rains. They wait and listen for their answers. My grandpa used to do that. He used to sit and watch the thunder coming in. You'd hear him say, "That's it. Aah." I don't know what he meant, but he'd say, "Aah." I'd ask him, "What's the matter with you, Grandpa? Are you going crazy the Diné way?" He'd just laugh and go back to listening to the thunder.

When people come to me with their sicknesses and problems, I sometimes have to go to a special place and say a prayer. When you help someone, you must be willing to pray all night and cry or laugh with them. That's what medicine's about. All that is within your patient must come to you, and when you work with them, they are your only concern.

A person who conducts a Trembling Hand Ceremony can tell you what direction you should take your life. For example, they can tell you where you should live. They'll start trembling as they pray or sing about it. They put pollen on their hand to indicate the different directions and put a mark that symbolizes you. They also put a rainbow on their hands and circle the palm all the way around to make it into lightning. They don't use the north because that is where the evil goes. They don't fool around with the north. That's why they only use three directions.

Some of those who conduct the Trembling Hand Ceremony will tremble lightly, while others will shake. I've seen all kinds of trembling. The way their hand moves gives them a diagnosis on their patient. The movements will tell the healer the patient's sickness, as well as where it comes from. If the healer's hand hits Mother Earth, it means death. If it hits something like a piece of furniture, it means that the sickness will get worse. Sometimes when the healer's hand is very shaky, they can help the patient by passing it over the patient's body.

There are still some powerful hand tremblers today. Once in a while when I'm trying to help my mom or aunt, I'll go to one of them. I really can't help my mom in the healing way. Even when she's very sick, I can't help her because I'm her flesh and blood. Any healing visions I try will not tell me anything about her sickness or make me feel how she feels inside. I tried it when she was very sick, and it didn't do anything. The same thing happened with my aunt, but I have helped her children and grandchildren. I asked a medicine man why I can't understand my mom's sickness, and he said the reason was that my mom had rejected me a long time ago. She's still a good mom, though.

Once a black friend of mine got cancer and asked my husband and me for help. We went into the woods and brought her some herbs. Sure enough, the medicine healed her. She didn't even need the surgery recommended for her. She lived and went on to have another child. She told us that the medicine got her horny. We had a good laugh about that. From then on, we decided to use our medicine on people of all colors. The medicine that cured her came from David's father, who taught David about the medicine.

There is a medicine man out there trying to get one of my medicines from me. One day he got sick and his face went crooked. He wanted a certain medicine that I have. We took it to him, but he wasn't home and we never had a chance to treat him. I went over to his house three times, but he was never there. I heard that his face is still crooked and he's still looking for his medicine. I know that if I go over there again, the medicine will backfire on me. He has to come to my house and ask for it again.

When my husband's mom was about to die, he saw a bright red-orange light outside our window. He remembered that his uncle had seen the same colored light when his wife was about to die. It's a sign of a death. I, too, have seen that light. I remember getting up at eleven o'clock one night to go to work. When I started the car, everything went bright red-orange around the area. I tried not to believe what was happening, but the next day my husband died. That colored light tells us that someone is going to die.

Native American Church

Medicine men and women deal with herbs, sandpainting, singing, and chanting. Some of them also deal with witchery and all kinds of hocus pocus on the other side.[5] In addition to medicine people, there are Roadmen. Roadmen work with peyote, cedar, sage, smoke, prayers, and songs. In Native American Church meetings, we eat peyote and concentrate on the cedar in the fire. It requires sitting all night through a meeting where we sing, pray, teach, and talk.

The Native American Church has been with me for a long time. The first time I ever tasted peyote was when I was about six. My mom said to come over and eat some coffee grounds. I went over and they sure didn't taste like coffee. She was using peyote and prayer for courage to face the difficult things in her life. That evening, about ten or fifteen minutes after she let me eat the peyote medicine, my body began to tingle. People say that's how the medicine starts to work. At the time, I was

---

[5] Medicine men and women can heal or they can cause illness. The Diné people refer to those who cause illness as witches or sorcerers. If they want to be discreet, they say "that medicine person works with the other side."

a hyperactive child and the medicine made me more hyper. I remember going outside and chasing a chicken. After a while, I went to sleep.

I continued to eat the peyote medicine as a child. When I was about nine, I attended a full peyote meeting. I wanted to see how it was, what they say, and what they do. I wanted to witness it myself. My sister and I hid behind some people and observed the meeting. The medicine man talked and afterward he started saying prayers while each person rolled up a smoke. With the smoke, they all started praying. When the medicine came around the third time, I grabbed a bunch of it and swallowed it without chewing. It was green and watery looking. Soon I started feeling something, and then we moved to the front to sit with the others. When the staff came near me, I grabbed it. Someone wanted me to sing. A man was playing the drum. That was the first time I started singing.

Even though I didn't know any songs, a song came to me automatically. I sang pretty well. The medicine man in charge of the meeting told me to come up front. He announced that I was going to be a medicine woman in the future and that I was going to have it all. He knew this because he saw it through my song. He then prayed, cedared me down very well, and gave me four medicines. He turned to my stepfather and said to me, "If he ever hurts you again, you come and tell me." Boy did I feel big and strong. That's when I started standing up for myself. My stepfather was mean. He used to hit me, and once he chased me with a horse. He also beat my mom with a stick. That's the kind of house I lived in.

I remember one vision that changed things for me. As a child, I was often sick. My brother finally paid attention. "Sister, I want you to have this ceremony done on you. I'm tired of you being sick all the time. I want you to get better." I was so sick that I wore a towel on my head. I used to get real hot. A meeting was held for me in the traditional Native American way. The medicine man conducting the meeting said I was visioning things I wasn't supposed to see. I would see a woman in the hospital and know where her pain was located. I would look at her and see an area of her body that was dark. Sometimes I'd see something black around her or I'd see a bug eating her.

I could also smell sickness and I could smell a person's blood. If a woman had sex the night before, I could smell it. My nose was that good, and my ears and eyes were also very good. I learned that all the smells and things I saw made me get sick. That's why they had a peyote meeting. The medicine man gave me a spoonful of medicine every thirty minutes. I was flying high, as you would say in the white man's way. The medicine was really working on me and gave me visions. I told the medicine man that it was getting scary because I started seeing graveyards where people were buried. I saw the bodies lying there and the marks on the coffins. The medicine man said that my sickness had to do with the Ghostway. It involved people who had died. I never found out who made that happen to me and I didn't question it.

When the peyote medicine started doctoring me, I felt puffy. I felt like I was sitting high in the sky. It made me feel the people around me, but I could only see their feet. The medicine fixed me up inside and my body hurt from it. I heard my heart beat and my liver move. I heard my insides moving and I saw my own fat. I was able to see myself in a true way.

After taking more medicine, my vision focused like a TV set and I could see into my past. I viewed the time when my sister and I butchered and cooked an old, small gray desert lizard. I don't know why we did it, but we didn't eat it. We had mistreated Mother Earth, and I learned that that was responsible for the soreness inside me.

Even after the meeting was over and the medicine man went away, the medicine continued to work on me for another week and a half. People came to my house asking for help because they believed I was under the influence of holy spiritual ways. I went and helped these people. I prayed and used the sacred knowledge I had been given. From that point on, many patients came to me.

Sandpainting

Sandpaintings are also used in our healing ceremonies. I first saw a sandpainting when I was a little girl.

Later as a child, I saw a sandpainting of the Lightningway. The painting was of a Thunder Person. I was able to watch that performance,

Figure 1.2

Traditional sandpainting

which was done for a newlywed couple. The man sat on the right and the woman on the left. The medicine man told the couple that the man is the head of the household and the woman takes care of the home. The young couple got up and I got up, too. The medicine man then allowed me to make my first rainbow there. He let me make a rainbow design on the sandpainting at the foot of the thunder, which was turquoise and red. Its border was yellow on one side and white on the other side. In the middle was a large Rainbow Person with a rainbow on his side.

The medicine man said that the rainbow symbolized the couple's hope and ambition. The young woman wanted many kids, so the rainbow surrounding the thunder had many kids. The husband wanted his kids to respect him, so the rainbow was colored yellow. He also wanted his kids to think positively. The color white was for that. The center of the painting depicted their aim to grow old together with no one but themselves. It was like putting the marriage together in a special way. The medicine man said that if they strayed from the marriage, something bad would happen.

After I made the rainbow, the medicine man said the people who helped him with the sandpainting would have more forwardness. He said that nothing would stop us from reaching our purpose. He then brought out his pollen bag. He went on to interpret the symbols and colors of the sandpainting. He made an X on each side of the thunder with his pollen. He told the husband to put his knees on a certain spot on the painting and the wife to place her knees on another spot. They had to do the same with their hands. They had to swing their bodies onto the sandpainting and sit down on it. That was the first time I ever saw such a performance. I was about ten when I witnessed it. It was a good ceremony. The couple is still alive and together.

Preparation

A sandpainting of the healing ways can be really detailed or it can be plain. It's up to the medicine person to decide how to make it. You look at the patient and see what is necessary. You then put the appropriate design inside. That's how the sandpainting gets designed. The details of each sandpainting are uniquely tailored to the particular situation. The general theme is always the same, but the details depend on the patient's situation. That's how I do mine with the Pollen Boy—by looking at the patient and then doing it. I put my own details into it based on how I think the patient can be helped.

I'm told that there are only nine medicine women who do sandpaintings for healing. One woman knows how to sing over the sandpaintings. I know how to pray over them. Another woman uses the whistle, while another uses smoke. None of us are alike because there are different ways of doing the healing and helping the patient. [To see a sandpainting created to help a woman become independent and strong, please see Figure 1.iii.]

As I mentioned before, the original designs came from the first world. Other designs came later from people who visioned things. All the details of my sandpaintings come from my dreams. The way I see the sandpainting and the way I understand it comes to me. Another medicine person may have the same general figure, but the design details come from my dreams.

Figure 1.3

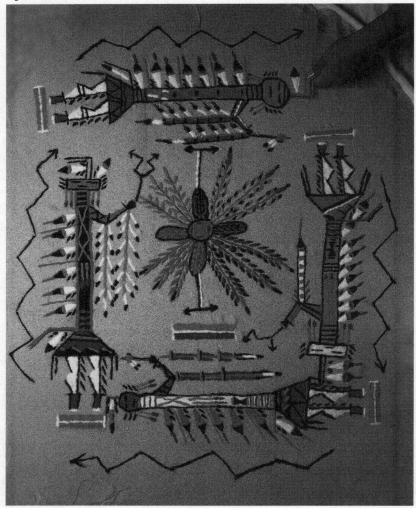

My favorite sandpainting, The Four Directions, consists of four Replanters[6] with lightning that move everything in a clockwise direction. This is used to help put a person's life back in order, particularly when they are under great stress from personal difficulty.

---

[6] The *Yei*, the Holy one who replants what you value, symbolizes replanting the creation. It is used to help replant a person's life lessons and accumulate their personal property. In general, it helps a person bloom like a flower.

When I'm going to perform a sandpainting on a person, I usually ask for a dream. If it doesn't come, I don't do a sandpainting. If I have to wait many days for that dream to come, I have to wait. Sometimes it can take five days. I follow what my dream tells me and I never question it. When I vision something, it happens. I don't play with it. Sometimes it scares me, but I have to go by what the dream tells me.

The sandpaintings I like to perform are the Whirling Logs, Thunder, and Sunbursts. Those three sandpaintings are my favorite ones. I also perform Walk in Beauty. There's a little song and a prayer for Walk in Beauty. The Courage Sunburst is for people who hesitate to do things; it gives you courage to do things. The Thunder Ceremony includes drinking herbs, meditating, self-understanding, praying, and using smoke. It is for someone who wants to accomplish something. One client wanted to become a school principal. I did the performance on her, and now she's the head of the school. Another patient wanted to be a councilman. He's now a councilman of the Navajo Nation. He's still my patient.

My Teacher Speaks

I am Don Hoskie, one of Walking Thunder's teachers. The people call me He Who Walks Away. I'm one hundred years old. I gave Walking Thunder the crystal vision and taught her sandpaintings and the Warrior Prayers and other songs. Now I want to teach her eight more songs and some more prayers. I want to get all of this together for her before I die.

You can't choose to be a medicine person. You must be chosen. If you are chosen, the medicine people should bless you. In my prayers, the only thing I ask for is healing. I never ask for money. I don't really care for it. I was taught that money is trouble. Doing things right is the only way.

I started learning traditional medicine when I was ten. I never went to school. I just followed the medicine people around and learned from them. My real teacher, however, is the Creator. I heal people by following what the Creator says. I don't believe in paper licenses for doctors. The Creator never had that. The paper is for those who don't have confidence in the Creator. When a patient comes to me, I am confident that the Creator is going to help me in healing that patient.

I don't want Walking Thunder to have a piece of paper. She should only trust the Creator when she helps a patient. A lot of people have done wrong things with the medicine way because they didn't follow the Creator. You must concentrate when you sing and pray, asking the Creator for help.

I passed on my knowledge to five people. Two of them have died and only three are left. Walking Thunder is one of my successors. I gave her the traditional ways for helping patients.

After all the performances and doctoring I've done, I now feel two hundred years old. Whenever I'm in a ceremony and it's strong, I feel a wind come into my body. The wind is with me all the time. Sometimes I feel like I'm going to become Jesus, that's how strong the wind can be. I know it isn't true, but that's how I feel inside.

Walking Thunder's Remembrances of He Who Walks Away

When I first met He Who Walks Away, I was very sick. I was not a healthy woman. My husband and his sister were holding me up when we walked into his house and asked him to help me. I told him that I'd been sick all the time and that I'd paid many medicine men, but I didn't get any better. He asked, "Do you know why?" He then told me to come and sit by him and he asked for my hand. I put my hand in the middle of his hand and he held it for about five minutes. Then he said, "Do you know what makes you sick? And do you know what people don't see? The true healer is in you and a spirit is making you sick. You are supposed to help other people, but you are rejecting it and you don't understand it." He then told me that he was going to perform a ceremony and that he wanted me to stay for several days.

I gave him the necklace I was wearing and told him that I had no money. He started singing and giving me herbs. I felt worse that first day. On the second day, I felt lighter, and by the time he was finished, I was cured and I walked out without anyone helping me.

He chewed on an herb and then spit it into my mouth. He said, "This is for you to understand the traditional way and for you to know the prayers and to understand the prayers." Each time he performed a prayer, he told a story that explained what the prayer was about. Each time he made a sandpainting, he also told a story. He roasted four sacred corns: white, blue, red, and a mixed color. He cooked them in hot ashes and when they were cooked, he put them in our mouths one at a time as he sang and did his prayers.

He made my husband, David, sit down and then he touched David's heart. David immediately fell over. He then started chanting, singing, and praying until David came back up. He Who Walks Away gave the trembling hand to David. You could feel the spirit throughout his ceremony. Sometimes it was cold and then it warmed and then it would get very cold again.

He knows the sandpainting prayer ways, crystal vision, the *Yeibechai* way, hand trembling, the Fire Danceway, the Lightningway, and all kinds of ceremonials. He also sucks things out of a person with his mouth. He always wears a red headband when he performs ceremonies.

He warned me that a lot of people would talk against me and criticize me when I took up the medicine way. He said not to mind them because I would be doctoring the people through the Creator. "If they criticize you," he said, "then they're criticizing the Creator."

He told me that all the holy people in the four directions will help me doctor others. He taught me that when you do a crystal vision, you're supposed to use your five senses. It's about smelling, tasting, hearing, seeing, and feeling. You must use all your senses when you do a crystal vision.

I first tested the crystal vision on my little brother. He had been missing from home for two weeks, and my mother was trying to find him. She had asked a lot of medicine people to help her, but they kept telling her that he was going to come back. My mom spent a lot of money trying to find him. Then she came to me and said, "You know how to do the crystal vision. Go find out where your little brother is."

We sat down, burned some charcoal, and then we started doing the crystal vision. I did my prayers as He Who Walks Away had taught me. I found out that he was in a ditch somewhere near a store. I said, "He's gone. He's not on this world. He's somewhere else."

My mother didn't believe me. Sure enough, someone found him in a ditch and called the Navajo police. His body was identified by a birthmark. If a person does not believe you and they think harshly of you, it can come back to you. This happened to me and I got my sickness again. I had to go back to He Who Walks Away and tell him what happened. He sang some songs and got me well again. I know who killed my brother because the crystal vision showed me. But I kept still and decided to leave things alone.

About a month or so later, my aunt's son got lost and the FBI tried to find him. My family asked me again to do a crystal vision. I agreed and in my concentration, I heard shoveling, coughing, and the sound of plastic being moved around. I saw my cousin being buried. When I told my aunt, she had the same reaction as my mom. She said I had put a spell on my cousin. I replied, "If you don't believe me, then go tell the police to dig up the grave." They dug it up and found him with no clothes, wrapped in plastic. Someone had stabbed him with a knife.

He Who Walks Away received his name because of the way he deals with his patients. If he has a feeling that a patient does not believe him or is testing him, he'll just gather his stuff and walk out. He'll simply stop in the middle of the ceremony and walk out without any questions. He'll walk away and won't help them. People will say to him, "Hey, why haven't you finished yet?" He will just turn around and say, "Why should I help you? You don't believe me. You just lost your money. That's it." No matter how far he has to walk, he walks. That's how they gave him the name. He is one of the great medicine men.

One day when David and I visited him, he told us we were going eagle hunting on top of a certain hill. When we got there, he told us to stand like tree stumps. We tried but couldn't do it. He said, "Be natural. Be yourself. You're a stump already." He stood there, held up his arms, and started singing. Pretty soon an eagle flew down and sat on his arm. While singing, he pulled out some feathers. He pulled out four feathers and then some little feathers to tie onto his gourd. He put pollen in the eagle's mouth while it made noises. He waved his hand and the eagle took off. We watched the eagle circle clockwise, all the way up into the

Figure 1.4

The mountains,
I become part of it . . .
The herbs, the evergreen,
I become part of it.
The morning mists, the clouds,
the gathering waters,
I become part of it.
The dew drops, the pollen,
I become part of it.

sky until we couldn't see him. He Who Walks Away taught me about the Eagleways. A living eagle feather is more holy than an eagle that's been shot or trapped. The eagle is a lifeline to the Creator. When you use the eagle feather and whistle, it puts a line between the Creator and you like a thread. You can't see it because it is invisible.

Some people were jealous of He Who Walks Away and said he was a witch doctor, but he never feared them. He was very powerful. He could use a robin feather like a lock pick to get inside any building. He could also use that robin's feather to go inside a person's body. He said that that was the hardest thing he learned.

In all the creation and all the life you will go through, know that the beauty is ahead of you. As you walk, the beauty is behind you, below you, and above you. That's the way you should think about yourself. Entering the beauty is realizing that you're in the beauty. You must fully appreciate the life that the Creator has given you and take care of it. That's entering the beauty.

HANDS OF FAITH
HEALERS OF BRAZIL

Introduction to *Hands of Faith*
by Bradford Keeney

Brazil is filled with healers of every imaginable orientation, practice, size, and shape.

Two elders, however, rise above the crowd. Meet Otavia and João, country healers who have never charged anything for their services. Both have led remarkable lives, surrounded by magical events that cannot be explained. Yet each believes that prayer, faith, and love are the only ingredients of their healing practice.

Of all the healers I have met in the world, João and Otavia stand out in the purity and strength of their faith and the love they are given by their families. I have never seen more love than that expressed in their families. That love alone is worthy of a story. While neither João nor Otavia claims to be anything special, their lives are filled with remarkable stories and testimonies.

Some of their stories convey a world filled with strange and mysterious experiences—happenings that cannot be satisfactorily explained to our rational minds. These unexplainable events may tempt us to beg for understandings that reveal an access to supernatural power and magical tricks. Yet Otavia's and João's nonordinary lives have nothing to do with spiritual mastery or elitism. Their glimpses of a world with expanded horizons are common for people whose hearts are open to a huge love, a love that breaks through all boundaries of reason and rationality. Yes, I am saying that when a person is in the purest love zone, extraordinary experiences take place naturally. It is a consequence of being open to spirit in a pure, heartful way.

Neither João nor Otavia regard themselves as more important than anyone else. In fact, João's children have learned one simple lesson from his example: each of us is no more important than a single, small pebble. If any person reaches for the "power" of the universe, spiritual or otherwise, the opening of the heart constricts. At best, or perhaps at worst, we end up exploding the atom or wreaking havoc upon our fragile ecosystem. The lives of Otavia and João show us another way: be small and love beyond the realm of measure.

In this chapter, you will find healers who modestly claim no expertise, but are able to successfully address many complex challenges. They teach us that the simplest faith and the humblest self-regard bring forth great mysteries and, more importantly, blessings of uplifting love and peace that surpass all understanding.

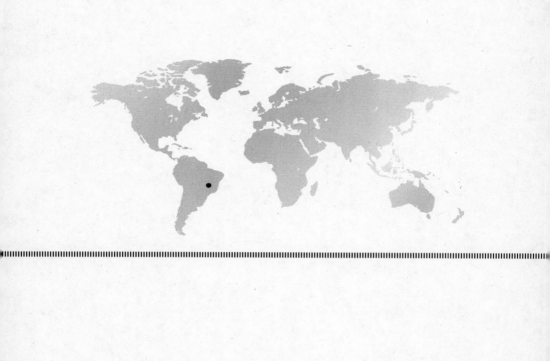

Otavia Alves Pimental Barbosa

Translation by Corinna Schabbel

> *All of a person's nature is shown in the design*
> *of their eyes. The past is printed in the eyes.*
> *On the other hand, the future is barely outlined*
> *and you are free to change the lines.*
> *Those lines are projected outward*
> *and help shape your life.*

I am ninety-six years old and I have spent all of my life trying to make people's lives a little better. I have given my soul to this task, and if I had more soul to give, I would do so without any hesitation.

I grew up on a farm in the north of São Paulo state in Brazil. I had five siblings and I was the oldest. My brother passed away years ago, but his spirit has always been on my side. He was younger than me. My brother had ten children, and now they are all married and happy. After my brother died, he became one of my spirit guides. He helps me and he's always with me. He didn't leave me alone. He is right here this very moment. He helps me when I bless[1] people. And he goes to other

---

[1] Otavia uses "bless" throughout her narrative as a way of referring to her healing skill. Therefore, she blesses someone to heal them.

people to help them when I ask him. There is a woman in town who is a psychologist. When she had surgery, I asked my brother's spirit to follow her to São Paulo, so he could assist her during the operation. He is able to go wherever we need him. It does not matter where the person lives.

Learning to Heal
Have you ever seen a bird trying hard to sing?
Birds never work to make a song. They sing effortlessly.
That's how they teach us to love one another.
We need to allow love to happen without any effort.
It is natural to love.

Love is the power of healing. If you love and if you have love, you are able to heal. I love everyone the same way. I have so much love that I often have to cry. It doesn't matter whether it is family or not. You have to live your love. To be in love is to be with the other. Friendship is one of the most beautiful things we can have. To love a person and to be a friend is fantastic! I live that way with my brother and my family.

I help people and ask my spirit guides to protect them. I want everyone to have brightness and happiness in their home. I always pray for this. I bless all the children who come to me. I am happy because I have children, grandchildren, great-grandchildren, and great-great-grandchildren. I am very pleased when they are okay. When they are hurt, I am unhappy. I'm always asking my spirit guides to help them.

Both my parents were blessed people who healed others. They blessed people and they helped heal their sickness. Poor families stayed at our place when they needed a home. My mother and father helped everyone who came to them. We had to build two more rooms to make enough space for those people.

One man lived at my parents' house his whole life. He came from the streets, and he helped us take care of the place. We didn't have just family meals. We had meals for everyone who was hungry. As a child, I learned that we are here on earth to help other people.

In addition to my parents' instruction, the African helpers who lived on our farm taught me how to use plants to heal. These Africans told me stories about an olive tree that existed in the spirit world. They said that you have to peel the fruit of that tree to make a remedy. I remember them talking about that special tree.

The women helpers in our family, Joan and Maria, had grown up in Africa, and they taught me the blessing I use today. They also taught me how to heal children. I remember when I had a headache and Maria put her hand on my head. I've never had a headache since that time. I learned to work that way with children. As a child, I had bad eyes, but Joan helped me get good eyes and taught me how to help people get over their illnesses and difficulties. She, too, put her hand on my head and prayed.

Joan and Maria used charcoal to bless the children. After saying a prayer, they would throw hot charcoals into a pan of water. If the charcoal sunk down to the bottom, they would say that the disease was going away. If it stayed floating on top, they would say that the disease remained and that the treatment must be repeated.

Joan and Maria were the first people to tell me about the spiritual stairs that lead to a special place in the spirit world called "the field of the birds." They told me how they climbed up to that field on one side of the stairs and climbed down from the field on another side. They were very old when I met them. I remember them dancing as much as they could and shaking their bodies during the dance.

The Spirit Priest

Once, a man came to our family and announced, "Go to the house of a certain baker and you will meet a priest who is invisible. You cannot see him, but go there, pray very hard, and ask him to come. If you pray and call him, the priest will come." My uncle went to the place and began to pray and called upon the priest to help him. He prayed and prayed to this priest, and one day he appeared. At first, no one but my uncle could see him. At my uncle's request, the priest came to us and removed the trouble, which he explained as something caused by evil spirits. He used a little whip and a quince stick. He beat the spirits until they recoiled.

Figure 2.1

The Spirit Priest

All became well and the priest joined our family. My aunt told us not to be afraid of what took place in the house because the dead priest was living with us.

The priest was called Aranha, but he didn't like that nickname because it meant "spider." His real name was Francisco. I was twelve years old when he first came to my family's house and sat in our room.

We talked all the time. When we turned off the light, he would come. He always ordered us to turn off the light because he would only come without the light. We did everything in the dark.

The priest talked to us and touched us with his hands. I believe that he died in a swimming accident. The story we heard was that he had gone off to a lake to swim with his friends, but they came back without him. He probably drowned in that lake. He was only in his early twenties when that happened. After his disappearance, he was first sighted at the local baker's house. He lived there as a spirit and helped solve their problems. When he was finished working with the baker's family, he joined us and became a part of our everyday life. It was my uncle who brought him to us.

The priest brought us everything we needed to do healing work. He brought us medicine that took care of the family. My brother watched the priest prepare the medicine. He saw drops fall into the water. Then we would all drink it. When we went into the woods, we never saw him, but we always felt his presence. We would talk to him and he would answer back, but we would never see him there. I saw him several times at other places. Once I saw him near the door eating an orange. Another time, a baby and I saw him eating an orange. When he saw me, he went away.

The priest taught me many things. He taught me how to prepare the sacred medicine that is used to bless people. He also taught this to my mother, sisters, and the entire family. The priest looked like a very young handsome man.

I remember when I was a small girl and a man came to hurt my father. He had stones in his pockets. The priest appeared to him and said, "If you want to use those stones, use them with the horses, but not with this man." That man never came back to bother us again.

The priest was able to gather other material things. For example, when we needed oil for the lamps at the farm, he would go to the village and get it. He did so on the condition that the next day my father would go to the village and pay for the oil.

He took care of us in many ways, including administering to our illnesses and injuries. I remember a time when I injured myself as a child, and the priest went to my mother and told her what happened. She came home and took care of me. On another occasion, my mother had a skin problem and the priest cured her in a blink of an eye.

He usually mixed the medicines that we needed in a small room near the kitchen. My brother would go inside that small room and find the medicine waiting for him. The priest taught us to pray. He gave us some unique prayers. My mother also taught us prayers, but the priest taught us even more.

The priest taught me other things about the spirit world through my dreams. The spirit world consists of a very huge field with beautiful grass. The "field of the birds" is the place that Joan and Maria had often spoken about. It is the field of the spirits. It looks like the most beautiful green blanket you've ever seen.

There is a stairway that I climb that goes up to the field and a stairway that brings me down. The stairway is somewhat like a white rope in the sky. When I dream, I go up and down the stairs. Although it's a dream, I am not able to forget it. I see the field of the birds and it's wonderful. I have learned that our bodies are just envelopes and when our bodies go away, when they go back to the earth, our spirits go to the field.

When you leave your body, you will be able to fly. When you pass on, you will be like a white bird. That's when you go to the field of the birds. There, you will find special railroad tracks. The tracks go both sideways as well as up into the sky. All the tracks are white. They are used to guide the trains and horses that can take you places. That is the way things work up there .

Blessings and Healings

When I started healing the sick, long lines of people would show up in front of our house. I started when I was still a child. The African helpers taught me what to do and supervised my first healings. I would put the sick children on my lap and give them the blessing the African women had taught me. I would sometimes put three pieces of hot charcoal in some water and say, "When the live coal goes out, the disease goes out, too." (See Figure 2.ii.)

I always used the special words of prayer that were taught to me. At times, I would use a special branch and rub oil onto the children's backs. I would repeat this for nine days in a row and they would get well. I recall a time when many children became sick and lost so much weight that their mothers became very worried. I cured them all and the mothers came back to give me special thanks. There were many people that I helped.

I have never charged a penny to heal anyone. I saw it as my obligation to do this work. This is God's will. When a sick person comes to me, I always begin by praying a special blessing for them. The way it works for me is simple: I pray for help and wait for a dream. In my dream, I see everything that is needed to help someone. In my dreams, different people come to me and tell me about the plants that I can use to heal others. That's how I learn more about the healing herbs. After the dream, I see the patients again and treat them as I was directed. My dreams tell me what is wrong with them and what should be done to make their life improve. Sometimes I dreamt so much that I fell off the bed!

I don't have many worries right now. I pray every evening before I go to bed. I pray for my children and I pray for my family. If I have any pain, I put my hand on it and ask Jesus to come bless me and help me. Then the pain disappears. This is faith. Everything is faith. The best cure is love. Everyone in my life loved me. Even the animals loved me. Yes, I even cured the animals. I did all of these things out of love.

When people read my story, I believe they will know me without knowing me. As a child, my brother and I spent most of our time with those loving African women. We played together and danced together. They helped me learn how to live in the fullest way. Today, I pass on their wisdom.

João Fernandes de Carvalho
Translation by Jose Carlos Vitor Gomes
As a child, I was only able to go to school for eleven months. That was the total amount of time given to my classroom education. Everything else I had to learn on my own. When my father became sick, I took over the family responsibilities. It was at that time that I dreamed of being a

doctor and curing people of sickness. Since it was not possible for me to be educated as a physician, it seems that Providence turned me into a healer, enabling me to help thousands of people.

I have given prescriptions and medical advice to multitudes of patients, and, early on, pharmacists were surprised that my instructions worked and that my prescriptions were powerful medicines for treating illness. They were curious about the doctor who was making these prescriptions.

I acquired informal medical knowledge by reading medical books and pharmacology catalogues. I also maintained some contact with traditional medical laboratories while I practiced my healing. Most important, I was helped in my work by a meditative state in which I received technical medical knowledge and deepened my faith in God's help and goodness. This special state of mind allowed medical information to pass through me. Those who came to me with faith were helped in this simple way.

My fame as a healer grew, and the streets in front of our house were lined with patients daily. They came by foot, horse, carriage, car, and truck. I waited for them with my pen and scarce pieces of paper. It was difficult for me to write due to my limited education, yet what needed to be written was always accomplished when I surrendered myself as a spiritual channel. What I did, I did voluntarily and without monetary compensation. I knew I was not a doctor, and I only gave whatever modest help I was able to extend to others.

I would always ask Our Lady to help the person who came to me, and then the prescription would enter my mind. I discovered that the size of the cure was related to the size of the person's faith. I also learned that God's mercy and miracles could cancel the effect of anyone's past karma, sin, and disease.

I found that the diseases of the world deeply offended me. I felt a rage toward disease and everything that caused human beings to suffer. I wanted to help all those that I could, so I wrote prescriptions, gave words of advice, and offered water, asking God to bless it. With each cure and success, I felt a joyous party in my heart. It brought me great happiness to help relieve the suffering of others, and it enabled me to sleep each night with deep inner peace.

Eventually the crowds that came to me became so large that we had to flee the farm in Brazil where we lived and go to the nearest village. There, the lines of people became even longer, and my reputation spread all over the region and other states. All the public transportation drivers knew how to get to my house. I became so well-known that I was invited to be a politician. However, I did not allow myself to be distracted from the healing work, and I found that I had to be careful because there were doctors alleging that my work was illegal. It had never occurred to me that I might be judged guilty of medical fraud or malpractice because my instrument of cure was simply prayer and a rosary.

The rumors of legal accusations unsettled me, and I found out that there were professional people who had vowed to harm me. You must realize that I never wanted to fight anyone. I never competed with any doctor and I didn't challenge the defined medical sciences. I only wanted peace for my family, so I decided to flee into obscurity as a way of protecting them. Many people of the village were sad when I left. My last words to them were, "Don't worry, I'm taking all the diseases with me." And now when I go back to that village after all of those years, I am still surrounded by people.

I suffered when I left our home. We abandoned our farm animals, house, and land. Yet I was blessed with a healthy family and wonderful grandchildren, and all eight of my children graduated from the university. This is a great source of happiness for me. (See Figure 2.v.)

I have learned that an authentic talent for helping people is a gift that cannot be bought or sold. It is a present from God and there is no price that can be attached to it. The pearl that is within me doesn't belong to me. It comes from a larger dimension and I am unable to give it to anyone else. It belongs to God. It feels like a force or electric current that moves through me when I pray. My rosary works like a telephone line to God. These experiences enable my faith to be reborn every day.

I once swore from the bottom of my heart that I would keep my secret, and I have been always afraid of revealing it. But now I am an old man, and it is time to tell some stories about my life and how I have helped cure others. I can say this, however, about my secret power: faith is the key. Faith is a personal tool that everybody possesses in larger or smaller degrees. It is not transferable. It is not a magical process that can be sold or taught. It is something that is always within you.

I have devoted my life to doing good for others, and I offer my words to you with the hope that they will bring some goodness to your life.

Early Memories

When I was a youngster, many strange things would happen around me. My sister and brothers like to talk about these things. For example, the sewing machine would sometimes operate by itself, luminous shapes would move in the backyard, voices would be heard, and a stove would light itself in the middle of the morning. I recall being thirteen years old and walking past a certain cluster of trees and seeing three crosses next to them. It is a custom of our culture to leave a cross at the place where someone died. It is a reverent act that affirms our respect for them. We believe that our departed ones sometimes return to the place where they died and we want them to see how we feel about them. At this particular place, I saw a woman dressed in white who was sitting next to the last cross.

The following day I went with my friend to the same place and saw the woman again, but this time she was dressed in plaid with a red crown. When I asked my friend whether he saw anyone, the woman with the red crown instantly disappeared in front of my eyes. I should add that the three crosses were located at a place where women would sometimes make a pilgrimage to pray for rain. This was my first contact with the world of spirits.

I am now eighty-two years old, and looking back on my life, I can honestly say that I never was involved with any kind of spiritualism and never did I ever ask to be a healer. I have only prayed with my rosary and found that God spontaneously gave me the gift to heal.

After that first vision, I started hearing voices while working on my parents' coffee farm. I would hear someone calling my name, "João, João . . . " When I stopped and looked around, no one was there. My desire to learn continued to grow, and I decided to study alone at night under the light of kerosene lamps. Fortunately I had a good brain and it was not long before I was reading the books of famous writers. Then I started reading books on medicine.

In the midst of this private learning, my brother acquired severe sores on his leg that no one could heal. I had a dream that I was seated at a table with a paper, a pen, and an image of Our Lady of Aparecida[2] on it. I wrote the names of several medicines on the paper and took it to a pharmacy. When I woke up, I remembered what I had written and actually went to the pharmacy to order the formula. It was a powder that my brother applied twice to his leg, which was quickly cured of the sores.

My faith grew with these kinds of experiences. I became a member of what was called the Occult Circle of the Communion of Thought, a very old mystical organization related to Masonry, the Rose Cross, and Theosophy. We studied spiritual texts and had fellowship with one another.

Faith and Prayer

With this new learning I made an amazing discovery. I found that my prescribed medications were not what necessarily cured people. It was their faith that cured, more so than any combination of chemicals that I could prescribe. I then began using water that I prayed over. This water was just as effective as my prescriptions. Again, I continued to do my work with no financial compensation. I used prayer to help relieve the suffering of others, but I never used my faith in God as a means to make money, and I always gave away everything that I received from Him.

God has always sent me what I need. In 1948, two friends bought me a ranch as a surprise gift. It was a ranch of fifteen hectares, and we plowed it to grow rice and coffee. The first crop was so successful that I was able to pay my friends back what they had paid for the entire ranch.

---

[2] Our Lady of Aparecida translates to "Our Lady Who Appeared," and is the patron saint of Brazil because of the number of answered prayers attributed to the veneration of her statue. She is an aspect of the Blessed Virgin Mary as a Black Madonna. This particular statue of her was given this name because it appeared in a fisherman's net as he was fishing in a deep river.

The Bird

There was a ranch that was owned by a very rich and powerful man. What was unusual was that the man never lived there. I finally decided to talk to him and find out what was going on. He told me that there was a moaning sound that came from his backyard, and he and his family were unable to stop it. The family had even tried praying for most of an evening, but still the moans continued.

I invited him to go to the ranch with me that evening, but he was too afraid. Instead, I brought some friends. They arrived with guns. I brought only a book entitled *Jesus Is the Way*. There was an old and tall tree in front of the house, and we stayed under it. At around ten o'clock in the evening, a huge bird started moving the middle branches, and my overanxious friends fired their guns at it.

Next, we went inside the house, and the moans began. Hard as we tried, no one could find their source. I started praying. I prayed a prayer similar to the one Joan of Arc spoke as she was burned. This is what I said:

> God, our Father, who is power and goodness, give strength to those who pass through trouble, give light to those who seek truth, and put compassion and charity into all men's hearts.
>
> God, give the traveler the guiding star, provide consolation for the afflicted and rest for the ill.
>
> Father, may your goodness cover those whom you created and may hope touch those who suffer. Permit your comforting spirit to bring forth peace, hope, and faith.
>
> God, you are a ray, a flame of love that can burn our earth. Let us drink from your fertile and infinite fountain.
>
> Dry our tears, calm our pain. Let us be one heart and one thought that reaches you as a shout of love. Our arms are open. Oh goodness! Oh beauty! Oh perfection! We desire your compassion.
>
> God, give us the strength to progress so that we may reach you. Give us the pure charity, the faith, the reason. Grant us the simplicity that will make our souls a mirror that reflects your image.

The more I prayed, the farther and farther away that moan sounded. I continued praying until the moan could not be heard, and it was never heard again. The family came back to the house and found, to their delight, that a bird sang near their house every evening. They told me about this bird and its special song. I went to hear it for myself one evening. As I walked in the woods toward the house, the bird came to me and sang its song. It sang it in back of me and then it sang it in front of me. The bird then gave me a spiritual gift. It filled me with a mystical fluid that helped my faith grow even stronger.

My Hands of Faith

Now I am retired because of my age. I don't want, nor will I accept any more interviews or research conducted on my talent. I simply want to be a friend with the most open and loving heart possible, and to join others for the cheerful moments that life brings us.

Nevertheless, my hands have not retired and they still have their abilities. It is a talent that I never learned and can't teach or donate to others. Nothing I have done was learned, because I never had a teacher.

Please know that it is enough to have God in your heart and to be a good brother or sister to others. Forget about personal gain and devote yourself to charity. It makes me sad to see people suffering from poverty while the rich and greedy absorb more than they need. I can't tell you how important it is for you to give freely with both of your hands.

Our hands are a sacred gift from God. One hand holds the secret wisdom while the other plants the faith. The highest power can come through our brain to our heart and out through our hands, spilling onto those we touch in prayer. Our hands can be used to serve greed and corruption, or they may be the servants of God's goodness. I am proud that my hands will always be directed to do good. My hands are the transmitters of my faith.

GARY HOLY BULL
LAKOTA *YUWIPI* MAN

Introduction to *Gary Holy Bull*
by Nancy Connor

Gary Holy Bull only speaks when he has something important to say. The rest of the time, he listens, even when no one is saying anything out loud. He listens for many things: to hear your true story from deep within you, to feel where your pain comes from, to understand the dynamics of the group around you, and to see whether there is anything he can do to help you if you should choose to ask. He says that most of us have forgotten how to really listen to each other and that is what is causing most of our troubles these days.

When he does speak, he speaks from the heart. He shares all of his life—the pain, the joy, the hardship, and the peace that come from doing what he is meant to be doing. He is willing to share the lessons he has learned from his difficult life and to help young men avoid the mistakes he made in his own past. He also tries to teach Sioux youth, as well as anyone else who cares to learn, what it means to be a good human being. We need more people on this earth with his heart and ability to care for others.

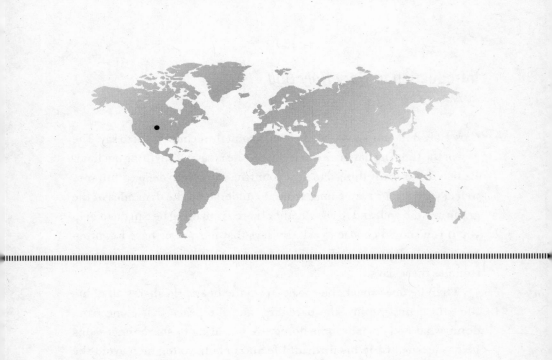

Gary Holy Bull

Ho!

My name is Gary Michael Holy Bull. My Lakota name is Ampohoksila. It means sunrise. My elders tell me that my first name, Ampohoksila, was given to me because I used to get up before sunrise and wake everyone up. It's a difficult name to live up to today because I like to sleep. Another name, Mahpiya Utateya, was given to me when my stepfather adopted me as his son. It means whirlwind clouds.

I was born on the Cheyenne River Indian Reservation and am an enrolled member of the Cheyenne River Sioux Tribe, Eagle Butte, South Dakota.

My parents were also born on the Cheyenne River Reservation. Both of my grandparents on my mother's side were descendants and survivors of the Wounded Knee Massacre.

My grandmother on my mother's side, Sophia Pretty Crane Voice, is the sister of the famous Lost Bird—the little baby who was found at the Wounded Knee Massacre and raised by a U.S. general in Beatrice, Nebraska.

My grandfather on my father's side was a descendent of Chief Hump, while my grandmother was related to the well-known Lakota figure Little Warrior, a close friend of Black Elk.

My earliest memory comes from when I was about two and a half years old. My mother was standing by the kitchen stove and washing dishes. I ran up to her and grabbed her apron.

She told me to be careful. Right in the middle of the one-room log house was a big pot-bellied stove, and the stove was red hot. I tripped and fell, and my hand landed on that stove. That was the first pain I remember in my life.

My mother took me to a medicine man named James Circle Bear. They made four nights of ceremony to try to save my hand.

My mother sat with me through the night in the medicine lodge and prayed for me. And my hand became well— healed by the prayers and ceremonies of our traditional people.

My mother had married a man called Andrew Red Fish. I remember many ceremonies and songs from that time of my childhood. One of the songs was sung by my stepfather's mother. She used to sing it to the children when we played around her lodge. It's about Iktomi, the "trickster."

Iktomi fooled all the ducks into dancing and then he told them to dance with their eyes closed. The ducks obediently got into a circle. Iktomi put himself in the middle and continued singing, while they started to dance with their eyes closed.

He then proceeded to kill them so he could eat them for dinner. One duck opened his eyes and was shocked to see what was happening. He hollered as loud as he could, "Run, he's killing us all!"

This story has always stuck in my mind, but I never understood it until recently. It's about the life we live today.

Once as a small child I was physically attacked by some teenagers. I tried to tell my mother what happened, but the teenagers came after me, saying it was all my fault. They beat me up again and blood flowed from my nose. My stepfather rescued me and he tried to comfort my little brother and me. He said, "You don't have to live in this." He put me in his car and we drove away.

Those were rough times. I blamed myself for all the violence that took place around the family. Even my mother would sometimes get beaten. I would cry for her and cry myself to sleep.

One day we took a trip to Mobridge, South Dakota, where my uncle lived. His name was Martin Holy Bull. I remember going over a bridge and being told that the bridge would sing to us. And sure enough, that bridge did sing. What I heard was the song that my grandmother used to sing about Iktomi.

When we arrived at my uncle's house, I couldn't believe how well everyone was treated. For a while there was true peace. And then the troubles began again. I became an angry child and I would throw tantrums, kick, and bite. I was taken to many ceremonies.

It seemed like we were at a ceremony every other night. A man named Romanus Bear Stop led many of them; he was a healer, and a lot of medicine men would come to his home, along Cherry Creek. That's where people went for ceremony.

Heyoka

Friend, I will send a voice, so hear me.
Friend, I will send a voice, so hear me.
Friend, I will send a voice, so hear me.
—Oglala Healing Song

When I was five years old, I found I could predict storms. I would often tell my grandparents when a storm was coming because I could hear it in the ground. Although it might be hundreds of miles away, I could always hear that storm coming and feel a slight shaking in the ground. When I'd hear or feel these things, I'd say, "Three or four days from now there is going to be a storm." At first they had a hard time believing me—until they noticed that it happened as I said it would. Whenever a thunderstorm would come through the reservation, I would dress up in funny canvas clothes. I made these clothes myself and would only wear them during storms.

My grandfather became very concerned about me, so he went to a very powerful medicine man. This holy man told my grandfather, "If you want him to live a life like you do, then sit with him on the hill for one night." After thinking about it for several days, my grandfather took me to a hill, where the medicine man fixed a special place for us to sit.

On that night came one of the biggest and strongest storms that anyone had ever seen. Lightning and thunder surrounded us, and every time the lightning came, the whole world lit up. I could see a lot in that lightning. I could see into the future. When I told my grandfather this, he would say, "No, don't talk like that. Don't say those things. Those are very powerful things."

That night I took care of my grandfather because he was scared. I wasn't frightened at all. I enjoyed it. I felt good, really good for the first time in my life. I had felt safe sitting up there in that storm. I could hear invisible people laughing, crying, and singing. I could even hear dogs barking and children crying.

My grandfather prayed throughout the night, asking the storm to set me free. He wanted me to be an ordinary person. He wanted me to live a life without the responsibilities that come to one who is taken by the Thunder Beings.[1] He sang, cried, and prayed for them to have mercy for my life.

I must have fallen asleep at some point during the night because the next thing that I remembered was coming out of the purification lodge.[2] (See Figure 3.ii.) My grandmother and parents were in this lodge. What my grandfather had seen was interpreted.

They realized that while we were up on that hill, powers from the storm were drawing me to live as a heyoka, a contrary person—a person who does things backward. But they more or less erased this influence, and put things back in order for my life. Otherwise, I would have had to do everything backward: saying "yes" when I meant "no," saying "It's going to be good" when I meant "It's going to be bad," or "You're going to live a long life" when I knew you were going to die. The medicine man told my grandfather that I was going to be fine. I would no longer dress up in strange clothes and run around in front of a storm.

---

1 The Sioux believe that everything in this world has a spirit, so they refer to the spirits of the thunder as Thunder Beings.

2 Sometimes called a sweat lodge, or *inipi* by our people, the purification lodge cleanses our whole being and enables us to feel closer to the Creator. The lodge is a dome made of willow branches that is covered by hides and blankets. The inside (where a circle of people sit around a pit filled with steaming hot rocks) is completely dark. In this sacred space, prayers and ceremonies are conducted.

After this ceremony, I became scared of storms like everyone else. I no longer wore those strange clothes. I no longer danced in front of the storms. But I still had my relationship with the Thunder Beings.

Hearing the Call

Not long after that we went into some purification lodges and things started happening to me. I started to see things, feel things, and hear things. For a while, I thought I was going crazy because I'd hear people talk and then notice that no one was around.

One day I went hunting. The sun was barely up and I spent the day hunting, not returning until around three o'clock in the afternoon. I brought back a deer. We were taught to clean our own meat, so I cleaned it and hung it up. My mother, stepfather, and grandmother were all there when I came home.

I then lay down under the shade of a tree and fell asleep. Somebody started shaking me, and I woke up to hear them say, "They're coming now, get up! They're coming, get up!" I got up and noticed that the sun was shining. I looked around to see who had awakened me and couldn't see anyone. There was no one in the house, the car was gone, and no one was anywhere near.

I went over to the edge of the cliff to see if anyone was going down the river. Nobody. Then I heard someone say in our Lakota language, "Hurry up, they're coming now. Hurry up, they're coming."

I went back to my spot in the shade and waited. After a while, a car drove up with my mother, stepfather, and grandmother in it. My stepfather looked at me in a funny way, like he knew something about what had happened. I got up and we walked toward the sweat lodge, which was close to the cliff overlooking the river. He said in Lakota, "When are they coming?" I looked at him and replied, "They're coming soon." That's all I said. He looked at me and did not say another word.

Nobody came that day. I kept thinking about who was supposed to come. I asked my stepfather who was coming. He just smiled at me and walked away.

That whole year, when I was twelve going on thirteen years old, I kept hearing those voices. When I slept, someone would shake me, sometimes grabbing my feet, and then I would hear it: "You need to hurry, they're coming now, they're coming soon."

I finally told my grandmother, thinking that she might tell me something. She looked at me, shook her head, and looked down at the ground.

I became very frustrated. Everything began to frustrate me, so I walked around wondering why I heard these voices. A year went by and nothing happened.

The voices I used to hear went away after I got drunk in the cellar of the chapel at St. Joseph's Indian School. But they came back the following spring, during the month of April. They said the same thing over and over again: "You need to hurry, they're coming, they're coming soon."

I finally couldn't take it anymore. I went to my mother and stepfather and said, "I keep hearing voices and this is what they're saying. I'm going to go crazy if someone doesn't tell me what's going on." Finally my stepfather stood up and said, "Well, we're going to Pine Ridge. When we get back, get the lodge ready and we'll go in." My parents got up and left.

I stayed and went out to pick some wood and rocks for the purification lodge. All day long I hauled wood and rocks. I got everything ready. All they had to do was say a prayer and light a match.

Toward evening a big cloud of dust could be seen in the distance. A car was coming up the dry creek bed. A little while later another cloud of dust with another car came up. Fairly soon there were three cars coming. When my parents and stepfather arrived, they had a man by the name of Two Sticks with them. As soon as he saw me, he put his hands together and said, "I see you all the time, Grandson, I see you all the time. Every night when I pray I see you, just the way you are standing, just the way you now look. I come to see you."

They took him into the lodge and there my stepfather adopted me as his oldest son. He prayed with me, cried with me, and apologized for all the bad things that had happened to me under his care. He said, "I'm going to call you 'son' from this day forward. You are my son."

And then the old man Two Sticks said,

> Supernatural beings, we call them Grandfather
> Spirits, have chosen you to carry on the bundle that your
> father is carrying. The voices you have been hearing are
> their voices. They are coming to be with you. I am here
> to prepare you.
>
> Two things are going to happen in your life. Some
> day you are going to meet a man who is going to help
> bring the four colors[3] together. He will be one of
> the four colors who will pray for this world. We are
> destroying this world very slowly. Technology is actually
> setting us back. Things are now going backwards. Every
> time they want to build something that runs quickly or
> gets things done more quickly, a part of Mother Earth
> is destroyed. The natural order of our environment has
> been hurt. There is a day that will come when this man
> will come to you. He will tell you his dream about the
> four colors and you will know when he is coming because
> you will see him in a dream before you meet him. You
> will make preparations to bring the four colors together
> and pray for Mother Earth.
>
> The second thing that will happen to you in the
> future is that you will visit a white house in the east.
> There will be a day when you talk at that place.

Old man Two Sticks and my father used to get together every month
and talk to me. They talked about the awesome responsibility that was
coming my way. They told me how the sacred bundle that I was to take
care of would help our people.

---

[3] The four colors – red, yellow, black, and white – make reference to various sacred
characteristics including skin color.

Figure 3.1

The following June, they took me to this hill, wrapped me in a blanket, tied the blanket up, and laid me down for four days and nights. When they came on the fourth night, I was told to do a healing ceremony that same night. That is when I conducted my first Yuwipi ceremony.[4] All the old people came.

There I realized what those voices were talking about. They were preparing me to hold the sacred bundle, the Yuwipi bundle, that my step-father would pass over to me after he passed away. When I came down from that hill, everything was explained to me. Those voices stopped. They had come after me, and I had given my life to them. From that time on, my life no longer belonged to me. It belonged to the Creator.

---

[4] "The Yuwipi ceremony . . . is an ancient Sioux ritual used to cure, to learn which herbs to use for curing, to prophesy about the future, and to find things that are lost . . . I can communicate with spirits and tell what they say."
—Fools Crow, Spiritual leader of the Teton Sioux

Figure 3.2

Three days later I walked away from everyone because I was scared. There were many more lessons that life had to teach me before I would be able to pick up the bundle again and accept my responsibility.

I went back to search for my identity and found out that my grandfather, Jobe Holy Bull, had a father named Peter Holy Bull, whose father was a Brulé chief named Sacred Buffalo. I guess that when he was put in a reservation, the war department changed his name from Sacred Buffalo to Holy Bull. They wanted him to have a male name. Someday we hope to change it back to Sacred Buffalo.

The buffalo teaches us honesty, kindness, sharing, and courage. It has been told that the buffalo gives all of itself to us; not just the meat, but every part is given to help us live. He was so kind to give himself. He was sharing. He had the courage to give himself. Every part of that buffalo teaches us something. The skull looks like a woman's reproductive organs. That's why it is used to represent life. It is our altar.

Rita

In June of 1977, I met two men, Willard Greeley and Norman Red Wing. They introduced me to some people from Sisseton, South Dakota. We were in the Standing Rock Reservation near Mobridge where an

American Indian Movement (AIM) gathering was going on. There Willard and Norman offered me a pipe and asked me to go to Sisseton to do a naming ceremony.

We traveled to Sisseton and I did the name-giving ceremony for them. There I met a woman named Rita, and the following year we were married. We struggled in those beginning years. I would drink too much and be abusive. I worked as a traditional counselor at a minimum-security prison that the Native American Rights Fund developed. It became a political football and then someone kicked it out too far and we were all fired.

Rita left me many times. I was often drunk and would get thrown in jail. She finally filed for a divorce. And then something happened: we sat down and talked all night. We were honest with each other and decided to enter the purification lodge. We went through four days of purification. Finally, on the fourth day, we understood who we were and we were able to forgive each other. I haven't had a drink for twenty years now.

I don't think that anyone can do spiritual healing work without a companion. To be honest with you, without Rita I would be dead or in prison. I'm very fortunate to be with her. She has incredible patience. My calling is too much to do on my own. I need her help and the support of my family. Their love makes it possible to believe in miracles and to move forward into the challenges of each day.

Because of my healing with Rita, I was able to share a lot of things with my mother. I apologized to her for my misconduct and asked her for forgiveness. I told her that it never was her fault. I was able to go through ceremonies with her during her wake and funeral. I had made my peace with her and I didn't cry when she passed away.

I know that she is with us today. Her spirit helps us with our children and with all the kids that we work with in the community where we live. I know that my mother is here, working with Rita. She's here every day, standing right next to Rita and me.

I try to help others realize this. If we really understand our ceremony, the keeping of the soul, we understand that we are shown how to use the spirit, the soul, to help us strengthen ourselves, our families, and our communities. That's what that ceremony does for us. There is no need to mourn or grieve when you understand that when someone dies it is a gain, rather than a loss.

Sun Dance

The dancer lay on the ground, and the man who performed the operation, bending over him, lifted the flesh of the chest between his thumb and forefinger; then thrusting an awl through the flesh, he followed this with the insertion of the pointed stick. . . . The thongs by which a man was suspended were usually of a length permitting only his toes to touch the ground. . . . While the men were dancing, they prayed for all in the tribe, especially the sick and the old.

The dance enclosure was about fifty feet in diameter, with a wide entrance at the east. The sacred pole stood in the center of this circle, and about fifteen feet west of the pole a square of earth was exposed, all vegetation being carefully removed and the ground finely pulverized. The square of earth was called *owan, ka wankan,* "sacred place," and no one was allowed to pass between it and the pole. Two intersecting lines were traced within the square of earth, forming a cross, these lines being parallel to the sides of the square but not touching them. After tracing these lines in the soil, the intercessor filled the incisions [in the ground] with tobacco which had been offered to the sky, the earth, and the cardinal points . . . he placed bunches of downy white eagle feathers. Very beautiful was the contrast of green turf, soft brown earth, shining white lines, and downy eagle feathers. West of this was placed a bed of fresh sage, on which the buffalo skull would be laid during the ceremony.

—*Frances Densmore, 1918*

Sun Dance was one of the ceremonies that was meant to bring pain to the warriors, the men. I tell my sons that every nine seconds there's a woman someplace who is pushing, pushing, pushing—going through some awesome pain. They are pushing, pushing, pushing, and through that pain a life comes into this world.

The same happens to you as a man in the Sun Dance. You pierce through that tree and you pull, pull, pull, until you break away from that wall of pain. Men a long time ago did this so that the Creator could put their lives back in order. In this way, their family's life was also put back in order.

Long ago men painted themselves black because they were ashamed to show their face to the Creator. They may have been ashamed because they took a life or maybe they hurt a life. In these four days of dancing, they try to break away from that shame and pain.

Sun Dance is a ceremony that also teaches us that in years past there was no such thing as an enemy. No one had an enemy. I speak fluent Lakota and in the traditional form, before it became a biblical version, there was no word for enemy. In the biblical version of our language, there's a word that is said to mean enemy—*tokah*. But this word simply means a people who are different. That is, they have different ways.

Today a lot of people use the Sun Dance to heal themselves from the enemies of disease, whether it be diabetes, cancer, tuberculosis, heart problems, and so on. People come to free themselves from these things in our sacred circle of dance.

Women also dance today for the same purpose. Years ago women weren't allowed to dance the Sun Dance, because they went through enough pain when they brought life into this world. It wasn't a rule or regulation established by men; it was just something that women understood. They felt that it was unnecessary for them to undergo four days of pain because they already had that lesson in childbirth. Today women dance because they want to be well, whether it is mental, physical, or spiritual health. And men dance for the same reason—to be well.

In 1978, Rita, my mother, and I went to Green Grass to participate in their annual Sun Dance—*Wi wanyang wacipi*. On the first day, they had a special pipe ceremony at the place where they keep the sacred calf pipe. They asked all the men dancers to line up on one side and all the women on another side. Then Orval Looking Horse, the keeper of the sacred pipe, brought out the bundle. An altar was made and they put the pipe on it. A medicine man named Martin High Bear did the pipe ceremony.

I sat down near the drum with the singers. We started to sing the songs that they wanted. During the second song, I started to have a nosebleed and it wouldn't stop. It just kept coming and coming. One of the singers, Ben Black Bear, Sr., looked at me and handed me some sage. He rolled it up and put it in both sides of my nose. I stood up with that sage in my nostrils and looked to the sky while saying a prayer. I saw the strangest thing: a white eagle was flying above. I then looked at the singers and they looked up and acknowledged that they were seeing it, too. That was the first time I ever saw an all-white eagle.

The next day, as we were getting ready to go to the dance, we gathered the sage to wear around our heads as a crown. My uncle came over to the camp and said that the old man Fools Crow wanted to see me.

I made myself ready and followed him over there. Fools Crow was sitting under the shade of a tree and greeted me as "Grandson." He went on to say, "I usually have a bunch of men to help me, but they're not here." He gave me a pipe and asked me to pray while I smoked it. He wanted me to help him run that Sun Dance. I became very scared. I was worried because the Sun Dance is a very, very serious thing, so serious that my family wouldn't even talk about it. I didn't know what to do.

Fools Crow had so much spiritual energy around him that it wasn't easy to get close to him. Whenever he looked at you, it felt like he was looking right through you. However, he knew who you were, and this helped make you believe in yourself whenever he asked you to do something for him.

He looked at me in a deeply reassuring way and said, "Do not worry, my Grandson." He stared into my eyes and slowly spoke these words: "When you were sixteen, you were already told that these things were going to happen. You were told that they were coming and that you must be ready. Grandson, they are here now." The next morning I brought the Sun Dancers in under the leadership of Fools Crow. He looked at me and said, "Okay, now take over. I'm going to sit down and watch you and the dancers. I'll pray with you and cry with you."

After that I helped him conduct that Sun Dance for the next three years, from 1978 through 1980. In 1981, after I came home to Sisseton, my friend Norman Red Wing and I adopted each other in a ceremony. We met with Dale Crawford and Ed Red Owl and decided that we wanted to have our own Sun Dance. We prepared throughout the whole year. I was afraid and scared to do it on my own and I told them, "I don't think that I can do this." They offered me the pipe and asked that I do it for them. I immediately went to see Fools Crow. I asked him, "Can I run the Sun Dance?" I told him what they wanted me to do and that they had insisted. He replied, "Go on the hill. Go on the top of the hill, sit there, cry, and pray. Talk to God. Talk to the Creator. That's where you will find all the answers for you. Only listen to them. I might tell you to go ahead and run off a cliff. It is they who have the answers for you."

I went on the hill the following spring before we had the Sun Dance. For two days I struggled with myself on top of that hill. I really struggled because I truly felt unworthy to do this on my own without someone like Fools Crow. He had helped me for three years at Green Grass. There I felt secure because I knew he was always there to answer or protect whatever went on in the lodge.

For two days I struggled deeply. I rolled around, sat up, stood up, got on my knees, cried, screamed, and hollered. And finally, on the third morning, I heard something from the north—I heard a man singing. He was singing a song about the Sun Dance. I knew the song was about the Sun Dance because when he started singing I noticed the morning star. The morning star started to dance when he sang.

I stood up and looked toward the morning star and tried to pay attention to the words of the song while noticing what the star was doing. The morning star was dancing across the whole sky. It would go toward the south bar of the circle and then come back up, all the way to the far north end of the circle. Then it would start going down and disappear, but only to come up again. It kept doing this. I began feeling good about what had been asked of me, to run the Sun Dance, and to conduct it for my brothers and sisters.

The previous fear—the feelings of being afraid, scared, lonely, and hopeless—went away. As I heard that song get louder and louder, I knew someone was getting closer and closer to me. I began to get scared again. This was a different kind of fear because I was afraid of who was singing the song. Perhaps it was a skeleton that was singing. I made my complete circle of prayers. I was standing west praying, and then I went to the north to pray. He started to sing again and I heard something talk from the east tree, the tree of life that we had put there as the altar. The tree spoke to me, "Look, my Grandson, look. Look who is singing. They are bringing you a song."

I looked and at first I didn't see anything. But then I noticed I was standing on a narrow ridge, the kind of ridge that is seen throughout the Badlands. The end of the ridge turned into a perfectly round hill. There I saw a coyote sitting there singing that song. When I noticed that it was a coyote, the coyote began hollering, the way all coyotes holler. The song turned into the coyote's holler.

That coyote faced north and then turned east toward me. When it turned, it had a black flap across its face, white on its eyes. Then a remarkable transformation took place.

A human form stood up and said to me, "This is the song you will use to conduct the Sun Dance. With this song, you will walk with your relatives into the sacred circle to take on an awesome responsibility. Know that there is a great price that you must pay to the Creator for the song that will help you."

Yuwipi and Other Ceremonies

Sometimes I think back to my childhood and remember all the ceremonies that took place. It seems that there was a ceremony going on every week and sometimes every night. There was one old medicine man who would conduct his ceremony with light in the room. They would leave an oil lamp burning while he did his work. A lot of things would happen in the room during that time. Gourds would be flying around and it used to scare me as a child. Yet I always felt comfortable and secure in the presence of those sacred elders.

When I was around eight years old, Charlie Kills Ree did a ceremony to bring back spirits. It was very scary. I remember when my grandmother Fannie Black Spotted Horse had a brother who passed away. After the funeral, we went to Red Scaffold and immediately held a ceremony. Charlie Kills Ree was the man conducting it. There, my grandmother's dead brother, Frank Black Spotted Horse, walked into the room. He talked and breathed in the same way that he had when he was alive. He was a heavyset man, and he had a wheezing sound when he breathed. It scared me.

Even though we got scared, when the ceremony was over we found that we had a very calm feeling, and everyone seemed happier. No one complained or was irritable. The ceremony had brought peace into our lives.

I also remember being worked on by Charlie Kills Ree. He would put a black cloth over his face, tie his hands behind his back, and then stand in the center of the room. As children we were told to be mindful of our elders. Charlie told us to take care of each other and to mind our parents. These things were told to us in ceremonies.

One of the most powerful holy men was Two Sticks. He was short and very old. He had a stick that he walked with. People had to help him get to the sweat lodge, the altar, and the ceremonies. When he came to me when I was a boy, I really felt loved and cared for in his presence. He gave me two powerful prophecies about my life. He also warned me about what would happen if I didn't follow the right road. He warned me about prison and that I would lose my first marriage. He said that prison and the loss of my marriage would happen if I didn't follow through with what the voices were telling me to do with my life. I didn't, so those things happened. Two Sticks was very strict, but he was also very kind. That's what I remember about him.

There are many kinds of ceremonies. There are those when our people come together to ask for certain help from the Creator, to help put their lives back in order.

There is a ceremony for the time when young girls who are going through puberty come into the lodge. Women come in and tell the girls about what's happening to their bodies. It lasts four days. The girls are told about becoming a woman, and many things are shared. Materials are brought to them to make dresses as they sit there in the lodge. They are told about how to be a part of family life. We celebrate how important each young woman is to the whole community.

There are ceremonies for making relatives, where you receive a name and are made a relative with someone. This also takes four days. During that time, men and women talk to you, telling you how important you are in the community. You are told that once you receive your new name, you will be given a special place in the community, and you will become a helper. You agree that no one in the community will ever be orphaned and that no one will ever go hungry. All these things are taught to you before you get your name.

There are other ceremonies. For instance, you can adopt a person when you see someone who has the same characteristics, personality, looks, or nature as your own relatives. In ceremony you ask them to become part of your family. Then you take care of them as if they were true relatives.

Yuwipi

Yuwipi is a form of ceremony where you call spirits to be part of the healing. They can be called to help us heal cancer, diabetes, leukemia, tuberculosis, and heart disease. These are very powerful, very ancient healing ceremonies, dating from before Columbus touched the East Coast. During the ceremony, in the old times, we used to wrap ourselves up in black-tailed deer skins, but now we use blankets. We used the black-tailed deer skin back then because you could breathe through its hide. That's why it's sometimes said that the ceremony is from the black-tailed deer (or the mule deer as it's called today).

It's not a ceremony that you plan. If we were sitting here and someone came to us who was very sick and wanted to have this ceremony, we'd do it right away. Whether it was light or dark in the room, we'd do it.

The first Yuwipi ceremony that I did for healing was for my wife, Rita. She was the first one. Before that I did the *Luwapi* spirit-calling ceremony where I was not tied up. There you simply call the spirits. In Yuwipi you are tied up and the spirits come and untie you.

When my wife was diagnosed with cancer in her womb, we were advised to send her to the University Hospital in Minneapolis. She didn't want to go. She wanted to go through Yuwipi. She was the first one that I got tied up for. I wasn't scared of the Yuwipi. I was scared for her. I did the best I could, and she is still with us today.[5] A week after the four-night ceremony, she went back to the doctors to get tested and they found that there was no cancer. She likes to tell this story.

Once a fourteen-year-old boy had a brain tumor and was told that he had six months to live. We did a ceremony for him. We worked on him for four nights. He lived, and three years later he fell down the stairs in his home while carrying the laundry. He was rushed to the hospital where all the doctors were busy talking and consulting their books. His mother became worried and asked what was going on. The doctors told her that the boy should have died three years ago with a tumor in his brain. They were trying to find an explanation as to why his tumor went away. She didn't want to tell them that he went through a ceremony.

The first time I conducted a purification lodge, or *inipi,* was at Bear Butte. Some people asked me to do it and I said, "I don't know if I can." "You could try," they replied. I knew the songs and I had watched my stepfather very closely. I did know all the necessary steps and proce-dures. So I did it.

However, I did so feeling very unsure and afraid of what might hap-pen. If the spirits came in, I wasn't sure what to do or what to say. We went into that sweat lodge and everyone prayed and sang. I didn't see anything, but I felt good. When it was over, we came out and prepared a meal by the camp. Everyone shared their experiences and mentioned all the things

---

5 Rita passed away a few years after the publication of the *Profiles of Healing* book about Gary.

that had happened in there. I must have been preoccupied, for everyone else saw many things. They heard voices and experienced powerful revelations. They saw the blue spark-like lights of the spirits as well as other things. I hadn't seen a thing because I was worrying over what I would do if something happened. All I did was sing and pray for them in the way that I had been taught as a child. That was my first experience.

Spirit often presents itself as a light, whether it be as bluish or white sparks or a mellow glow of warm light. I've been told that this is lightning. The lightning that comes to the ground is blue, whereas the lightning that comes off the ground is reddish yellow. And then there is that light in the clouds, the light that glows. It's showing its power in a way that lets us know what it can do.

In the Yuwipi ceremony, people sometimes get touched by flying gourds. Sometimes we are picked up by the shirt collar or feel feathers brush our skin.

There are different spirits that come into the lodge: some are in human form, others are in the form of the eagle, hawk, owl, robin, blackbird, and meadowlark. And then there are the four-legged ones such as the black bear, buffalo, elk, black-tailed deer, and sometimes the coyote. Some people see them in ceremony. Usually small, innocent children have no difficulty seeing them. Some adults will see them, while others won't. Little children will often say, "Uncle Gary, all those little buffaloes were running around again."

There are a lot of things that I want to say to my relatives, particularly my Lakota people. Every one of us has a spirit. We have to bring that spirit together to make a ceremony happen, to make medicine for the sick ones. Know that your life does not belong to you. Your life belongs to the Creator and every human spirit out there. Whether it's black or white or red or yellow, it belongs to the same Creator.

Today my father is present as a spirit in my ceremonies. Thirteen years ago he wasn't because I didn't allow him to be there. I was still too angry at him. But today, yes, he is there. I hear him sometimes before we start. I'll hear him singing his favorite song. Then I'll start the ceremony with that song.

Figure 3.3

The pipe is one of our most sacred instruments. Our word for the sacred pipe is *Chanupa*, which means two sticks. It refers to the stem that comes from the tree of life and the stone that represents Mother Earth. The stone that turned itself into this world is held by the tree of life. It is very sacred to smoke through this pipe. The tobacco that we use is from the bark of the red willow tree. There's also a root that we dig called bear root, and it really smells sweet. Then there's a little green tree with a shiny green leaf. You take these three things, put them together, and you get our tobacco. This smoke gives you a good feeling. It is not hallucinogenic, but is a natural medicine that helps us pray. It doesn't give you a head rush like Marlboros do, but it provides a good feeling that makes you feel very comfortable, relaxed, and more mindful of the presence of the Creator. This is the sacred quality of our tobacco. It helps bring all good spirits together—your spirit, my spirit, everybody's spirit is connected when you smoke this.

One of the most sacred instruments in our culture is the drum. We use it at all of our gatherings and ceremonies. The drum has to be there. The drum is made from a sacred four-legged animal, whether it be the deer, the elk, or the buffalo. The hide has a spirit so that when you make a drum out of a hide, it becomes a very sacred act. The drum beat is the spirit of the animal and it helps bring our spirit out. It carries the voice of God because it is from God's creation. The four-legged one gave its life so we could use its hide and spirit to bring forth a good feeling for our ceremonies.

Sacred Wisdom

Hanbelachia is a time for fasting, praying, and literally crying for a sacred vision that will give your life direction and help bring healing to your community. When you go off to do a vision quest, be wholehearted, open-minded, brave, and very patient. The most important preparation you can make is to remain mindful of God's creation. Simply be mindful that this world is a sacred creation. Everything has a spirit and everything can talk to you while you're out there all alone.

I learned to pray by listening to my grandparents and my mother. I always tell people that I learned a different kind of prayer than the prayer normally heard in the lodge today. The kind of prayer I learned was the kind where you felt that you were actually talking to somebody, sending a voice to someone. Today I hear prayers that sound like begging—they ask for pity from the Creator. The prayers that I grew up hearing were different. They said, "This is me, and I am asking you to do the best for this man or woman who is lying there because he or she is sick."

In this kind of prayer, you talk to someone rather than beg for something. My father, mother, stepfather, and grandmother could really pray. I heard them pray every morning and every evening. Their prayers often were answered. I used to hear them say, "Although there are so many white men and they think they have us in their hands, we will survive."

And their prayers were answered. Their way did survive.

Before a ceremony, I tell each and every person there that they should talk to their spirit and ask it to talk to the Greater Spirit. These things are sacred. The Greater Spirit and each person's spirit move by themselves. Like the wind, spirit moves by itself. When people bring their spirits together, there is great movement, great energy. It's one of the most awesome feelings we can experience. When you bring spirits together, things will move by themselves, things will happen, you can see into the beyond, and hear the unheard.

I think that everything is sacred. Old man Fools Crow would pray in the basement of a metal shanty, and it would be like praying in the middle of the most beautiful place in the middle of the prairie.

We should never forget that wherever we pray, that spot becomes the center of the universe for that moment. Sacred sites, however, are those places we consider particularly sacred. We go there to replenish ourselves and to revisit their prophecies. These places include Bear Butte and the Great Medicine Wheel.

When we go there, the animal spirits are there. Everything that grows there—the plants, the flowers, the roots—can be used for medicinal purposes. The mountains at a sacred site talk to us and help us revisit the old prophecies that were told thousands of years ago. They help us live in a way that will not destroy the world. That's why we need to preserve these places. Our people need to go there. Our ancestors' bones are there and many of their medicine bundles rest with them.

I have never disrespected a white person's church or temple. We ask the same respect—that our natural churches, the sacred sites of earth, be respected as the holy temples that they truly are. When you visit them, say something that acknowledges this holiness and you will walk away with a better understanding of who you really are. The next time you come back, you will find a part of you waiting for you.

Many of our sacred instruments are being sold or kept in museums or private collections. Healers use them to bring spiritual energies for healing. However, there is a powerful price that must be paid to have these things. This price has nothing to do with money, but has everything to do with responsibility. Its price is not a million dollars, but your life. Your life is always the cost with spiritual things. Ask the higher power how you should respectfully relate to a spiritual instrument.

Keep it in a very special place. Do not desecrate it by public display. It is for healing.

No matter how much you pay for these things, natural law will affect everyone who is near to it. Natural law is the law that we don't see or feel until it comes to us. It is the Creator who corrects things. This is natural law. Look at what happens when storms destroy what people materially value—their boats, houses, cars, and things. They are destroyed by natural law.

I remember when I was five years old and a storm came that forced us to go into a cellar. The Yuwipi men stood outside, praying with their pipes. They sang songs while the storm came toward them. Storms like that are very destructive. They can create conflict within yourself. But at the same time, if you talk to that storm, the storm can be kind. That's what we were taught, and from this I have learned kindness.

Caring for a bundle is a spiritual calling. It's something that you are chosen to do, and with this responsibility is the custom of not asking for payment. Sometimes this causes great hardship for our families.

Prior to 1942, everyone took care of their healers and medicine people. They understood the sacrifices that they made. Today, unfortunately, too many people feel that giving a K-Mart blanket is a sufficient offering for seeking spiritual help. It's a very difficult life that we live. We have to pay bills, have a home, drive a car, and place groceries on the table.

I was always told to ask for nothing. If a person asks you to do a ceremony, they will give you what is needed. The Creator helps you in this way. When you seek the help of a spiritual person, think about the price they pay to help you.

I was taught that you should give to others because the Creator will return it to you. You will get twice as much back as you put out for others. You give because you have compassion for children and for families.

Here's the advice I give to others who want to know how to approach a medicine person. First, don't call them. Go find them, no matter how far you have to drive. Then offer them some tobacco. This is called a binding ceremony. Then tell him or her what you need. Don't insult him by leaving a skull of an animal, a seashell, or a feather, because his family doesn't

Figure 3.4

eat animal skulls or seashells. If you don't want to leave money, then buy some groceries, or some fuel oil for his stove. Don't insult him with five dollars. Give in proportion to the value of what is being done for your life. Show your sincere appreciation. Demonstrate your compassion to the Creator through generosity and sharing. In the old days, a family would give up several horses to be healed. What price is enough for your life?

Natural law teaches us that there are four basic values that we must embrace. They are taught to us by the four winds: kindness, honesty, sharing, and courage. It's so simple that it is difficult. This is because so many things try to convince us that there's more to life than these four values. Simply be kind, honest, sharing, and courageous. That's it.

GUARANI SHAMANS
OF THE FOREST

Introduction to *Guarani Shamans of the Forest*
by Bradford Keeney

The Guarani of Paraguay and Brazil live in some of the largest subtropical forests in the world. Most of the Guarani population—around fifteen thousand of the total—live in eastern Paraguay and are anthropologically divided into three groups: the Chiripa, the Paitavytera, and the Mbya. The Chiripa, who are the subject of this book, call themselves *Ava-kue* (men) and *Kuna-ngue* (women), or simply *Ava-Guarani, Guarani,* or *Ka'aguygua* (inhabitants of the forest). The Guarani live in eastern Paraguay, in the area between the Jejui Guaza, Corrientes, and Acaray rivers. Their present population is estimated at five thousand individuals.

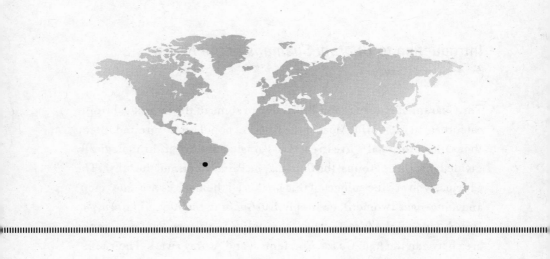

Ava Tapa Miri

My soul-name or Guarani name is Ava Tape Miri, which means little seagull man. The name white people know me by is Florencio Portillo. I live in Communidad Fortuna in Paraguay. I am the community's chief shaman.

One of my earliest memories is from when I was five years old. I remember my father as an important shaman. In my mind I can still see him dancing. That is my first memory. He was a community leader who tried very hard to make our culture survive. He wanted to have our culture stay alive in our minds so that it will be passed on to our future generations. My father was a spiritually strong man and he made me strong. Traditional Guarani culture is strong in me because of my father.

During his time, the Guarani had more freedom. We did not face other cultures invading our way of life. Prior to the revolution, sometime before the late 1940s, all we had was the dance and our ceremonies. And that was all that we needed.

In 1947, my father became sick. His belly grew very large. After a year of illness and suffering, he died. At that time I truly felt abandoned. I was in a village near the Jejui River. All the families living there suffered a great loss because he was their protector. He was the main shaman of the village.

My uncle also lived in this area. He came and took us to his home. He knew we were all alone and feeling sad. In our culture, when someone dies, we know that their family must be relocated so that they can heal from their grief. We moved because of my uncle. There, my older brother built a house. My mother and brother also moved there, and we lived near a small river called the Ibicui. Later, the land of our new home became Communidad Fortuna. An old shaman named Ciriaco Vera lived in this place.

I was the last son of my father's family. I deeply missed my father after his death. I felt a deep loss, because he had spoiled me with much attention. It was a new beginning for us when my mother, brother, and I started out in our new home. I lived with them for about six or seven years.

When I was nearly fifteen years old, I went off with a Paraguayan man who took me to work in the herb fields. I left home and threw myself into physically challenging work because I felt my life had no meaning. In the fields I met someone who became a good friend. He listened to me as I talked about my sadness for the first time. He was an Indian man and he understood what had happened to me.

Some Paraguayan men would occasionally come into the wilderness. Two of them were very bad. They were professional killers who killed for money. A woman who owned a liquor store told me about them and warned me to take care of myself because they were dangerous. At the time, I owned a machete and an ax, but I began thinking about how to get a shotgun and a knife. I figured out a way and I got hold of these weapons.

One day many people sat together in her liquor store that was also a bar. One of the bad men walked up to me and said, "I need to talk to you. Come with me." I was very afraid because I knew that anything might happen. I followed him, and then I noticed that the other bad man was following us. I walked with my hand on the gun and said to them, "What do you want?" I pretended to be brave.

The first bad man said, "Take it easy. We've been watching you and we like the kind of man you are." After telling me that they liked me, they told me that they were killers. They said that they rob places and kill people as a way of making lots of money. They then asked me, to my great surprise, to join them as outlaws. All I could think was that I knew nothing about their way of life. I was simply a child of nature. But I liked the feeling that came over me when they told me these things. It made me feel strong like a grown man, and at that time, macho men ruled. I accepted their offer and I went off with them because being around them, I felt like a strong man and I liked that feeling.

They told me to watch a certain person so they could figure out how to kill him. I did it. If they had wanted me to kill, I was ready.

This was how things were, and on one Saturday afternoon, we went to the hangout where alcohol was sold. Looking around, I saw a guitar and a violin on the counter. Musicians with their instruments gathered because the people wanted to dance. The three of us walked in and sat in separate places. We were watching over the entire place and keeping a protective eye on each other.

During the dance, one of our men got up to dance with a beautiful woman. Within minutes her boyfriend noticed and he jumped up and took her away from the dancing. A big problem was beginning. After the next song, the man returned to the same woman, even though her boyfriend was standing next to her. The boyfriend refused to let him dance with her. At that point, everyone could feel that something was about to happen there.

On the third song, the same thing started to happen again. The boyfriend did not back down. He refused to let the outlaw dance with his girlfriend. The outlaw took out his gun and shot him dead. The bullet went right through his heart. As I watched, I prepared myself for a big fight.

Four men who were friends of the murdered man came over and asked who the killer was. We said nothing. And then it began. Bullets flew all over the place. It seemed that everyone in the bar was shooting. I don't know whether I killed anyone or not that day, but many people died.

My partners and I knew that we had to disappear. There were only two choices for me—flee across the Paraguayan border and live in exile in Brazil or go back to my village. I went back home to my village. I returned home when I was eighteen years old and I've never left.

I want to mention that when I was living with the outlaws, I started feeling the call of the spirits. My father began appearing in my dreams.

He set a crown of feathers on my head—the corona that all shamans wear. He also placed all the shamanic ornaments on my body and a sacred rattle in my hand. It was in dreams that my father taught me how to make these things. Sometimes he sang to me and said, "I am leaving this song for you." My father always came from the East, where the song originates and where it is also the home of God.

My father told me many things in my dreams, even how my family was worrying about him. After this I knew that I was a changed man. I was taught not to eat particular oils and meats. These dreams also brought me sadness by reminding me of the original commitment I had made to my father and to my culture. I felt completely alone.

I cried all night long during this period of intense dreaming. It was the beginning of my new life. I was now a young man and, after I returned to the village, I began dancing and singing all the time. I was filled with the spirits and a new life.

Weeks passed, and my father came to me in another dream. He said, "Your entire family must support you, so you can do the shamanic work." I wasn't sure what to do next, but I felt a strong inner sense that said I should go on a journey to a certain village far away. There I met the four shamans of that community. I did not know them until I arrived. Of the four men, the most powerful shaman was Ascurra, whose Guarani name means, "he who comes from God."

There were many people in that community, and every afternoon they went to the temple to pray. These shamans helped me a lot by talking to me for long periods of time. When a shaman is talking to you, he or she is giving you soul. Their words are soul, and this is what the Guarani Indians call "word souls."[1] The four shamans also had me drink

---

[1] *Ayvu*, "word soul," is the principal aspect of Guarani life. Word souls are realized when your heart is touched by the spirit and you are moved to express yourself through speech. It is so pure that when it comes to you through your body, it gives pure wisdom and truth. If you don't act right and you break the harmony between your body and the word souls, community, and nature, you may possibly die. The source of the word souls is the main God and the minor gods. The ancestors do not carry the word souls. The word souls of the shaman bring harmony. Each person can and should bring word souls to one another. This is the life of the community.

the juice of the cedro tree and *chicha*[2], the sacred drink we use in our ceremonies. They also wet my chest with these juices, because it is one of the ways of getting closer to our souls. These shamans prepared me for my new life of living by the guidance of the spirits.

After I began praying and dancing a lot, I had a dream that four dead shamans came to me from the West, where the sun goes down. When I say that they came from the West, I mean that their spirits came from that sacred direction. Each spirit gave me a song. I didn't know these shamans when they were human beings on earth. They only came to me in my dream.

These shamans spoke to me: "We come from where the real father lives. He is the one who sent us to you." Among the Guarani gods, one God is the principal God. He is like the president of all the smaller gods. He is the one who sent the shamans in my dream. They went on to say, "We have come from the Big God. We are here to carry you with us." Then they took me to another place. I felt as though I had died and I was seeing things from another world. I was taken to a large field not of this earth. It is in another place in space. There were many birds that ate special fruits. The shaman spirits said, "Now that you know this place, you should listen to this song." They then sang a sacred song as I watched the sunset.[3] A very bright light came to me, and then spirits who had human-like bodies arrived. These spirits were the word souls of our culture. They took me to the chief shaman, who showed me how to baptize people. He gave me the power to be a strong shaman. Finally he said, "We will now send you back to earth where you will stay awhile to help others." Then the four shaman spirits brought me back home.

After this vision, I started baptizing people into the Guarani spiritual life. I baptized all children, as it is necessary. To a shaman, anyone who he or she loves is his child. We shamans want to baptize everyone

---

[2] *Chicha* is a fermented beverage that has a mild intoxicating effect and is often used in Guarani ceremonial life.

[3] Without exception, a Guarani cannot be a shaman without receiving a song from a sacred vision.

we love to protect them and bring them into the spirit.[4] My big dream taught me how to baptize others and made me ready and wanting to do this for my people.

After this big dream, I ate very little. The impact of the dream made me feel like fasting. I only desired wild roots, berries, *chicha*, corn porridge, honey, and water. During that intense time, only these simple things are meant to be eaten.

I am now going to tell you a very sacred story. It is usually told in song. It is a very powerful story. It is dangerous to hear if you don't listen carefully. This story carries much spiritual truth. It is not nonsense. It speaks in the most ancient way.

The spirits told me about the beginning of the world. I heard how the plants, animals, and oceans were made. The spirits also told me about the first shaman. His name was Paragua. He lived near the region now known as Asunción, Paraguay. He was a great chief and shaman. This renowned shaman left the world the way it was in nearly perfect condition. He wanted to stay on earth, but he was not allowed to remain. He had too much of the divine inside him. He had so much love in his heart and light in his head that he could not remain on earth. He also knew that the earth would become ugly and filled with problems caused by humans.

Paragua started our sacred singing and dancing. Paragua said, "We have to live the sacred way and walk to the East." This is where he and the spirits went. Before he left, Paragua said, "If you live according to the sacred tradition, you won't lose planet earth."

He left many lessons for all people—white, black, yellow, and Indian. We should follow his advice, but we are not listening. When we don't follow the path, many bad things start to happen. This happens to the missionaries who come to us with silent hatred in their hearts. They

---

[4] The Guarani baptism is a ceremony, sometimes lasting most of an evening, in which a person is given a soul-name or Guarani forest name. This name enables you to be recognized by the Guarani spirit world. The ceremony varies from shaman to shaman, but typically it includes being sprinkled by holy water and holding a burning candle while the community dances, sings, and prays.

divide our communities and disrupt our old sacred ways. Now we must start from a new beginning to see if we can make things better. The world is getting worse, but if we dance and pray, there is hope. We can recover if we dance, but otherwise, the world will end. Through our dance and prayer, we can help clean up the world.

According to our cultural knowledge, white people poisoned the waters of the world. Indian people did not poison the water. White people don't understand the earth as we do, and this ignorance leads to earth's destruction. All the bad things that human beings do to earth also go up to the sun and cause harm to it. The bad things we do always hurt the sun. When we do something wrong, we may not feel it, but the spirits know it. This is because the spirits are more sensitive than we are.

If we don't improve ourselves in the next fifty years, the world's problems will become extremely critical. It is important that the shamans around the world be contacted and asked what they know. It is the shamans who can guide us. There is not enough contact between the shamans. They carry the pain of the world and they need each other for support. Shamans know how to help each other. They help initiates by blowing on them in a special way. This cleanses them and leaves them with a spiritual gift. When something comes to a shaman in a dream, it leaves them with something. Perhaps it's a sacred song, a way to find a medicine, or how to make something sacred. This is the spirit's gift to us.

Those who carry the pain of others hold the power to heal. It is the price of being a healer. It is an impossible role, but it must be done so that others may survive. Please pray for us and know that we are here to help the earth continue.

Tupa Nevangayu

My soul-name or Guarani forest name is Tupa Nevangayu, which means "the one that comes from the Gods." My white name is Guillermo Rojas. I live in Communidad Acaraymi, where I am the community's chief shaman. It is not far from the great waterfalls, which was where the Mbya Guarani once lived. Their temples were like ours except once the doors were closed, no air could get inside. The smoke became very thick in their ceremony because they used a lot of tobacco. They wouldn't let you into their temples unless you had a good heart. You could not enter their temple unless you were asked to do so. This is the Guarani way.

Like Ava Tape Miri, I am an Ava-kue-Chiripa Guarani. In our tradition, we must follow the teachings of the shaman. Some people are chosen to be a shaman, while others do not have this destiny. The shamans carry the word souls that are made for everybody, but only some are ready to receive the word souls.

I can remember back to when I was five years old. I used to wake up in the morning and drink maté, our special herbal drink.[5] We drank it every day. We didn't have any schools back then. Every morning my mother and father gave me the lessons I needed. This was true for all Guarani children.

On Saturdays, we would gather together in a temple. The shaman placed us in two lines — one for women and the other for men. He then talked to each group. Then we danced for two to three days in a row. There used to be very big temples. There are fewer Guarani today, so our temples are smaller. The shaman would make a farm close to the temple. The whole community worked on the shaman's farm, and the food was shared by the entire community. The single men and women were told by the shaman to look for our firewood. The grandmothers taught the others how to cook. The shaman lay in his hammock and told everyone what to do. He was in charge of all the daily life around the temple.

We would make chicha, our sacred drink, with corn and sweet potatoes. Honey was added to make a meal. When I was a little boy, we didn't use spoons or forks. We also didn't use any salt in our food. We used part of a coconut shell as a spoon. I also remember using a corn cob to dip into honey. That's how we ate that sweet delight.

Again, the chief of the village was always the shaman. Back then there was no political leader like there is today. The shaman gave instructions

---

[5] This tea is made from a native plant, called yerba maté (*Ilex paraguayensis*), which contains a large amount of caffeine. The Guarani often add medicinal bark and leaves to it and boil the mixture in water.

in how to live. For instance, he might tell four to five people to go into the forest to hunt for some meat or search for some honey. We always danced before a hunt so we could see if it was good to hunt that day or whether we should wait.

Through the sacred song, we were able to see and guide everything. Because of our simple way of life, we were closer to nature. It was easier for the spirits to bring the sacred songs to us. This was the way God wanted us to live. Now we are the last people left living this way. The elder shamans of today are the last ones who are carrying the old culture. Unfortunately, now we can no longer reach the same spiritual level that our ancestors attained. We are only a remnant of the way they used to live. We are the last ones of an ancient tradition.

In the past, villages used to regularly visit each other. Each community took turns making chicha, and then everyone came together for a great gathering. In this way, the villages knew one another by meeting on a regular basis. I also remember that as a child, I was taught to make and set up a trap to catch animals for food. The grandmothers taught the children how to make hammocks and other handicrafts. It was the grandmothers who taught how to pound the plants into powder and to cook our meals.

Everyone was invited when there was a wedding. During the wedding, there was a lot of dancing. The shamans gave advice to the couple during the dance. The grandfather shaman and grandmother shaman told them that they could only be separated by death. "From now on," they said, "you are responsible for your life. You must make a small farm because your children will want to eat all the time." Back then it was our custom to have the boyfriend set up a small hut on a farm ground before he got married.

It used to be that all community meetings were held in the temple, and all activities were organized and supervised by the shaman. Some of the villagers were told to check the traps every day. All kinds of animals, big and small, were caught for food. Once the animals were caught, they were brought to the temple. Each animal has its spirit protector, and the shaman had to oversee the spiritual situation. Afterward, the community came together to dance, and then everyone ate.

No one hid their food. It was always shared. If a neighbor did not go on a hunt, they would still get a piece of meat that others caught. As a child, I lived near a river, and we speared for fish. When we caught a lot of fish on a stick, we went from house to house giving everyone some fish. But always, we had to dance before we ate. That's the way we did things back then.

When we did a blessing for the fruits, all the fruits were brought to the temple, even those we didn't eat. We did this every year and we still do it today. We don't use any chemicals on our farms. Instead, we pray and respect nature. During this particular ceremony, the shaman tells the community how to tend to the plants. He tells us how to live with nature and with each other. We do this to attain *mbiroy*—harmony with all. Mbiroy is the ideal ecological balance we strive for. This is the purpose of our life—to reach mbiroy. With this understanding, we realize that all the fruits we eat are both a food and medicine.

When I dance and shake my rattle, I am able to see things. Even the act of holding a rattle helps me to see. When I hold my rattle, I am holding a piece of the great holy rattle of the sky. When I pray, I hear what is going to happen to another person. Chicha is also very important, because it gives a deep holy goodness to our body, helping us to achieve mbiroy.

When I put myself into a prayerful attitude, I speak with great humility, acknowledging that I am nothing as a person. I confess that I am simple flesh made of dirt. This attitude helps to make me a cradle for the soul. For the Guarani, the word souls are the main thing. I am only a medium for the spirits who carry the word souls. We bring forth word souls for the good of the world.

I always need four helpers to pray with me and four women to sing during our ceremonies. *Takua ry'apu*, the hollow bamboo instrument, makes a very holy sound during the dance when the women pound it on the ground.

When I pray, the great God listens and tells the minor gods to pay attention to what I am asking. I must be very strong in the moment when the minor gods come to me. That's when the helpers must be there to support me with words and physical assistance. The gods always let me

Figure 4.1

know when something will happen. For example, they may tell me that a song is coming from God before a thunderstorm. This is how I live with the spirits.

Many shamans leave their songs because of the way evil interferes with their lives. It is not easy being a shaman. You must always wrestle with the interference of evil. It is too much for some people to bear. To survive as a shaman you must never forget to talk to your God a lot and continually ask Him for the necessary strength to move through each day. This is the only way a shaman can find peace.

You must ask the Great Father, God, to protect you from evil. Directly ask Him not to let the bad things touch you. And never forget that you must keep a high level of attention and awareness to receive the songs from the four winds and from above. It is the songs that bring you deeply into the shaman's world.

After you receive the sacred song, you can begin baptizing others. You baptize all the children. In our community we call everyone a child, no matter how young or old they are. When you baptize someone, you ask God where the child comes from—East, West, North, or South. God tells you where the child is from, and then He tells you their Guarani spiritual name. When you were conceived, God gave you a spiritual name. God gives this to you. The shaman asks God what He named you, and in our baptism ceremony, this name is announced to the community. We dance and celebrate such an event. Most people know me as Guillermo, but this is not my real name. I only use it for my relations with white people. It doesn't say anything to me. It doesn't say where my spirit came from. My Guarani forest name is my real soul-name. This is true for all Guarani Indians.

In the baptism dance, I blow the spirit of the person and tell them their real name. I knew it the first time they asked me because I asked the Great Father at that time. However, I don't tell the child until the public baptism ceremony.

When the shaman finds out a person's name, he also sees the future of their life. The shaman knows whether that person will become a shaman. There are two types of people: shamans and those who have an empty body or, simply, just a body. In other words, there are people with a sacred song and those without a song. If I see that someone will become a shaman, I tell their family to take care of them. What I say to them is true for all people, not just the Guarani. Even though the child may be a baby, if I see that they are going to be a shaman, the family must make them the sacred ornaments—a feather wrist band, rattle, corona, and so forth.

The shaman's wife has to be an example for the other women. She has to live by the rules God gave us. She has to dance and teach the other women. My wife can also heal. She has her own song and with this song she heals. She has received several songs from sacred dreams. She has some important things to say.

Takua Kawirembeyju

I received my songs from the center. I was home and something powerful happened. My husband was with me when I received the songs. I have an uncle who is a shaman and he is still alive. In my dream, my uncle brought me a big pot from heaven and put it in my house. It was a sacred pot. I knew that it gave me the power to heal.

In the dream, one of my daughters brought me a grandson who was ill. She asked me to cure him. I told her, "Go and take him to your father. He is a shaman. After you go to the grandfather, bring me back the son." After my daughter went to the grandfather, I lit my pipe and smoked the whole house. Then my daughter returned and brought the child with her. I looked at the child and told her not to worry. "Don't worry, my daughter, tomorrow he will be playing with the other children." Then I said, "If your son gets sick again, I won't be able to help him." After the dream, the child got sick and was taken to a white doctor in Asunción, and there he died.

The future is up to us. We all have to be together. There will be fire, big water, and darkness. The big rains and changes that are happening now are a warning. We can make things better. It is up to each one of us, because we have always been one people.

Right now the worst thing non-Indian people are doing is destroying the earth. We all have to take care of the earth. We must face this responsibility together.

Also, the world must begin sharing again. We need more kindness. Whether rich or poor, we are spiritually the same. Everyone has the God-given right to eat. The poor must be fed. They cannot be forgotten. When we share, we are doing what God wants us to do on earth. This is all that He asks. We must act in this way.

VUSAMAZULU CREDO MUTWA
ZULU HIGH SANUSI

Introduction to *Vusamazulu Credo Mutwa*
by Nancy Connor

Credo Mutwa has a place among the best storytellers ever known. He heals with stories, he tells of African history through stories, he teaches lessons with stories, and he makes everyone around him laugh with his stories. If you arrive at his doorstep, he will demonstrate his hospitality by telling stories all day, if you let him. He has told his stories on radio, in newspapers for adults and comic books for children, and on film for television documentaries.

But Credo Mutwa is much more than his stories. He teaches traditional African healers to prepare herbal cures for everything from headaches and allergies to cancer and HIV. He teaches the healers divination to diagnose patients, to help find lost objects, and to help a patient learn which path to follow in order to make the best of their future. He teaches the healers to go into deep trance, shaking and sobbing, where they learn where the patient's pain comes from so that they can share that pain and help the patient heal from it.

Many important people—among them the Dalai Lama and several former presidents of South Africa—have spoken with Credo to hear his stories, to gain his insight and advice on their problems, and to ask him to heal them. He does so with humility, grace, and humor, giving generously of his time and energy. He never turns away anyone who comes to his door, no matter how great or small their concern. He is often considered one of the more notable shamans of our time, and this honor is greatly deserved.

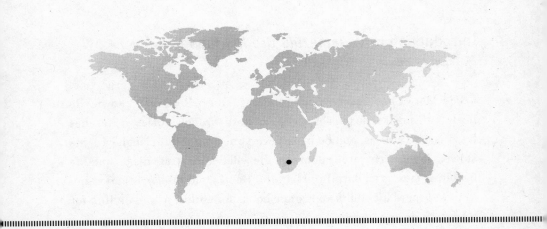

Zululand

I was born on July 21, 1921. I was my father's seventh child. My father, Allen Fana Mutwa, was a Christian, a confessing Catholic. My mother, Nomabunu, was a pagan and the daughter of Ziko Shezi, who fought in some of the bloodiest battles in South Africa. My grandfather also fought in the great Zulu wars, in which the Zulus tried to throw the English out of Natal. He was a veteran of the battle of Ulundi, which ended the Zulu Wars.

In those days, there was a horrendous enmity between non-Christian blacks and Christian blacks. In fact, this enmity was aided and abetted by the missionaries. If a Christian black man was caught talking to a pagan woman, the church authorities horribly punished that man. They received a punishment called "taken out of the flock." A special bench was set just inside the door of each church, and all those who had been "taken out of the flock" were made a public display and forced to sit on the bench and not on the pews. Everyone who entered the church would see you, an outcast, sitting inside the entrance of the church. Being shamed publicly was how the missionaries punished Christian blacks for associating with non-Christian blacks.

My mother was a pretty woman with a silvery voice and the powerful legs of a dancer. When she met my father, they fell madly in love. And then one day my father sent a message to my mother's father. My father appealed to my grandfather that he grant permission for his daughter to convert to Christianity. A messenger, sent by my father, carried a framed picture of Jesus Christ in his saddlebag to show to my grandfather. When the old warrior saw this picture, it was like a red flag to an angry bull. My grandfather took the picture and threw it on the ground, smashing it, and then with his sandaled feet he danced on the picture, shattering it to many pieces. "Who is this son of a diseased daughter of a dog who dares to come and tell me that my daughter must, on her knees, worship at the feet of the god of the English?" he exclaimed.

Thus, my father and my mother were separated. But an accident, if one can call it that, had already taken place. When my mother visited my father at his construction camp, they made love, and I was on the way.

In those days in Zululand, there was nothing more shameful than for a girl to be pregnant with an illegitimate baby in her father's home. So while my mother carried me, she was the target of curses hurled at her by all the village girls. She became an object of shame to my grandfather's eleven wives. Everyone was disgusted with her, and it was even worse, that she, the daughter of a prominent man, was about to give birth to a child fathered by a traveling Christian.

My mother had no choice but to hide. She had to go to a small town to live with relatives. It was there, in Dundee, South Africa, that I was born.

I am told that my mother, traumatized by her day-to-day life, tried to kill me several times. My grandmother, Sikhowe, told me of one such attempt. I was asleep on a mat, under a sheepskin blanket just outside our hut. My mother returned from the river, where she had gone to fetch water. She was weeping because she had been beaten with belts by a group of local girls who called her a mother of a bastard. She laid down the pot of water she was carrying on her head, and then with a scream of rage, she picked up a stone. As she was about to smash my head with the stone, my grandmother staggered out of her hut and wrestled my mother to the ground. "What are you doing?" cried my grandmother. "How dare you to commit such a crime in your grandfather's village? Do you want to bring more disgrace to the shame that you have already brought us?"

After that incident, my mother tried to kill herself and had to be taken, for some months, to a home of a *sangoma*.[1] She had to take me with her.

My grandmother Sikhowe spoke to my mother for many days while she was in the home of the sangoma, where she was being treated for severe trauma and depression: "Don't you understand that this baby might be someone? Don't you understand that one day this baby might uplift the Zulu people just as another illegitimate baby once did?"

When I was a baby, everyone shunned me. I grew up in isolation. One day I was sick and crying, and people in the sangoma's home yelled at my mother to shut me up because I was disturbing their sleep. So my mother named me "Vusamazulu," which means "he who cries and awakens the sleeping Zulus."

The fact that I was illegitimate followed me everywhere. Children were told not to play with me. Even when we were looking after cattle together, the other boys did not talk to me. So I was always alone.

As I grew older, I began noticing unusual things about myself. The first thing I noticed was that I was very good at sculpting and wood-carving. Sitting alone, I carved beautiful spoons using a rusty old pocketknife. I also had strange dreams of unbelievable vividness and clarity. Right before my seventh year, I noticed that if something of major importance was to happen in my paternal grandfather's village, I first dreamt about it. I saw exactly what was going to happen and who would do what and why. This disturbed my father so he punished me for talking about these dreams.

Nevertheless, the people in our village began respecting me for the dreams, and my strange dreams reached the ears of our local chief. He

---

[1] A *sangoma* is a traditional African healer, typically a female diviner and clairvoyant who uses the drum to arouse the spirits. Hence, they are referred to as "drum persons." *Inyangas* are traditional healers who sometimes use herbs. They are traditionally regarded as "moon persons." The *sanusi* is the highest class of African healer. They are regarded as priests by millions of African people. The sanusis know all the ancient secrets of protection and healing, and they also serve their communities with psychological help. The *sanusi* is regarded as the uplifter—the one who causes things to ascend. The highest of the *sanusis* is known as the High Sanusi.

called my father and said, "Your child is gifted, Mutwa. You must stop discouraging him. He is not possessed by the devil. If anyone is possessed by the devil, you are, you Christian. Now leave your child alone."

One day I became very ill. I was so sick, I could barely walk. And after a while, I couldn't walk at all. I was in constant pain, day in and day out. My uncle took me to European doctors and Christian faith healers. The doctors gave me injections, pills, and treatments of all kinds, and Christian faith healers prayed over me, talking in tongues and dancing like baboons all around me. But I was not healed.

And then the people began to whisper that I was suffering from a healer's disease because my visions intensified when the disease came. All of a sudden, I was able to see through people. If a person had a sickness in their body, I could see it. Don't ask me how, but I could. It was as if their body had turned into a moving statue of glass, and all their ailments were dark brown or dirty green blotches inside the transparent body.

Each time I saw people with sicknesses in them, I had a strange urge to crawl toward them and touch them. I just wanted to touch them and take their sicknesses away. And then one day my Aunt Anastasia, who had come from Durban to look after me, entered the house where I was lying helplessly on a grass mat. As she came toward me, crawling on her knees into the beehive hut, I saw a huge, dark red blotch in the center of her chest. I also noticed that her big, plump, motherly face with small eyes that could light up with girlish mischief was gray and dull with pain.

A strange and burning urge came over me. It was an urge to touch this woman to take the pain away from her. But in those days, even among the Christian blacks, a child was never allowed to touch an adult for any reason, and traditional laws were strictly held. But as Aunt Anastasia came toward me, I saw the huge, pulsing blotch where her heart should be, and I felt this irresistible urge to touch her. Aunt Anastasia said to me, "I see you, Credo."

I had been baptized by this time and was ridiculously named Credo by the priest. I hated this strange name. My name was Vusamazulu. I let everybody know that. This name, Credo, was totally alien to me. I hated it.

A	"How have you slept?"
CM	"Auntie, I slept well. I only had the pain before sunrise. But, Auntie, what is wrong?"
A	"What do you mean, Credo?"
CM	"Auntie, there is pain in your chest. There is pain in your left shoulder down to your elbow. You are not well, Auntie."
A	"And how do you know that?"
CM	"Auntie, I can see, I can see your pain."
A	"You are not a sangoma. Are you, little heathen, taking after your mother?" she laughed.
CM	"No, Auntie. I am not a sangoma, but I can see."

Then Aunt Anastasia did a strange thing. She placed the bowl of porridge she had brought next to me.

A	"Can you take my pain away, Credo?"
CM	"Auntie, I don't know."
A	"Little Mutwa, listen. Can you do what Jesus is said to have done? Can you take my pain away?"
CM	An incredibly foolish and daring answer came to my lips on that strange and cloudy day: "Auntie, if you allow me to touch you, I will."

She came close to me and took my hand and placed it on her ample chest, between her large breasts. As I touched her, my hand became strangely hot, and my fingers tingled. I don't know how long my hand rested on her chest. But, suddenly, she sighed deeply and shook her head.

A	"You know what? The pain in my chest is gone. How did you do it?"
CM	"Auntie, I don't know."
A	"Have you ever touched anyone before?"
CM	"No, Auntie, I am afraid. Please, don't tell my father, because my stepmother will kill me."

My Aunt Anastasia was a woman who could not keep a secret. And in no time, the fact that I was able to take pain away from people by simply touching them spread throughout the land. And one day, who should come to my father's village but the local chief, who was still angry because he was bitten by one of our dogs some weeks before. I first dreamt about it and tried in vain to warn my elder half-brother against it. I dreamt that our dog bit His Majesty, so I told my half-brother that if His Majesty visited our home, the dog must be tied up. But my half-brother said that there was no chance of the chief visiting our home, so why worry? However, His Majesty did come to collect money for his daughter's wedding, and our dog went after him and bit him, which did not endear us to His Majesty at all.

This time, however, His Majesty wanted me to touch a certain part of his body, which he said was not working properly. My father was furious, but His Majesty firmly put my father in his place. He stayed for a number of days, and each morning I had to touch a very royal part of him. I was amazed when a fortnight later he sent two beautiful cows as a gift for my father in gratitude for the sick boy's healing hands.

Once, I was brutally raped by a gang of miners and I immediately got sick and found shelter in a dirty shack outside the mines. I stayed there with some Africans and Hindus, who all lived on beer day in and day out. Trying to find peace, I began drinking again, but my sickness worsened.

My sister and uncle found me and took me back to Zululand, the home of my biological mother and grandfather. They left me in a beehive hut village, where I had briefly lived as a child. Here my grandmother, Sikhowe, huge and with snow-white hair still done in the style of the ancient Zulus, walked about topless, her breasts bare under the sun. She wore a huge skin skirt and a large beach towel. Her legs were huge and swollen, one with a running sore on which she had put a poultice of herbs. She had a ready, booming laugh, and she told me stories from long ago. Her name, Sikhowe, meant "the place of the mushrooms."

My mother had a lean, high-cheekboned Zulu face with flaring nostrils, small eyes, and a mouth that was always set in a hard line. She was smeared from head to toe in red ochre. She wore a white cloth, also dirtied with red ochre. And she wore a skin skirt as well, with wire bangles around her calves, ankles, arms, and wrists. She smelled of wild herbs and homemade Vaseline.

Then there was her half-sister, Mynah, who was a slender statue in living ebony. Mynah was a full-fledged sangoma, even then. Her hair was smeared with red ochre, in what you call dreadlocks today. She was barebreasted, and strings of pulped and dried herbs crisscrossed her body. Around her neck were necklaces of seashells and a band of ancient copper. She also wore a skin skirt smeared with red ochre, and its hem was trimmed with seashells. When she walked, the rattles around her ankles made a haunting sound.

My grandfather, Ziko Shezi, had a traditional ring around his head. His beard was torn and tattered like that of a mountain goat, and his blood-red eyes were deeply set and searching. On his left arm was a terrible scar made by an English saber from a battle of many years ago.

Those were the people to whom I returned. They all said to me, "We are going to help you get well." My grandfather asked harshly, "Do you want to die in the arms of an alien white man's god or do you want to live in the arms of our people's ancient gods?" These people, who were loving but firm, told me about a side of Africa that I knew nothing about. From them I learned that our people had a religion when the white man came to this land. The white missionaries did not bring religion and belief in God. We were already religious when the first white man's wagon creaked through the veldt drawn by a span of oxen. "We believed in God before your Jesus set his dainty white feet in our land," said my grandmother.

Aunt Mynah was my teacher. She grew up far away from my grandfather's village, where as a girl she was very sick and weak. She was eventually taken to see an old healer because they believed that a heavy spirit was crushing her life force. One day, to everyone's surprise, Mynah started laughing. This was very strange to the people in the village. She said that her grandmother had appeared to her in a dream and instructed her to laugh and to make other people laugh. Her grandmother also said that if this happened, Mynah would be able to heal many people.

She subsequently began dreaming about the things that were going to happen in the future. For example, she had a dream in which one of her half-brothers was covered entirely in cow dung. She sent a warning to the young man that something very bad was going to happen to him. In the dream, she was told that he must stop playing with fire-making equipment. Unknown to my grandfather and to the rest of the family, the young man had bought himself a very old fire-starting apparatus.

Before Mynah could reach Grandfather's village, her brother started playing with the equipment and his grass hut caught on fire. He was so badly burned that he received the traditional treatment of taking calf dung mixed with herbs and rubbing it all over the burned body. When Mynah finally arrived, she found him covered with dung, exactly as she had dreamt. Soon after, he died of pneumonia, presumably brought on by the burns he had suffered. Mynah never forgave herself for failing to get to him on time.

When she was sixteen years old, Mynah was initiated by Senzeni, the mother of my mother. She was the last surviving daughter of the Zulu king Dingane. After various initiations, various ancestral spirits began manifesting themselves. She eventually reached a very high stage of initiation and became a *mulozi*—that is, one who is guided by the whistling spirits.

My aunt Mynah has had a strange and incredible life. When the time came for her to be married, she met a man who fell deeply in love with her. Unfortunately, he died in a mining accident before they could get married. The next man who proposed to her lost the cattle that were to be the dowry. This was seen as a message from the ancestral spirits that they did not want her to be married. Mynah, therefore, devoted her whole being to becoming a great healer.

One day when she was out in the bush with some other girls, they saw a terrible creature standing among the trees. It looked like a crocodile with a very short snout and very large teeth. It had the body of a man, but the body was as white as chalk from head to foot. Mynah was the only girl unafraid of the creature, and her friends saw the creature call her and then talk to her. To this day Mynah has never told anyone what the creature said to her. Afterward, she became a sangoma of the highest order, and her healing was in demand from as far away as Swaziland.

Her traditional name is Zamekile, and it means "daughter of good effort." Spirits talk to her through a whistling sound. The whistling can occur even when she is not around, which can only happen to a powerful healer.

My grandfather had a secret medicine bag. When he became very sick, he appointed Mynah as the custodian of the bag. It was then taken and hidden very far away. She had to locate it and bring it home before it was destroyed. Mynah fasted for a number of days, and then one afternoon she ran out of the village and traveled for a long distance looking for the bag. Unassisted by anyone, she found the bag inside a termite hill. Luckily the termites had not begun molesting the bag. Today, she is still the keeper of my grandfather's medicine bag.

The bag's contents are one of the most secret things in the family. Only the keeper of the bag may open and breathe into the bag to speak into it. As a sangoma heals people over the years, he or she is told by the spirits to break away pieces of *muti* (traditional medicine) that have successfully treated the sick. Then the muti is dried and added to the contents of the bag of communication, as it is traditionally called.

Mynah also made her own medicine bag. Medicines sometimes are shown in dreams, as are the directions to locate them. Usually the bag is made from a bull's thick hide or elephant skin. If the healer is a woman, it is made into a drawstring bag. But if the healer is a man, the bag will have a flap, almost like a briefcase in appearance.

When Mynah makes a medicine to protect a person from harm, she uses various ingredients, all of them protective. They may be from plants, animals, or no material at all, such as words spoken into the bag. You can put words into the bag or you can put stones, minerals, animal flesh, dried insects, or different kinds of grain into it. The spirits show you what to put in the bag.

For Mynah, the whistling spirits give a diagnosis, telling her the nature of the patient's troubles. They also tell her what medicines, if any, can be used. It may be a verbal medicine or a material medicine. Mynah often heals by touch. She also heals by water and she even heals by urine. She may advise a person, for example, to drink a half cupful of his or her own urine at the beginning of each day. Sometimes it's the patient's own urine, while at other times it may be someone else's. She might use baby's urine, for example, if a man has serious trouble with his prostate. However, she only uses her own urine for very high initiations.

When she touches someone, she often shakes and trembles. For some sicknesses, she will shake mildly, while other illnesses make her shake violently and bring forth very powerful sounds. At times she bites people to get the sickness out. She doesn't lick them with her tongue, but I have seen other high healers in her class do that, especially in Swaziland. Other high healers may also lie on top of a patient, usually in the north/south direction. My grandfather and his brothers used to do that for people who were gored by cattle and lost a large amount of blood.

Mynah is a great healer and teacher who helped me learn the ancient ways. I am grateful for all that she has taught me. She is one of the last of the old breed. (See Figure 5.iii of a ritual using medicine bag.)

Initiation

When I was a young man, the day finally came when Mynah placed the pot of initiation upon my head, as a first step in training as a sangoma. A new world opened its arms to me: heathen Africa which, even at that time, was slowly beginning to vanish. A new vista of knowledge beckoned me like distant mountains. I began learning about our people and our ancient laws. And as I went through the rituals of initiation, I was told many, many things.

In Africa when you are an initiate, you must obey your teachers without questions. You must never talk back to them. You must gather firewood in the forest and bring it to your place of initiation. You must never think of anything outside the circle of initiation. .

You had to dance strenuously to communicate with your body, your muscles, and your mind. Mynah told me that when a person dances, he or she speaks to every vein, artery, joint, and length of muscle within their body. "Above all," she said, "you receive power from the earth, our mother. The power flows from the depth of the earth into your feet and up your spine to the top of your head. That is the power of the sangoma, the person of the drum."

From time to time, I had to go into a special steaming hut, called the *isifutho*. And after each steam, I ran out into the cold to roll on the dewy grass, even in midwinter when the summits of the great mountains in west Zululand were snow-capped. My aunt told me: "Your body must receive benefits from the two great powers, Vusamazulu. Heat and cold must both claim you like girlfriends. And you must dance and dance to remove all the evil sweat from your insides."

I underwent internal baths. I had to drink a large quantity of medicine each morning to fill my stomach. Then, using a feather to tickle the back of my throat, I brought it up again. And I endured enemas that would have made an elephant run away screaming. Have you ever had a traditional Zulu enema? It's done with a large cow horn, which is pierced at the tip. The whole thing goes into your back passage. Typically a big leather bag is used to hold the rest of the medicine, which is poured in with a calabash. And you can hear it glug-glugging into your intestines. Then you must be a good runner to get out of the hut and into the bush and you know what happens next. It's as if every bowel inside your stomach suddenly escapes through your rectum like snakes.

We were forbidden certain foods but had to eat certain other foods. Also, on the back of every initiate's head was a loop of beads called "the loop of beggarliness." We had to go from village to village begging for food, begging for grain. It was a ritual of self-debasement that is part of our initiation. We were told to meditate and to seek the hidden power of eternity and the force that lay hidden amongst the stars. We call this the "hidden bride."

Now what is this power? It comes to you in a strange way. When you dance, you dance in a circle, stomping your feet firmly against the ground and kicking your feet. You must kick your feet high and shake every inch of your body. When the dancing reaches its height, a strange spell comes over you. It feels like you are no longer dancing but floating in air. You are at one with the earth and the sky, at once. You continue to dance. And then a strange thing bursts from the small of your back. A pot full of hot water suddenly jets up from the small of your back between your buttocks right up your spine to the top of your head, where it explodes into space and seems to float toward the stars. Your vision changes. Your mind suddenly flies. You are covered in sweat but don't feel any pain as you continue to dance. Sometimes the powerful force of the hidden one, the *ncumu* as it is traditionally called, will come a second time, and suddenly you will feel a part of you leaving your body. You will see yourself in the air helplessly lying on your back while the other you dances maniacally beneath you. The you who is lying above the dancing you will float into a region of eternal peace. I can't describe it any other way than to say that you feel as though you are one with every animal, tree, river, stream, and mountain on earth. You feel united with creation. And when you fall down, you want to get up and do it again, but your weak body can no longer bear the strain, so you lie with your face in the sand, gasping hard like a fish on land trying to breathe.

One day after dancing nearly to exhaustion, I was ordered by my other teacher, Felapakati, to go into a hut. As I knelt inside the hut, there came what I can only call a strange explosion inside my head. Like a silver fog, a strange and totally inexplicable burst of joy filled me. I didn't know what I had to be happy about. My body was aching, with every muscle protesting, but suddenly I was filled with this great joy. A joy so intense that I wished I had arms long enough to embrace the whole world. I felt as one, but yet I felt as many. I was one human being, and yet I was many, many more. Suddenly, my heart also felt a deep sorrow. I heard people crying from far away. I also heard people, thousands of them, laughing far away. And later when my teachers, Mynah and her friend Felapakati, entered the hut, I crawled on my hands and knees to them.

CM "Makhosi," — that is what an initiate must
say — "Great Kings." (We refer to our ancestral
spirits and those who teach us as great sovereigns.)
"Makhosi, Great Kings, lions of the world."

F	"Look at his eyes, look at the stupid one's crossed eyes."
M	Mynah looked at me, "What's wrong with you? Have you been stealing our beer in the dark while we were away?"
CM	"No, my aunt, you know I do not touch beer," my eyes downcast.
F	"Which is unfortunate." Felapakati was testy. "If you got nice and drunk, I would have the privilege of kicking your ass. Now what's up with you? Why are you looking as if you had just made love for the first time?"
CM	"I do not understand, Great One."
M	"Oh, you don't understand, do you? What do you hear? What do you feel?" Mynah was always a serious woman.
CM	"Great Mother, I feel a stupid joy. I feel I could run outside and embrace that tree or that cow grazing next to it."
M	"Of course. Tell him, Felapakati, what this is that he feels." Felapakati leaned against the grass wall of the hut, and his bleary eyes mocked me from under the shade of his jackal-skin hat.
F	"For the first time, Christian boy, you are experiencing something that your people talk about."
CM	"What is it, Great One?"
F	"You are experiencing love, fat little bastard. You Christians talk a lot about love, but when it comes to you, you don't know what it is. Tell us, how do you feel?"
CM	"Great One, as I have said, I feel like embracing everything outside this village. I feel like embracing both of you. But I hear people crying in my ears, and I hear people laughing. What is this? Am I going mad?"

F "Oh, it would be of great help to me if you could go mad. What you are feeling, boy, is love. And what you are hearing, boy, are the cries of millions of people who tragically died long ago with their lives unfulfilled. What you are also hearing, Christian boy, are the sounds of happy souls who lived this earthly life to the fullest and died peacefully."

CM "But, Great Father, why do I feel as if I should embrace everybody?"

F "Because you are everybody. That is what a true sangoma should be. You should feel that you are everyone and anyone. You are a white man, a black man, and a colored man. You are an Indian. You are a priest. You are a thief. You are everything. Now you are a true sangoma. You have taken the first step towards what we call *ukubamunye nezwe*, 'to be one with the land.' Listen again, and again, sit still and listen, stupid."

I listened. At first I heard nothing. And then I heard something from a distance: savage animal sounds, sorrowful and ecstatic sounds of animals. I heard lions mating in the bush. I heard crocodiles rejoicing in the rivers. These sounds were familiar to me. I heard birds, and I heard growls and roars of unknown animals from a distant time. And then I heard something so incredible that I lack words to describe it. Imagine, my friends, a roaring fire. A huge fire. A thunderous fire. A fire the likes of which no one has ever seen. It was a great fire. I heard the crackling of its huge flames. I heard flames licking high into the air and splashing down again in huge roars.

"Great One, what is that?" I asked stupidly. Felapakati answered, "You are hearing the sound of the sun. What you are hearing are the fires of the sun. The fires that caused the creation to be. Listen again, Vusamazulu, listen."

I listened again, and this time it was a familiar sound. It was the swishing of great waves, screaming sea birds, and some strange sounds of mighty animals. I learned many years later that these were the sounds whales make in the depths of the sea. It was magic. It was pure golden madness. It was total insanity.

I also heard mighty waterfalls cascading in the centers of forgotten forests. I heard people's voices: happy people, little people hunting in the forests. I heard the voices of Bantu people, speaking in a language that I knew. I heard voices of people from faraway lands.

Figure 5.1

Then different smells began to assail my nostrils. First, I smelled a primitive, primeval fire, hot enough to melt metal into vapor. I smelled the sea. I smelled the desert and unwatered sand in my nostrils. I smelled birds, animals, and even the ants underground. For one magical moment, I was one with all creatures.

Inside each soul are two worms, a red and a blue worm, and they are always in conflict with each other. Mynah told me that the red worm represented evil, all the vices and weaknesses of a person. And the dark blue worm represented all the good, virtues, and strengths of a person.

Every soul must have both good and evil—the blue worm and the red worm. Without a perfect balance, the soul will die. If, for instance, a man should only be good, he would have no reason to exist. If he were only bad, he would automatically be destroyed. Overly good people never live long. The two worms are always quarreling inside each soul, and if one worm seriously damages the other, the soul becomes unbalanced and can no longer survive in the world. Survival requires a balance between good and evil.

The great soul, the *moya*, is the sphere with the worms fighting inside. There is also a little soul, the ena, which develops as the human being grows from childhood to old age and death. Whereas the *ena*, which only starts to come into being as a person is being born, is sometimes seen as the ghost of a dead person, the moya moves through all the incarnations from a human being to animal, reptile, bird, rock, tree, fish, and ultimately to the star. The enas of our ancestors must be fed in order for them to stay alive. If we do not sacrifice cows and goats to offer their enas to feed our ancestors' enas, our ancestors will cease to exist.

I also learned that the bulky creature that I see as myself is really not me. My real self is a tiny little human being or a humanoid who resides inside a burning little star. This little star, brighter than the sun but smaller than the point of a needle, is deep inside my brain at the back of the skull. My teachers, with another sangoma named Nomaswati who had come from Swaziland, taught me that if I had a problem which I could not solve, all I had to do was to go to bed early thinking about the problem. Then before falling asleep, I was to think of the little star all alone in the colossal void of unimaginable blackness. I was to imagine this star, this tiny point of intensely bright light, and call upon the very small me who lives inside that star. This would awaken the solution to my problem.

To be a sangoma, you have to learn various forms of healing. You are taught how to give a sick person a carefully prepared tea from many herbs. You are taught how to prepare the different teas and administer them properly. In Western medicine, a doctor will prepare an herbal brew or a medicinal brew, say a cough mixture, and he will instruct the patient to take this medicine three times a day. But in African medical practice you don't give a person an herbal preparation and tell them to take it three or four times a day. African herbal medicine is taken only at specific times during the day. For example, when a patient with a chronic stomach ailment is brought to you, it is your duty as a *sangoma* to find out the person's star sign and their time of birth, when they first saw the world. We observe a patient carefully for a number of days before we administer any herbal medicine. When you watch a patient who is moaning on the sick mat, you will observe that there is a time during the day, in the morning or in the afternoon, when the patient feels better. You will discover that this happens every day at the same time. The great teachers know that this is the time when the patient was born. We believe that there are two times that are important for a human being: the time of their conception and the time of their birth. Those are the times to administer medicine to the patient. We can find those times by observing the patient's condition over a number of days. We are told that the time when the patient begins to feel better and show signs of improvement is when the patient was either born or conceived.

We also know that many children are conceived on their mother's birthdays. We watch for this because it is very important. We say that the mother energy, which rises within the person, is trying to help the patient out of their ailment. This is why we administer the medicine at that time, so that the herbal medicine with the great mother energy can hasten recovery.

If you find two patients, one born under the lion star sign and the other under the dolphin star sign, and they suffer from the same illness, you must realize that their bodies are not the same. The person born under the lion star sign will have to be treated differently from that of the dolphin star sign. The lion star sign patient must be given more medicine in powder form and not in liquid form. And for the dolphin star sign, the patient must be given a lot of liquid medicine and not powdered medicine. In other words, if a person is a water sign, he must be treated with liquids, with various kinds of water—brackish water, fresh water, or any other water. On the other hand, if a person is born under a land sign, such as the various goat signs and the lion sign, the treatment must rely more on powdered medicines than liquids.

You have to know all this and much more. One of the methods of healing that a sangoma must know is called "drinking the sickness." In this method, you place your hands about one inch above the surface of the patient's body, and you run your hands up and down, shaking your fingers, until you feel every one of the patient's symptoms in your own body. You absorb the patient's illness, and then, using the power of your mind, you expel the sickness from your body by elimination. For example, if a patient suffers from a kidney disease, you hold your hands over the patient until you feel pain in your kidneys. Then you wait until you have to urinate. And as you urinate you think deeply about the patient's illness and visualize the patient's illness being expelled.

I was taught another amazing thing. With modern medical doctors, the patient comes and tells the doctor as much as possible about his symptoms. But in Africa, a patient does not tell the doctor anything about his sickness. The doctor must, with divination instruments, such as the bones of divination, accurately find out the patient's problems. People also consult sangomas because of distressing dreams or because they have lost something or someone. People may come to sangomas on behalf of other people. For instance, a mother will go see a sangoma because one of her children is in trouble, and you, the sangoma, by throwing your bones, must tell her why she has come.

Even after your "coming out ceremony," which tells everyone that you are now a full-fledged *sangoma,* it is by no means the end of your education as a *sangoma.* Your teacher must examine you to see if you are ready to start working for the people. In the old days when I was initiated, a *sangoma* had to be initiated and still remain an initiate for a full year under the tutelage of one teacher. After that, the sangoma became an apprentice healer, and he was allowed to heal and consult people, but under the strict supervision of the teacher. This was the stage of the *uhlaka,* "the apprentice healer."

First you become the *twasa,* which means "initiate." Then you are an *uhlaka;* you heal people under your teacher's supervision. Finally, you become a full sangoma. Now you are independent, but you are still expected to keep in touch with your teacher to learn more from him or her.

African Journeys

Chikerema was a chosen one. He was a high sanusi and was the custodian of an ivory arm. It had been made many centuries before for a great king who had lost his left arm battling a man-eating crocodile. His people made this ivory arm, and the great king wore it for the rest of his life. It was now an heirloom, a priceless treasure kept by Chikerema's family. Chikerema's father was murdered by a white man in Salisbury, a city now called Harare. Chikerema inherited his father's profession as traditional healer.

Chikerema was destined to open another amazing door for me in my quest to learn about my people's ways. "You must spend two nights in the cave of the ancestors," he said to me. "Because this is the only way we can find out if you are really fit to bear the important task that is about to be entrusted to you. If you show fear, you will fail at your task. But if you successfully spend two nights in the cave of the ancestors, we shall declare you fit for the great duty we are to put on your shoulders."

I said nothing as Chikerema and a number of his friends escorted me through the dense bush toward the cave of the Varozwi people. We came into the cave, and I noticed that the floor of the cave was studded with what I first thought were many round stones. Some of these were broken, with their tops missing. My blood went cold. When looking closely I found that all these stones were, in fact, men who had been buried with only the tops of their skulls above ground.

I am not a particularly brave man. In fact, many times I have found myself to be a coward. But there is something about a cave that fascinates me. When I am inside a cave, I feel closest to God. I fear nothing and no one. I spent not two nights but three in the great cave of the Varozwi. At the end of that time, Chikerema came and placed both his hands over my head and told me with a smile that I had passed the test. A cloud of suspicion filled my mind when I heard him say that. He then told me that I must stay in the cave for yet another day and that food would be brought to me. Food was indeed brought, and it was a very untraditional meal: a small tin of corned beef, a stale piece of bread, a loaf of bread from a trading store, and a tinful of water. Into the cave I went.

Next day at sunset, Chikerema and his people came to fetch me back to their village. When I arrived, I noticed that the villagers were staring at me. When I looked back they avoided my glance. In Africa, this is a sign of deep respect. When an African meets you eye to eye, he is showing contempt for you. But when he avoids your eyes, he is showing respect — something I would like outsiders to understand when they come to Africa.

When I arrived at Chikerema's house, I was told that on the following morning my training would begin after a sacred meal. I spent a restful night in that land, far away from my native Zululand. The following morning I was given a ritual steam bath, followed by a cold water bath, and then a long dress was given to me to wear. Then Chikerema's young wife, one of four, led me to Chikerema's hut, and I was told to enter. A smiling woman beckoned me to go inside, and there a peculiar sight met my eyes. There were dishes of food placed all over the floor of the hut, as if many people were going to eat. I noticed that there were different foods: food only for chiefs, food only for rich tribal people, food only for warriors, and food that travelers eat. Then I realized that I was being tested. Luckily my aunt Mynah had told me about this tradition, which uses food to test an initiate. I looked at all the food. There was stiff maize porridge, of the type called *sadza* by the people of Zimbabwe. There were porridge, yams, and sweet potatoes. I was no warrior, so which food was I to choose? I was amused and amazed looking at all the food. There was sadza with boiled chicken and boiled wild spinach. I rejected that since it was woman's food. Then I saw a round clay bowl about the size of a football next to a wooden dish heaped with mashed sweet potatoes. Inside the bowl was a chicken, which was roasted under clay. What kind of a person would eat such food? It came to me: a gourmet, a person who loved food. There was fried impala meat with sadza, a food of a warrior, but I was no warrior. I chose a dish of sadza with dried beef and placed it at Chikerema's feet.

C   "Is this the food that you have chosen?"

CM   "Yes, Great One, it is."

C   "Do you know the meaning of this food?"

CM   "Yes. Dried meat has been the food of travelers in Africa for many centuries, and sadza is also a food that a traveler eats. So being a traveler, sir, through your land, I've chosen this as my breakfast."

Chikerema's young wife had prepared all this food. She smiled at me.

W1   "This foreigner is a wise man. What tribe did you say you were?"

CM   "I am a Zulu, Great Lady."

W2   "You are a barbarian. You belong to a nation of thieves and killers. Do you accept that?"

CM   "Yes."

W2   "Your people used to attack my people and massacre them and steal our cattle."

CM   "Great Lady, I wish with all my power that I could heal the ancient wounds of Africa. I wish there would be forgiveness between your people and mine."

Chikerema smiled at his wife and dismissed her with a nod, and she bowed briefly and ran back to her hut. I ate the meat and the *sadza,* and Chikerema walked over to me and shook my hand.

C   "I want to know what you felt when you slept in that cave. What did you feel? What dreams did you have?"

CM   "Great One, as I slept in that cave I saw great chiefs, great men and women sitting on stools inside the cave. I heard many gunshots, although I saw nobody being shot."

C   "Yes, yes. In that cave white people trapped some of our ancestors and slaughtered them like animals. In some of the caves in this land, English soldiers threw sticks of dynamite onto the heads of our people who were hiding from them. Please remember that."

CM   "Great One, I will."

When Chikerema finished speaking, I noticed that sangomas had gathered around us. They were in full regalia of feathers, animal skins, and some in shoes or in traditional sandals. Chikerema told me that I was to go with these sangomas. They took me under a very big tree in the bush and sat me on a stool and danced in a great circle around me. As they danced, they must have passed a force from the earth to where I was seated because something seemed to be leaving my body. Suddenly I found myself floating on my back, close to the branches of the great tree, while a figure I recognized to be myself sat against the great tree trunk below.

Strange sounds, like whispers of people far away, filled my ears. Knowledge of some kind was being given to me.

In search of high initiation, not the trivial mumbo jumbo that is easily found, a true initiate has to undergo such radical experiences. When you complete these ordeals, you feel reborn. And you will never forget what you were taught.

Another mystery involved my mother, who was my grandfather's favorite daughter. He loved her and hoped that she would marry a wealthy man with many cattle. In 1918, after a terrible influenza epidemic that killed many people in her community, my mother mysteriously disappeared and reappeared a number of days later. No one believed her story about the disappearance, and she was thrashed with a hippo-hide whip for it. She said that she was taken away by a little old man with large eyes, who showed her many strange things. My mother, when she came back, carried a peculiar smell, and the wise people in our community told my grandfather to believe her because she carried the smell of a *Mantindane*. This is a Zulu word too often incorrectly translated to mean a fairy or a nature spirit. More accurately, it refers to what some people call the gray aliens. After I was born, my mother and I both disappeared and came back a few days later. This time she returned completely gray, looking like someone who had died, and everyone believed her story. These encounters with unknown entities are common among Africans, and I have experienced them several times in my life. It is another mystery that we will never fully understand.

I believe that the human mind is capable, under certain intensely emotional circumstances, of achieving what one might call the impossible. For example, if the powers of your mind are aroused enough, you can actually create ghost figures that other people, no matter how skeptical, can perceive. Actually, these figures are carvings of your own mind, but to protect the people you love, you can call upon this entity, which exists in your mind. When assisted by others, these figures can be projected on an enemy, who will see them and flee.

It is also possible for a group of human beings sitting in a circle to become one mind. This happens if everyone is filled with deep love and respect for one another. Such a gathering can create a beautiful energy that can bring good and healing to anyone entering its field.

African Healing

All the great healers of Africa use the wisdom of their ancestors to heal the suffering. Any time an African sangoma heals, they voice the wisdom of their ancestors. I will now provide some examples of how we accomplish this.

There was a man in Soweto who was about thirty years old and who truly deserved to be called a mama's boy. He was a car mechanic and a taximan who wanted to live a normal life. His mother worried that she would die without seeing her son married. He had never formed a healthy relationship with a woman his age. If he found a woman who wanted to marry him, he would stay with her for a while and then run back to his mother. Incredibly, when he lived with his mother, he behaved in a very odd way. He would urinate in bed like a baby, although he was a man in his thirties. We discovered that he had an obsessive love for his mother. He saw his mother as something more precious than any wife could ever be. His mother worried: "My son must get married, but he won't marry anyone we find for him."

When I met the young man, I decided that he was being haunted by a vision of his mother. He had grown up close to his mother, and they lived alone in a hostile world surrounded by murderers, pickpockets, and other criminals. They had found safety with each other.

For me, it was an easy problem to solve. I advised the young man that he must find a woman about five years older than him. Furthermore, she had to look like his mother in face and in figure, as much as possible. We were lucky. His mother found him such a woman. She even proposed to the woman on her son's behalf. We told this woman that she must behave toward this young man exactly as his mother had always done. When I last heard from these people, the mother had passed away and the son and his wife were living a happy life.

This type of treatment heals a person by using another person. We substituted another woman for his mother. This is called "moving the mask." It's found in almost all the tribes.

Sometimes you find a person who is a terrible thief who simply cannot stop stealing. What you must first do is bring her to the home of a *sangoma*. When you bring her home, you must let her live in your house, but you must encourage her, without her knowledge, to steal things in the house. You can take a piece of cow dung, cut it nicely with a sharp knife, and wrap it up in a chocolate wrapper. Then you must place it where she will find and steal it. When she steals it, you must openly accuse her of theft and scold her. This cannot be done in public, where she would lose face in front of other people. You must scold her gently, like a child who has been caught in an act of wrongdoing. Then you must order her to bring back the thing she stole. When she does, unwrap it and show her what she has stolen is a fresh piece of dung, not a piece of chocolate.

What a person like this really needs is parental love. They steal because they are lonely in their hearts. They grew up without receiving the attention they needed. Therefore, you must create a situation that gives them the attention they missed as a child.

Although there are sicknesses of the spirit that just require love, there are others that require more drastic treatments. For example, if a man, a homicidal maniac, kills people like rubbish, you must do something very unique. You must take him far away to a place where a woman is about to give birth. There, have him wash his hands seven times with ashes, soap, and water. As the child is about to be born, blindfold him and bring him into the house where the birthing is taking place. He must have no idea what's going on. When the woman, about to give birth, is screaming, two men should hold him tightly by the shoulders and the arms. They should hold out his hands as if he's asking for something. The moment the child is born, have him feel the baby, placenta, and everything, still warm and wet. Then take the baby away from him. He will immediately become very sick, and he will puke his heart out. After this experience, he will never kill another human being.

In Africa, we are aware that there is a time when some human beings reject life and become killers. To shock this person back into life, you must expose him to life in its most primitive form, like making him play midwife to a goat being born. In some dramatic way, you must reacquaint him with life again.

In the olden days, when a warrior returned from the battlefield, he was not allowed to approach his wife or wives until he underwent a ceremony of purification. Only afterward was he allowed in the company of normal society. At times when I was young, this purification was even extended to people who were just released from jail. A young man who had been imprisoned was not allowed in his father's village until he underwent a very stringent purification process. He was given enemas to cleanse him, in case he was sodomized while in jail. He also had to go through a sweat treatment and afterward he was forced to wade up to his neck in a river. All the things were done to restore and to reintroduce him to normal life.

In the cases of drug addiction, I discovered that the best way to help an addicted person is to help them discover the God within. They must find talents inside themselves. A person becomes a drug addict because they feel a burning inside, which they don't understand, and because they don't know who they are. They think that by taking drugs they will get rid of that fire and the deep loneliness they feel inside.

With a clear and open mind, you must stay with a drug addict to observe them very closely. If a drug addict doesn't want to give up their addiction, they will fool you, so you must find their true self and their unique talents.

There was a married woman who drank very heavily and she went great distances to visit friends in the most dangerous parts of the township. She deliberately put her life in danger, which deeply distressed her husband. He saw that his wife actually wanted to die; she wanted to be murdered. She loved her husband passionately, but he turned around and started abusing her and called her a drunkard. He did and said things to her that deeply hurt her. For this reason, she kept going about looking for death.

I was this man, and the woman was my late wife, Cecelia. I eventually noticed that my wife was deeply gifted—she sang, danced, and loved to read. What was I going to do to help my wife get out of this terrible death wish? I didn't want her to know that I was trying to cure her because she would resist me. I had to be cunning.

I sent a friend to a secondhand bookshop to find comic books about romance and love, which she loved. She eagerly read them. I said, "Why don't you make your own comic book and let me illustrate it?"

We did that together. We started a little comic with the story of her life, and she poured out all her heartbreak in it. We depicted the birth of her children, how the man she married rejected her, and how her friends pressed her to go to parties and drink. When it was completed, she sat down and read her own comic book.

Cecelia asked, "My God, did this really happen to me? Did I lose my job as a teacher because I drank too much?" I replied, "Yes, Cecelia. But tell me, why do you drink?" She didn't want to tell me at first, but she eventually told me that she was hiding something. She said, "There is something burning me inside. It is something that I feel I must do but I am afraid of doing it." I asked her what it was. She replied, "I want to pray over people and take them by the shoulders and shake them until they are well." When I asked her what was stopping her, she replied that she was a Catholic and they don't do that to people.

In those days, the Catholic Church was very formal and very stiff. At the services the prayers were still said in Latin.

I arranged to take Cecelia to a free church in the township and there, for the first time, I saw her as she really was. She danced, sang, and shook people by the shoulders as she prayed over them. Then she stopped drinking. Later, Cecelia bought a bottle of beer and said to me, "Mutwa, I want you to mark this bottle and mark it well."

I put tape on the bottle halfway down its neck. I also painted it yellow, and we put it inside the refrigerator. That night I realized that something was wrong because Cecelia, who was not drunk, was trembling and crying. She was having the sickness an alcoholic has when trying to give it up. It is a terrible sickness to witness; the whole body trembles and the eyes become glassy, and the person is out of this world in many ways. I watched my wife fight and conquer her drinking habit, and I also saw her struggle when she gave up cigarette smoking. I tried my best to help her, but she was the one who did the fighting. For over thirty years, her drinking did not trouble us, but after she stopped drinking, something else emerged from Cecelia. She developed the *sangoma* sickness and became a healer.

Struggling to Survive

One of the most important lessons from our ancestors is the importance of getting rid of negative thoughts and memories because they hinder spiritual progress. You can't heal others if you have painful memories or heartbreak. We say that a rotten net cannot catch a good fish. A healer who has memory of painful experiences must forget their unpleasant past. Simply stop remembering it. You must forgive those who harmed you and forget their harm. You cannot let the past pain poison your present.

We must realize that we human beings have been damaged, either by creatures from the stars or by ourselves. We were split into two. Out of the split emerged the inhibited intellectual who refuses to accept certain truths about our humanity. On the other side is the ecstatic human or the savage within us. Contrary to what the intellectuals teach, you are not the master of your own destiny, and your control over your own life is actually quite limited.

Human beings were not intended to be sane and intellectual. We were supposed to be wise and made of feelings. Again and again, I have come across both white and black people who try to have their cake and eat it, too. You are either a shaman or an intellectual. You are either a green person, who lives according to the chaotic rules of the moon and the earth, or you are a dry and dead thing that believes that two plus two makes four.

Again, I emphasize that you are not your own master. What little free will you were given is to help you avoid death. For example, if I see a crocodile in the river, I have the free will to either go toward it and be eaten or to back away and live another day. That is the only free will we were given.

There are intelligent forces that live through us in strange and illogical ways. If you are a shaman, you must leave yourself alone. Stop judging yourself. You don't know what's happening to you and you don't know why it is happening. Furthermore, you must never find out. When something strange happens to you or to a friend or to the world, you want to go and find out why. But in the end, you come back filled with superstition. In searching for answers to the unknowable, human beings ended up in the pool of superstition. In the process of trying to get out of it, they only got deeper into it. From the pool of superstition, they escaped to the desert of skepticism where they died very lonely and miserable deaths without knowing anything about this amazing thing we call life. Let the power ebb through you.

In our teachings we say that you must never question the gods. You must never doubt what they are doing. You must accept. If you are capable of healing, then go ahead and heal. Don't look to find its mechanism. It's not there. Simply be what you are called to be. There are things in this world that have no explanation, not because there is no explanation, but because our minds are not designed to find out.

Let me sing this last song, the song of peace I sang one troubled night when guns filled the skies with the whine of bullets. My mission is to create understanding between human beings of different nationalities and races. I shall sing this song to close my story:

> Let it shine, oh let it shine, oh let the lamp of peace shine.
> Oh let it shine, oh let it shine, oh let the lamp of
> peace shine.
> In the North and in the South, let the lamp of peace shine.
> In the East and in the West, oh let the lamp of peace shine.
> Between white men and black men, let the lamp of
> peace shine.
> Between humans and animals, let the lamp of peace shine.
> Between men and women, let the lamp of peace shine.
> Between nations, let the lamp of peace blaze.

At the end of time when the fading universe recalls each fugitive galaxy and runaway star, when the planets are once more called to become one with the great mass where a new universe will be born, let the lamp of peace be the only thing in the eternal dark, until the voice of God is heard again and creation is reborn.

Makhosi. Makhosi. Peace be with you and health and enlightenment and plenty and happiness and justice. *Makhosi.*

BALIANS
TRADITIONAL HEALERS OF BALI

Introduction: Balinese Healing, Magic, and the Sacred *Lontars*
by I Wayan Budi Asa Mekel

I saw my first *balian*, or traditional healer, when I was a boy. There was a very famous balian whose name was Kak Pranda. I used to watch people go to him and receive treatment. This grandfather looked at what kind of sickness the person had and then made them a certain herbal medicine. Some people came to him and asked for an amulet. He would make it for them and place prayers and mantras upon it.

Whenever I became sick, like having a bad headache or a fever, I would ask him to cure me. He would then give me the kind of medicine to cure my sickness. Once I asked him to take me to a certain place at night where a particular dance was performed in a cemetery. The performance was made by the people who practiced black magic, or what we call "the left side." He said he would take me to that place, but I kept waiting and waiting. I guess he didn't want me to see that kind of ceremony because he never took me to the night dance. He explained that it was dangerous for me to see the dance because it involved *leyaks*, the people who practice on the left side.

To this day, I have never seen that kind of dance. Now I don't want to see it because I know it is dangerous. The more I learned about leyaks, the more I realized I should not play around with them. It is a very serious matter.

If you want to see the black magic, you should walk alone in Bali at night. There are many Balinese people who walk alone at night and see something they didn't expect to see. They might see a leyak disguised as a dog that is as large as a cow. Or the leyak may look like a huge tower. Sometimes they see Rangda, the creature with long protruding teeth, a tongue of fire, and bulging eyes. You must know what to do if you see these things. Otherwise, your life will be in danger.

There is usually a sign that takes place before you see a leyak. It may get unusually dark or you smell something that is very sweet and fragrant. When you receive those signs, you must protect yourself.

To practice black magic, you must sacrifice someone you love in your own family. You don't kill them with a knife, but do it by spiritual means.

This is why it's difficult to prove that someone was killed by black magic. These things are very secret. No one tells you the name of this kind of practitioner. They'll just say something like, "Somebody over there, a tall person with blue sunglasses, goes out late at night." You have to go to a medium, who under trance can verify whether someone is a leyak.

To protect yourself from a leyak you have to make special offerings and receive some holy water from a balian. The balian might give you a certain kind of drawing or amulet to take home. You will be instructed to place it in a certain area so its power can be effective in making the leyak weak.

As I mentioned, there are two orientations of balians. Black magic is called the practice of the left. The balian on the left (balian pengiwa) is permitted to make bad situations, sometimes making a situation that helps kill a person. The practice of the right is more concerned with healing. Balians of the right side (balian penengen) do not make bad situations. They try to cure people of their sicknesses and problems.

Healers on the right are divided into four groups. Balian *kapicans* have received a gift from a god. This gift is sometimes an object in the form of a bird or an animal. The name of the divine given material used for healing is *pica*. It may look like a piece of jewelry, stone, bone, ring, coin, and so forth. The magical substance is used to both diagnose disease and as a therapy for treating the patient.

Balian *katakson* refers to the capability of a balian to allow a god to talk through him or her. Here the god, the *taxsu*, enters the balian's body and speaks to the person who comes for help. In other words, the balian goes into a spiritual trance in order to help the client. They usually ask the family or patient to write down what they say in trance because they have no memory of what they say when they come back to everyday consciousness.

Both the balian katakson and balian kapican usually undergo a series of mystical experiences as a means of becoming a healer. Sometimes this takes place against their will. These people may become balians in a very short period of time. They are seen as having a magical power either as a taksu or as the owner of a pica. Their power may only last two to five years, so many of them start learning about medicinal herbs so they can continue their career as a balian through prescribing medicines and giving therapeutic massages.

A balian *usada* is a healer or shaman who learns their practice from the sacred writings called lontars. They look up information in these lontars as a means of finding out how to cure a problem. This orientation to healing is somewhat akin to a Western medical doctor whose medical knowledge is based on textbook learning. Their cures emphasize the use of herbs and nonherbs, based upon the medical lontar book called *usada*. It is a modification of Ayurveda, the traditional Hindu textbook of medicine. Since it is written on the dry palm leaves of the lontar, the book is usually called lontar Usada. It is estimated that there are about five thousand lontar Usadas in Bali and in collections abroad. Some belong to libraries and others are under the care of priests and traditional healers.

Balian *campuran* is a mixture of all the other balian groups. They can read the lontars and have communication with the gods. Some of these balians make magical drawings that have been recorded in the lontars. These drawings come from Bali's past. They are associated with the gods of Bali.

The lontar books were first recorded during the eleventh century, and were readily available by the fourteenth and fifteenth centuries. They were written and read by the educated priests. A priest first has a sacred vision and then writes it down on the long narrow leaves of the lontar palm, a common tree found in Bali. He scratches the leaves with a knife and rubs burned candlenut (macadamia) into the etched surface to make the letters more perceptible. These leaves are tied together to make a book that enables information to be taught to other priests. Every thirty years the usada has to be rewritten because the lontar leaves become fragile as they deteriorate.

The lontar manuscripts of usada consist of two parts, the *Tutur* and the *Usada*. The Tutur has a more theoretical and philosophical orientation. It explains health and sickness and teaches a physiological understanding of the human body with a mystical undertone. The Usada is more focused on medical prescriptions and methods of treatment. It is more of a how-to series of books. There are usadas for the sicknesses of children (Usada

Rare), eye diseases (Usada Netra), and other specific problems and their remedies. The *Usada Taru Pramana* is a plant medicine textbook.

In 1978, a study conducted by Dr. Ngurah Nala discovered that there were more than two thousand balians among the approximately one thousand villages of Bali. Most of them practiced their healing part-time while they continued working as farmers, traders, or fishermen. The most common name of these healers is balian, but they are sometimes called *jero dasaran* or *tapakan*.

The highest level of balian is the person who receives permission from a god to do his or her work. When a god shows you a vision or gives you a gift, you will be the most powerful kind of balian. Sometimes the gift doesn't last very long. The power may remain for only several months or a few years. After that, the people stop going to that balian. The power is capable of moving from one person to another. If the balian cannot keep him- or herself pure, the power may decide to leave. A balian has to be careful about what he or she eats and about sexual relations. If a balian makes a mistake, he or she can erase the mistake through the appropriate offerings, prayers, mantras, and ceremonies. A balian has to take care of him- or herself to keep the power.

We have rules in Bali for keeping ourselves pure. For example, you shouldn't walk under a clothesline, and you should never rub someone's head. The person whose head is rubbed loses his purity. You're also not allowed to lean over somebody's head. We have many rules for maintaining our purity.

Whereas the balian katakson and balian kapican receive their initiation through direct intervention of a god, the balian usada must undergo a long learning process. He is tutored by a senior balian and goes through a training course comparable to Western medical schools. Many Balinese people view the balian usada as identical to a doctor of modern medicine.

The details of how someone can become a balian usada are found in the lontars called *Bodha Kecapi*, *Usada Kalimosada*, and *Usada Sari*. Before being accepted as a student, he must take an oath to his teacher that he will share the good and bad times. Readiness to obey all rules of the master teacher is necessary. After a series of ceremonies, the student

Figure 1.i

Walking Thunder, Diné Medicine Woman

Figure 1.ii

Walking Thunder's family

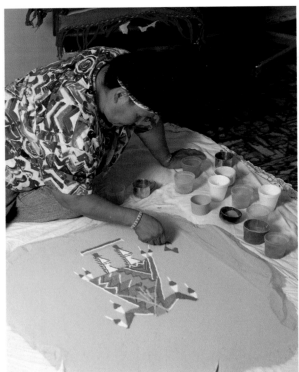

Figure 1.iii

A sandpainting created
to help a woman become
independent and strong

Figure 1.iv

Walking Thunder's favorite
sandpainting,
The Four Directions

Figure 2.i

Otavia Alves Pimentel Barbosa and family

Figure 2.ii

Otavia using charcoal:
"When the live coal goes out,
the disease goes out, too."

Figure 2.iii

João Fernandes de Carvalho

Figure 2.iv

João with one
of his spiritual
prescriptions

Figure 2.v

João with his family

Figure 3.i

Gary Holy Bull,
Lakota *Yuwipi* Man

Figure 3.ii

The dome framework of a purification lodge, made from willow branches

Figure 3.iii

Covered purification lodge

Figure 3.iv

Gary Holy Bull

Figure 4.i

Ava Tape Miri, Guarani Shaman

Figure 4.ii

Tupa Nevangayu, Guarani Shaman, and family

Figure 4.iii

Takua
Kawirembeyju,
Guarani Shaman

Figure 5.i

Credo Mutwa singing with South African boys serving prison sentences for rape and murder

Figure 5.ii

Credo Mutwa's Aunt Mynah and initiates prepare for a ceremony

Figure 5.iii

Divination ritual at Cliff of the Vultures using a medicine bag, with Credo Mutwa and Mutwa's assistant Sangoma, Nobela, in trance. The *Fearsome Gorge* lies below.

Figure 5.iv

Zulu ceremony

Figure 5.v

Credo Mutwa

Figure 6.i

Mangku Alit,
traditional healer
of Bali

Figure 6.ii

Jero Mangku
Srikandi,
healer of Bali

Figure 6.iii

I Gusti Gede Raka Antara,
healer of Bali

Figure 7.i

Ikuko Osumi, Sensei

Figure 7.ii

Osumi's Aunt
Hisa Hayashibe

Figure 7.iii

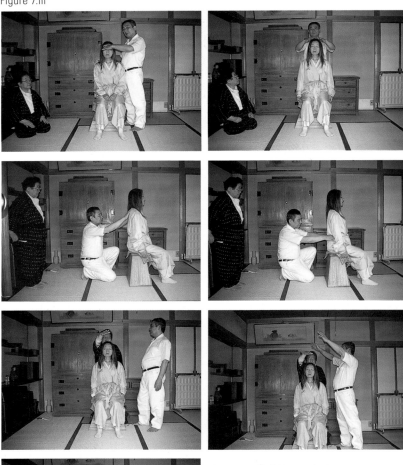

Japanese Seiki transmission

Figure 7.iv

The daily exercise of Seiki

Figure 7.v

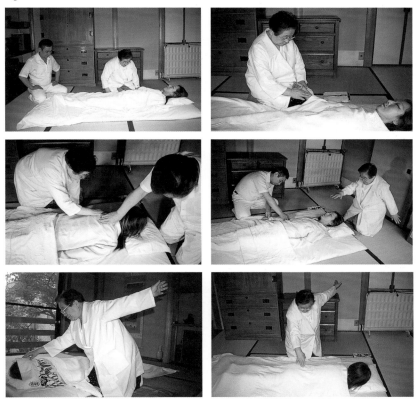

Seiki therapy

Figure 8.i

Shaker "Prayer House"

Figure 8.ii

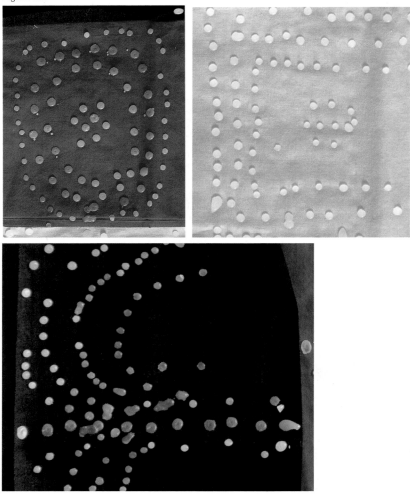

Cloth bands with wax markings for Shaker mourning ceremony

Figure 8.iii

Mother Ralph praying in a Shaker "Praise House"

Figure 8.iv

Mother Haynes

Figure 8.v

Shaker spiritual service

Figure 8.vi

Mother Samuel, Shaker leader

Figure 8.vii

Mother and Father Pompey,
Shaker spiritual elders

Figure 8.viii

St. Vincent street scene

Figure 8.ix

Archbishop Pompey,
Shaker healer

Figure 9.i

Mabolelo Shikwe,
Kalahari Bushman
healer

Figure 9.ii

Kalahari Bushmen

Figure 9.iii

Rasimane,
Kalahari
Bushman
healer

Figure 9.iv

Motaope Saboabue,
Kalahari Bushman healer

Figure 9.v

Xherma, Kalahari Bushman healer

Figure 9.vi

Kalahari healing dance

Figure 9.vii

Komtsa Xau,
Kalahari
Bushman healer

Figure 9.viii

Xixae Dxao,
Kalahari Bushman
healer

Figure 10.i

A redrawing of rock art from Eastern Cape showing bent over postures of dances

Figure 10.ii

Figure 10.iii

Ropes to the sky (from Bleek, 1940, plates 18 and 19)

The "flying posture"—a common motif in Kalahari rock paintings

is given the oral teachings. Years of study follow, and the student acquries mastery in anatomy, psychology, pathology, and pharmacology. Today fewer young adults are training to be balian usadas. Western education, which is beginning to influence the educational institutions here, does not consider the knowledge of the lontar usadas to be scientific in the modern world. Hence, the present generation is more interested in pursuing modern medicine. At the same time, the number of lontars is declining due to decay and lack of maintenance by successors. Finally, the raw materials for the medicines are becoming more difficult to find because the land in which they used to grow is disappearing due to agriculture, industry, and housing development. Yet Balinese people still seek balians for help, especially when the sickness or problem is believed to be *niskala* disease, something caused by supernatural forces.

When you need help you must choose the correct balian and the correct god for your situation. The same god can be used to help or harm another person. If you want to create something, you have to call upon Brahma.[1] If you want to preserve something, you have to call Wishnu. For destroying, you call upon Siwa. Each of these gods is a part of the whole. Each balian has her or his own way. What is right is that they follow their natural way. Some balians must follow the left side. That is not wrong to us. It is simply their way. We think of good and evil in a different way than traditional Western philosophy. We believe that God can be evil if he makes something bad. On the other hand, we recognize that evil can make something good. When that happens, evil becomes a good.

One of the reasons to see a balian is to find your way—whether you are to follow the left or right way. Most people don't understand this point of view. Instead, they go to the balian to get medicines for their sickness. Behind the medicine is a lot of explanation about the way of life they should live. This is the wisdom that helps people live a good life. We have

---

[1] In the Indian Hindu religion, the three primary gods are Brahma, the creator, Vishnu, the preserver, and Shiva, the destroyer. Wishnu and Siwa are the Balinese Hindu spellings for the Indian Hindu gods Vishnu and Shiva. Since this is a book on Balinese culture, we have maintained their versions throughout this chapter.

many stories that help us understand that there are many views of each situation. We learn that good is always bad from some point of view and bad is always good from another perspective.

There are two kinds of diseases. Those caused by natural physical means are called *sekala* disease. The second kind of disease is brought about by supernatural or nonmaterial things. These are called *niskala* disease. We see sickness as representing an unbalanced situation. The balian sets out to find what is unbalanced. It could come from any level—from a witch's spell, family business matters, physical events, and so on. Most healers probably use a mix of good and bad. You have to have both in order to achieve balance. If you erase the bad, you couldn't have good. You must always have the balance. In a way, this means that some balians need to make sickness while others must cure the sickness.

Power comes from the tension between the left and right, evil and good. We call this power *sakti*. Western scholars mix up this concept. They think it means the life force or vitality within a person. When there is a battle between opposing forces, the power is in the difference between them. When one side wins, the power or sakti is said to go to that side. At that moment, there is no sakti for the loser. But the sakti began as the tension or difference between them before there was a victor. This is a complex understanding. No one really has sakti in the sense of having a force or power inside them. It is more accurate to say that a spiritual person is fighting for sakti rather than say that they have sakti. If we say that they have sakti it really means that they are in a battle for it. If there is no evil attacking you, there is no sakti in the situation. But if someone is trying to kill you and you are still alive, you are in sakti. This is an important concept to us and outsiders who study our culture don't understand it. You never win a battle because the important fights keep going on. You may be winning and then there is sakti. We might say, "Don't go over there because he is sakti." This means he is winning. He is alive as he confronts forces that try to destroy him. Sometimes you win and sometimes you lose. All of our stories are about these cycles of winning and losing sakti.

A person who practices black magic can also be sakti. This person is using his power to kill and harm others. He is winning. We might say,

"Don't go over there because he is sakti." This time when we say it, it means that the person practices black magic. He could give you a bad headache or cause trouble for you. However, we also know that the strong practitioner of black magic is necessary for the creation of strong balians of the right. Those who heal need those who make others sick. The tension and fight between them makes the sakti necessary for the balian to be an effective healer. Balinese wisdom understands that on the big level—the enemy is necessary, but you must still fight him or her as hard as you can.

Practitioners of black magic like to turn themselves into other creatures because they want to test themselves. They want to see if they are sakti or not. When they are successful they feel great, saying, "Oh, I can do that." This sort of playing around has a cost. Once they start doing it and feeling the power of their skill, it is hard for them to stop. It's like smoking. Once you get addicted, it is hard to cut off. You have to be careful.

In Bali, if you talk about our way of life, you are talking about our religion. And if you talk about our religion, you are talking about our everyday life. Our religion and life cannot be separated. Like the human body, our religion has a head, body, and feet. Philosophy is considered its head, ethics its body, and ritual constitutes the feet. All of these parts must make up a balanced whole.

For the Balinese people, Jero Gede Macaling is the most important god. Jero means the highest level, *gede* means big, and *macaling* refers to a big tusk or fang. This god is considered to be controlling all of the villages and people. Many people aim their prayers to him and consider him to be the most important manifestation of the supreme god. He can make both bad and good things happen in your life. In order to benefit from him, we must make prayers and offerings and remember him in whatever we are doing. This god, or *barong*, is very powerful, and many people are afraid of him. Many balians use his powers to cure illness and help others. When balians pray to him from far away, they make special offerings and call him along with other manifestations of the supreme god. Some balians will ask this god to do something, show them a sign, or speak through them while in trance. Both balians of the left and right appeal to this god. He is just power that can be used for purposes of the right or left.

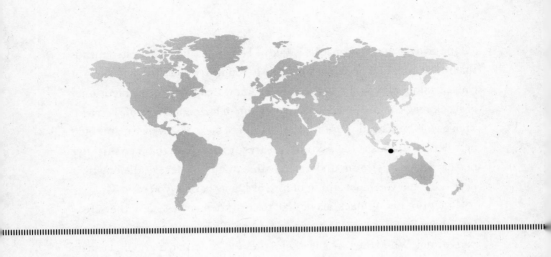

Balians

Mangku Alit

My grandfather was a balian and now this is what I do. All of this began for me when I was fourteen years old. At that time, I was in a very bad automobile accident. I was the only one who survived the crash. Soon after that calamity, I almost drowned in a river. I went under the water several times, but was rescued. That wasn't the end of it. After the near drowning, I fell down from a mango tree and should have been injured, but walked away without a scratch. These three things happened one right after the other when I was a girl.

Then the spirits started disturbing me. This would happen each day at 8:00 in the morning and at 12:00 midnight. I was unable to go to school for a while because I was so disturbed and confused by these spirits. When I sat in a chair, they made me feel like I wasn't sitting. Instead, I felt like I was floating above the chair. When I was able to go to school, I always knew the answers even before the teacher had taught the subject. This frustrated the teachers because in Bali a student is not supposed to be seen as above the teacher. This behavior was regarded as a sign that I would become a balian.

I was told that I needed to be taken to a balian. My family and friends were worried that if I didn't start the appropriate rituals to become a balian, the spirits would make me sick again or cause another accident. That's the way these things work. I refused because I didn't believe any of it. My older brothers and sisters weren't balians, so I thought I didn't have to be one. I then became mysteriously ill again and collapsed into an unconscious state for three days. I was asleep and no one could awaken me.

When I woke up and found out what had happened, I knew at that moment that I had no choice. I had to be a balian. If I chose to not believe or not to do the work, then I would be refusing what god was giving me. That would be dangerous. At eighteen years of age, back in 1980, I began helping others as a balian. From that moment on, I allowed the gods to direct what I do. My learning is not from books and teachers. I am an instrument of the gods.

When I do my work as a balian, my body feels very light. I feel no attachment to my body. When I sit on my platform, I feel like I am floating over it. My body hair stands straight up when this happens. My head feels like it expands and gets larger and my body feels like it is also stretching. Then my head starts feeling very cold. That's when I take burning, glowing hot charcoals and put my face in their smoke. It

Figure 6.1

Figure 6.2

should feel very hot, but to me it feels very cold. Burning coconut shells produce very high heat, but it always feels cold to me. I always use the smoke when I help people.

When I started, I had very white skin, but now my skin is brown because I hold hot charcoals all the time. I have been using them for twenty years. When the smoke is blown to and fro around my face, I am inviting the god Siwa to enter my head. I breathe the smoke through my nose and mouth. This happens automatically and I have no explanation for why this happens. Then the gods may speak through me. Siwa,

Buddha, and other gods come through my voice. They give help to the people who ask for it.

People come to me for help with their sickness, personal problems, and business issues. The gods help them with all kinds of challenges and difficulties. Sometimes the gods come to me in my dreams. They usually do that if I made a mistake in a ceremony. They will correct my words or show me what I did wrong so it can be corrected. Sometimes they tell me a different way of helping a person. If I dream of someone getting sick and see a grave, then I have to hurry to cure them. That means there is little time to help them get well. If I dream of a huge flood or see the river wash away the houses and trees, then I know that a big storm or monsoon is on the way.

When the gods communicate with me, I receive a special feeling in my body. I don't see or hear them. I feel something come over me and then they speak automatically through my voice. The gods will tell what kind of sickness a person has and explain why a person has it. The gods usually speak no longer than ten minutes at a time.

Once a family brought me a young man who was going crazy. People were convinced that he had been the victim of black magic. However, the gods told me that he simply needed to go to school. That was the medicine for him. He went back to school and was no longer crazy. There had been no black magic and he did not require a plant medicine or a ceremony. The gods use many different kinds of treatments and medicines.

When people come to me, they do not tell me anything about their situation, problem, or illness. They just come and sit down while I make a prayer. The gods tell me everything. There is no need for the patient to say anything. They bring their offerings and expect the gods to tell me whatever I need to know.

Jero Mangku Srikandi

I am connected to the magic of Buddhism, Islam, Hinduism, and Christianity. The gods of the world now use me to help others. The gods have given me their certificates of approval. When people come to me with a problem, my job is to release the problem so that the person's

Figure 6.3

life becomes peaceful and prosperous. If someone wants to do healing work in Bali, they can come to me. I have the authority to grant them approval from the gods.

I never went to school. I became a balian when I was seven years old. The gods spoke different languages through me. I have been helping people ever since.

I started as a balian when a god came to me. The god told me to die three times. I experienced what felt like death and I went to heaven. There I was given permission from God. When I told people about what had happened, they made a cremation ceremony for me. I was wrapped up in cloth just like a dead person. The ceremony was held in a special temple. All priests should experience themselves dying and becoming reborn again.

After this took place, the gods would enter me and dance and sing through my body. There is a Chinese goddess that enters me. She taught me to dance and move my hands in a magical way. This goddess is named Dewikwanin.[2] I do whatever the gods and goddesses tell me to do. If a god comes down and tells me to lie on the ground, I do so without

---

[2] Dewikwanin is the Balinese name for the Buddhist goddess Quan Yin, who is the embodiment of compassionate loving-kindness.

hesitation. If I am told to move my hands, my hands instantly move. I always do what the gods want.

When a patient comes to me, I ask my god what is wrong with them and what kind of medicines will help. When the goddess dances me, I feel like I am flying. I am very light. I am the only balian who dances like this.

Last November I went to Java because a god there wanted to be inside me. It spoke a different language. Now it helps me work with other people who come for help.

The gods tell me about the people who come to me. I know who is practicing black magic. The god has me ask them what they think they are doing with it. However, I don't use any special protection against them. I only use my gods. I can also see who is practicing white magic. I help them do their job.

I Gusti Gede Raka Antara

My grandfather was a balian who healed the sick. After he died, people started coming to me asking for medicines. Since my father didn't want to be a healer, I felt the responsibility was coming to me. I then had a special dream where my old grandfather came up to me and said he was going to take me to a certain place. The place in the dream was very strange, and we had to go through different areas because many of the routes were blocked. It was difficult to get there in the dream. In the dream, I saw myself being purified with holy water when we finally arrived.

After that dream, I would often hear a voice just before I fell asleep in the evenings. I would be half asleep when I heard someone say, "If you go this way, it will be like this." I kept hearing these same words over and over.

In my dreams, my grandfather taught me how to heal others by passing my power or energy to someone. I also learned that I could see a person's sickness when I looked at them and that I would automatically know what to do that would help their situation.

I am a scholar of the lontars. The lontars in my family have been handed down for fifteen generations. They have to be recopied every sixty years or so. The lontars teach many things, including how we can take energy from nature. First it comes into the body and then it can be aimed at other people.

It brings great pleasure to feel high vibrations in the head. To feel this you must press down your anger. Anger must first be controlled. If you can reduce your anger, all the power of nature will come to you without any effort. Let me sing you something from the lontar:

The biggest enemy we have is anger. Our closest friend is knowledge.

When nature's energy flows through you, you will feel your body having many hearts. They will all beat their rhythms. These hearts can pump an energy that brings forth the sacred light. The most powerful light is blue.

We balians have many kinds of sacred knowledge recorded in the lontars. Some of these hold magical drawings that can be used for many different purposes. I will now show them to you and tell you what they may be used for. They can be used for health, protection, social advantage, and many other purposes.

If you learn about the right side, you must also learn about the left. Otherwise, if you just learn about the right or white side, someone who is practicing black magic will try to confront or fight you. It's like a magnet. Opposites will draw one another out. If you already know the power of both sides, you will know how to avoid drawing out the left or black side. The lontars teach us about both sides. You must learn both sides to protect yourself.

People who practice on the left side also use the magical drawings. Most of the black magic happens when you are sleeping. You have less control during your sleep. People usually learn about the left side from a black magic practitioner. The teacher will give you some magical words and then step on your head with their foot. This is the same initiation that is done by the gods who help you do good things for people. In this case, a human being steps on his or her student. There used to be many black magic teachers in Bali, but not anymore. I learned about the left side from the lontar teachings.

I learned that the good always comes with the bad. They are in the same home. If some good happens, look out for the bad. I have learned to respect both sides and to work carefully within the space that holds both of them.

Figure 6.4

I have seen an evil spirit. It was associated with a black magic practitioner. However, my patient, who looked in the same direction, did not see anything. Black magic involves making someone see an illusion; that is, seeing something that is not really there. What I saw was a projected image. It was not real in the physical sense. It was something sent by black magic.

Sometimes when you protect yourself, you must send an image to keep people away, but there is actually nothing there. You can use an image from the drawings to send something that's not real. However, it will be there as an experience and other people will think it is real. It's like a shadow. It can walk, but it is not separate from you. The magic works by how you use your concentration to focus on an image and project it somewhere. A black magic practitioner can turn himself or herself into another image like a tower or a bull.

Figure 6.5

Whenever you see a shadow that upsets you or you see and hear something that looks and sounds like it is evil, sit down, close your eyes, and fully concentrate. Immediately open your eyes in one direction without blinking and it will disappear. This action is like shining a strong light or fire on the darkness. It makes it go away.

If you want to be close to someone, there is a certain mantra you can use with a drawing. You may have to spread it on the ground and add some salt. If the person you want walks on it, he or she will want to be in touch with you.

Before you see the magical drawing, I want you to remember that the left and right sides, or good and bad, are always joined. You must learn from their interaction and not be overconcerned with either maximizing or minimizing either side. This is the way of wisdom. It is also the secret to power and the very essence of the deepest love and compassion.

An offering should be made to all drawings every day. If an offering isn't made, it shows the spirits that you aren't paying attention, and the spirit, in turn, will not pay attention to you.

Pematuh Agung

Draw this image onto a piece of gold and place it in your bedroom. It aims to create peace and harmony in your life.

Figure 6.6

Ikuko Osumi, Sensei
JAPANESE MASTER OF SEIKI JUTSU

Introduction to *Ikuko Osumi, Sensei*

by Nancy Connor

Osumi, Sensei is among the most energetically powerful healers I have met. In fact, her healing sessions with me left me overwhelmed by her power. She and her assistant channel energy in a way that is directed and purposeful in order to heal those who come to her for treatment. She has a very long list of clients, ranging from ordinary people from her village to corporate executives from well-known companies. Each of them has a story of her ability to heal, her concern for her patients, and her connection to spirit.

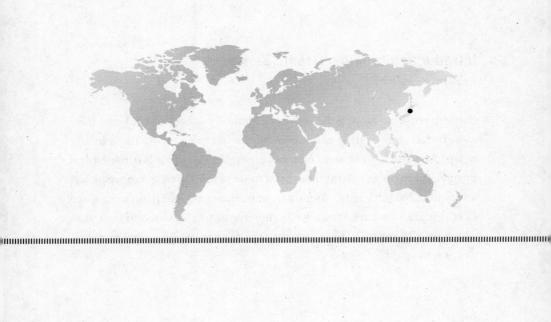

I WAS BORN on the fifteenth of May, 1918, into an ancient samurai family called Katagiri, in the village of Gamo, near Sendai city in Miyagi Prefecture, Japan. Gamo was a seashore district about 190 miles north of Tokyo. It was quiet and rich in nature, and the people were fishermen and farmers. It was my childhood habit to stand on a small hill called Hiyori Mountain and listen to the wind and observe the animals. Those were days of wonder. I discovered and learned about the harmony of nature, the rhythms of the four seasons, and the variety of flowers and natural life.

My childhood was haunted by the story my grandfather told me about a great tidal wave. It touched my dreams. I experienced the roar of the Sanriku tidal wave, a devastating event that occurred before I was born. I still dream of it today.

My grandfather, who owned the local fishing fleet and several large rice fields, told me how my grandmother and aunt had crouched in the corner of the twelve-mat room on the second floor of his immense home. He watched them bow again and again toward the sea, praying to every Shinto god and Buddhist saint for deliverance. The fearsome tidal wave that Grandfather had predicted would strike our coast was bearing down upon them.

"This is exactly why I had a two-story house built!" my grandfather shouted out. In my imagination, I could see his silhouette against the night sky, straight and firm. "It's a gigantic crest moving toward us!" my grandfather soon proclaimed. And as my aunt tells the story, he "didn't move a centimeter away from the window." She admired his courage. He stood leaning forward and peering unafraid at the roaring sea as it advanced toward him.

The enormous wall of water crashed into the village and crept right up to the foundation of his house. He watched stoically as the sea swirled around and carried almost everything back out to sea with it—houses, trees, and people. The village was destroyed in front of his eyes.

My grandfather practically rebuilt the village himself. He gave money, goods, and property to rehabilitate Gamo. He is most famous today for his generous investment in the construction of a permanent harbor for the nearby town of Shiogama. Before the tidal wave, Shiogama had a natural harbor that provided the local mooring for the region's fishing boats. Unfortunately, the tidal wave destroyed the harbor and caused the loss of many lives. Grandfather told me that he wanted to be sure that life, property, and fishing boats would be protected in the future. Out of his own resources, he undertook the construction of a massive break-water project.

Even at that early age, I was struck deep in my heart by the thought of those fishermen dying in that terrible mountain of water. I often thought about the fishermen and the village people. I was also very aware of the difference between the luxury found in my grandfather's great house and the humble, almost poverty-stricken existence of the villagers.

Although I understood how much he cared for the fishermen, I observed how custom required that the fishermen be met in the kitchen, while other guests with family crests on their kimonos, indicating their lineage in a great family, were ceremoniously ushered into the living room. My grandfather was the head of the fishermen's organization and was therefore respected by both rich and poor.

The fishing people loved my grandfather and respected our family, and I always had a warm feeling for them. Whenever I met them outside of our house, they bowed and said, "Ah, it's Katagiri-san's grandchild." If they were in a cart, they always offered me a ride. I was moved to tears when I saw someone who had lost a leg or an arm at sea, or heard how someone had died due to the lack of proper medical treatment, since there was no doctor in the village. As a child, I set the goal of becoming a doctor and helping people with such suffering.

But the fortunes of the Katagiri family soon began to decline. Expenditures for the reconstruction of Shiogama harbor were more than my grandfather had predicted. He was never able to recoup the huge amount of money that he invested into that project. That, in addition to other philanthropic expenses and various ill-advised ventures, cut deeply into his finances. He was losing his once-enormous fortune.

My grandfather never complained during this time, but he began to age more quickly than I thought he should. He was no longer able to walk with me through the orchard or go to the hill where we would look out over the ocean. In better times and health, he would take me to that hill and teach me how to chant Chinese poems and perform sword dances. And when the weather was bad, we would stand there and wave white or red flags to the fishing boats, indicating the direction the wind was blowing. My father, with his long, thin arms, also helped us wave those flags. I was no more than five years old at the time.

Early Signs of Power

When I was eight years old, I knew that I was an "unusual" child. I had strange visions that often amazed the villagers. I knew the sex of an unborn baby who was being carried by a pregnant fisherman's wife. I was also a veritable weather forecaster for the village. I never failed to predict the weather for the following day, and the fishermen counted on me to help them in their work. I also became well-known to the surrounding area for my clairvoyance.

One time a driver of a cart picked me up and gave me a ride to my grandfather's house. I thought I saw a sick man lying in the back of the cart. He was wearing an unusual pair of green pantaloons. I asked the driver who the man with the bright clothing was, and he turned around and looked puzzled. He didn't know what I was talking about.

"The man right there," I said, "the one wearing those funny green pantaloons." The driver looked very perplexed, but managed to say,

"That could be my brother because he is mighty proud of those panta-loons, but where is he?" He did not see anyone in the back of the cart. I then gasped because I turned and saw that the man I was describing was dead. I told the driver, "Your brother is lying in the back and he is dead."

He let me off the cart and turned around to go home as fast as the cart could take him. When he arrived, his wife met him with the news that his brother had fallen on his fishing boat, become caught in his tackle, and fallen into the water and drowned.

Finding *Seiki* Within

Seiki has benefited people in every corner of the world, although it is called by many different names and is exercised in many different ways. In Japanese, "seiki" is composed of two Chinese characters, sei and ki. Sei means "life," while ki means "spirit," "mind," as well as "air," "atmosphere," "breath." Seiki is an old Japanese word used to refer to the vital life force.

When I was fifteen years old, my grandfather had lost almost every-thing, including his house. We moved to Shiogama and lived with my great aunt. My grandfather died soon after we moved, and we mourned his passing for a long time. I kept hearing my father's last words to me: "Go to Tokyo, Ikuko, and be of service to the villagers." The desire to do something for others grew within me. I decided I would leave Shiogama, go to my mother in Tokyo, and become a doctor.

My mother brought me to Tokyo, but her family decided that I was to stay with my mother's second-eldest brother, Mr. Hayashibe, and his wife. They had no children and lived in a large two-story house in the western section of Tokyo. I didn't see my mother for the next three months, and then she showed up at the house. She spoke with my aunt and uncle, but I did not see her. After she left, my aunt told me that my mother was engaged to remarry and that it had been decided that I would permanently live with my uncle and aunt. I was devastated and shocked. I had lived with the fantasy of living with my mother while studying to become a doctor. My dreams were destroyed in that moment.

My uncle and aunt didn't send me to the university to study medicine as I had hoped, but arranged for me to take private lessons in such traditional refinements as tea ceremony, sewing, calligraphy, and flower arranging. I knew that they were preparing me for a future marriage. However, I was unable to stay with any class for more than three months, and the teachers gave up on me. Life became a terrible, thick, black cloud through which I had to push myself every step of the way. I felt very disappointed with the direction of my life, and I refused to listen to anyone.

My uncle took me to various Western doctors and Chinese specialists who prescribed both drugs and herbs. I did not improve and my world became a hazy fog of half-remembered and half-forgotten dreams.

What stood out to me in those confusing times were my aunt's strange daily visits to a private room in the house. I noticed how she would go upstairs, dressed in full kimono regalia, and disappear behind the door of a small three-mat room in the Hayashibe home. She was quite austere, had chalk-white skin, and was very healthy for a sixty-year-old woman. (See Figure 7.ii.)

One day she asked the servants to bring tea to us. "Ikuko," she said, "I want you to listen to me. I have something I want to tell you. Perhaps you have wondered what I do every day in that three-mat room. I can't tell you directly because it is too difficult to explain. I feel that what I do in there can cure you of your problems. Medicine isn't working, and I want to propose something that I want to keep strictly between you and me."

She paused to take a sip of tea and then went on: "I'm well aware that a young woman has to present a modest face in the world, but yours is too modest. You show no spirit, although I feel that there is much hidden within. I am aware of your hidden disappointment over your mother's marriage. But these things can't be helped. Your mother has married into the Osaka family, and they do not want it known that she was ever previously married. Your mother doesn't dislike you. She wants you to live your own life. You should also know that she had been married into the Katagiri family very much against her own will." She then offered me a rice cake and some daintily wrapped delicacies. "Take it all," she urged me. "You must eat. You look like a skeleton."

I slowly took the cake and felt the impact of my aunt's words. Why hadn't someone told me this news about my mother a long time ago?

My aunt had more to say. She leaned over and said, "Every day at three o'clock, as you probably know very well by now, I close myself in my three-mat room. There I do my seiki exercises. I can't explain seiki to you, but I believe that seiki is the only thing left that can cure you. I'm sure I can cure you with it. Are you willing to try?" I nodded my head, without understanding anything that she had said. And then she added, "Not a word to your uncle because he isn't a seiki enthusiast."

My aunt then said that she would "instill" seiki into me the next afternoon. She told me that she had originally had a weak constitution and had been very sick after marrying her uncle. She had seiki instilled in her, and after carrying out daily seiki exercises she regained her health. She gave me a warning: "Don't ever try to instill seiki in other people. It's a dangerous act and you can become so exhausted that you can easily die."

The next day she instilled seiki into me and I was horrified to see that her arms and hands had turned purple. She remained in bed for several days to regain her energy. She had risked her life to help save mine and showed me how much she cared for me. I still remember her words: "Ikuko, if you can get well this way, I don't care what happens to me."

I didn't understand how my aunt instilled seiki in me. She simply sat me on a stool in the "seiki room," as she called the three-mat room upstairs. She stepped behind me, and I couldn't see what she was doing. I remember that after a while I found myself moving around in an endless rocking motion. That movement pleased my aunt, who subsequently said that I now had seiki inside me.

"You could even become a seiki teacher," my aunt said, and laughed a rare laugh. She was extremely pleased with what had happened, but quickly frowned and warned, "Under no circumstances are you to teach any kind of seiki therapy. It's too dangerous." I still didn't understand what she was talking about.

The next day she spoke about a "follow-up" to the seiki instillation. "I want you to sit on the stool that's in the seiki room at least once a day for twenty minutes. When you sit down, put the tips of your fingers together and bring them up to your eyes. Touch your fingers against your closed eyes. Then wait and see what takes place."

I went dutifully up to the three-mat room and sat on the seiki stool. I touched my eyes as she had instructed and nothing happened. I felt somewhat foolish, and then all of a sudden I began moving slowly in a circular fashion as I had done when seiki had been instilled. My body continued to move on its own, and I felt that I was not instigating its movement. I became intrigued with this self-propelled motion and found it to be a pleasant sensation. I did this for twenty minutes and then stopped the rocking movement by my own will. That was my first seiki exercise session.

After receiving seiki, I sensed the seeds of some well-being within my body, and I made a commitment to do this exercise every day. My aunt was pleased with what had taken place, and she told me that the next time I should touch my body in various places with my hands. I found that the force of seiki drew my hand to touch my heart, eyes, and lungs. It was strange, but I began appreciating the power my aunt had placed within me.

Over the following months, my health began to improve. I began thinking that I would not become a doctor, but would become someone like my aunt who could instill seiki into others. In that way, I could help other people with their health. I followed the way my aunt did her exercise. I, too, approached it as an austere ceremony and dressed in a formal kimono to practice it. The relationship with my aunt became very warm and abiding. She showed me how to make the exercise more effective and taught me to remove all thoughts and emotions from my mind. With seiki, I had a new life and purpose in life.

I learned that the daily practice of seiki throws off exhaustion and unwanted elements from the body and replaces them with a surge of new energy. It was the key to daily health and well-being. I started doing my seiki exercise every day and felt myself absorbing energy from nature itself as my body moved around and around on the stool.

At that time, I began intense self-analysis. I contemplated the inter-relationship between nature and the human body and how our health functions within that context. I pondered the relationship between various body movements and the workings of our glands and nerves. I considered how it was possible to relieve various kinds of pain. In this deep period of contemplation, I lost contact with the everyday world and felt as if I had entered another dimension of the universe. I could look inside my own body and observe its inner workings. I learned to be one with the seiki movements that took place in my body during my exercise time.

Learning to Help Others with Seiki

Within three months, I was completely myself again. The neighbors would come to visit me again, often bringing fresh vegetables. If some-one was sick, they came to me for treatment. I learned how to heal with the power of seiki that overflowed within me. People were astonished at this unexpected power, and many came for treatment. Those days spent in the country were the most memorable of my life. Surrounded by natural beauty, I conversed with nature and my own body. There my relationship with seiki matured.

One day a cousin came to visit us. He had been diagnosed as having heart disease. Even the act of walking was difficult for him. He com-plained about not being able to sleep at night, and I noticed how he always carried many medicines around with him.

My aunt began talking with him about seiki, and he showed an intense interest in the subject. My aunt then stood up and walked to the window. She quickly turned around and said to him, "Do you want to get well?" "Of course I do," he answered at once. After a moment of silence, my aunt announced, "Then let us instill seiki in you."

I looked at my cousin and my aunt with great surprise. That word "us" truly startled me. What did my aunt mean? It was the first time she had ever implied that we were some kind of team. I was then even more surprised to hear her say, "Ikuko will instill seiki into you. Is that all right?"

This sent a thrill through me and I looked at my aunt, but she looked away. The sound of confidence in her voice assured me that my time had come. Whatever doubts and fears had been associated with giving seiki were immediately dissipated. I knew I was ready to do this kind of work.

My cousin put himself in my hands. I told him what I knew about seiki, and I expressed my belief that he would get well if he undertook the treatments. Within two days, he threw away his medicine and devoted himself to being under my care. His preparation for being instilled with seiki took time. I wanted his body to be free of the medicines he had been taking. I also wanted him to rest. During that time, I couldn't stop thinking about the day when I would be faced with the challenge of instilling seiki within his body. I felt inexplicably confident about doing this.

When the day arrived for him to receive seiki, my aunt stayed downstairs in the living room. She did not say a word as I led my cousin upstairs into the three-mat room. I sat him down on the seiki stool and stood behind him as my aunt had done when she gave me seiki. I began moving my hands in the air. Somehow I knew I was supposed to do that. The essence of seiki was in the hands and fingers.

I then moved my hands over my cousin's head, groping toward something invisible to others. While my arms were moving about, I accidentally hit the wall. The sound of this impact sent a strange resonance into my head. I then knew that this kind of noise was necessary. I spontaneously began taking in deep breaths of air and blowing them out as I hit the wall with the palms of my hands. The noise precipitated certain kinds of vibrations. A fluttering sound moved past my ears. The room was electrified with sound, vibration, and movement.

And then, quite suddenly, my hands felt drawn to the top of his head as if they were magnets. They clamped so immediately to his head that I was somewhat taken aback. My cousin uttered a slight sound of surprise, but within a second or two I felt something like a bolt of electricity move through my hand into my cousin's head. I knew that this was seiki. I wanted to shout with happiness! At that moment, my cousin's head slipped away from my hand due to the back and forth movements that had come upon him. It was the same kind of movement that I had experienced during my own instillation and during my seiki exercise. I was delirious with excitement, for I knew that I had instilled seiki into someone for the first time in my life.

As my cousin rocked back and forth, he cried out in ecstasy, "It's like walking on a cloud." I moved toward the doorway and looked back to see him rocking with complete contentment. I went to get my aunt and show her that I had succeeded in instilling seiki.

Without a word, my aunt followed me upstairs and looked into the three-mat room. She immediately broke her silence and with a big smile on her face she exclaimed, "That, Ikuko, is seiki. You have mastered it at last. You have done a marvelous job. Congratulations! This is exactly what I have been teaching you."

I looked at her with bewilderment. My aunt had taught me nothing. Then I realized that she had been my teacher all along. Most important, she had taught me confidence. What more can you ask from a teacher?

My aunt then went to my cousin and lightly touched his tailbone with the tips of her fingers. He immediately stopped rocking. That was the first and last concrete thing about seiki that she ever showed me.

Figure 7.1

"Congratulations!" she said to him. "Ikuko has instilled seiki within you. She will tell you what you are to do next." And then she left the room.

I told him how to sit on the stool and do the seiki exercise each day. To this day, my very first patient is as healthy as a horse. His heart problem completely disappeared, and he walks about with the gait of a thirty-year-old man.

With this initial success, I began treating relatives and friends of the family, instilling seiki into those who showed interest.

Eizon Hoin

More than ten years after I became a seiki therapist, I returned to Gamo to visit my native land. I went to express my appreciation to my relatives, acquaintances, and ancestors for my being able to help others. I went to the shrine of Eizon Hoin on top of Maki, the sacred mountain that I often visited as a child. He was one of my ancestors and is very important in my work.

My grandmother had taken me to Mount Maki when I was five years old. There she told me about our famous Katagiri ancestor Eizon Hoin, who was a seventeenth-century Buddhist priest. My grandmother told me about a white snake that lived near his shrine and that protected the family. No one had ever seen it, but its cast-off skins were gathered each year and used by my grandmother as medicine to treat wounds and warts.

Once I was playing with a ball and it rolled into the area of the shrine. When I went to get it, the white snake suddenly appeared in front of me, raised its head, and began to speak. It said that it was tired and could no longer help the family. "You must do it now," it said to me.

The white snake, a messenger or manifestation of Eizon Hoin, had called me to be a helper of the family. Eizon Hoin was known for protecting people with his spiritual power, and because of this he was given the title Hoin, which is the highest rank of priesthood.

When I returned as an adult to visit his shrine, I felt his presence in the left side of my physical body and realized how he still protects me.

My Practice

At the end of her life, my aunt insisted that I study anatomy in order to qualify as a professional massage therapist so that I could legally open up my own seiki clinic. On the day that I returned from submitting my application for the exam, my aunt died.

On March 10, 1966, I officially opened my house as a clinic.

I have made the instilling of seiki the one and only goal of my life. I found that before it can be successfully transmitted and instilled, there is a preliminary period required to prepare the patient's body. Patients often say that this preparation results in the disappearance of their illnesses, aches, pains, exhaustion, and suffering. This takes place because my own seiki penetrates into the patient's body as I prepare them for instillation.

Word began to spread about my treatments. Patients often told me that they had tried various doctors and therapists without success. Many people came to me for help, including university teachers, musicians, politicians, company directors, architects, writers, and medical doctors, among others.

Other than what my aunt taught me, I never received any lessons or instruction about seiki. My knowledge has been self-taught. It came from my observation of nature and through the difficulties of my own life. I have always believed that difficulty and hardship was my way. Any kind of difficulty that happened to me was useful for my future. My husband died early in our marriage, and even his death was a blessing because it freed me to give my life to seiki, something I would not have been able to do in a traditional marriage.

I later studied anatomy at a renowned medical school and it gave me more confidence in my work because it confirmed what I had learned about the body through my intense periods of contemplation.

I came to realize the importance of the ancient Eastern idea that it is wise to annihilate the ego and to detach from emotions. Only through wholehearted devotion and concentration can anything important be accomplished. With my hands and fingers glued to my patient's bodies, I unite with them and find that treatment takes place in its own natural way.

Before my aunt died, she gave me a small book by Jozo Ishii entitled *The Essentials of Seiki Self-Healing Therapy*, published by the Seiki Institute in 1928.[1] It states that "seiki stimulates the exhausted nerves of the body and causes a reflex movement in the muscular system," referring to the automatic rocking motion which seiki brings about. Through this movement, seiki serves the physiological needs of the body. In this way it cures any disorders that may be present. Through daily seiki exercise, pain and sickness may be warded off.

Jozo Ishii wrote, "If elderly people make use of seiki, it will revitalize them and help return them to health, ultimately promoting and maintaining long life." Furthermore, "seiki stimulates any afflicted part of the body and sparks the cells in that region into activity. This influence spreads to surrounding areas until finally the cells of the body are aroused to action. This fires activation of the metabolism, quickens the flow of blood, brings forth active secretion, piques strong respiration, and induces proper and steady secretion. The result is that stagnation within the body is washed away. Seiki excites the nervous system. The nerves of any afflicted organs react. This produces the physiological movement of the nerves that are required for rehabilitation."

I am not a doctor, but I know that all organs and systems of the body are interrelated, each helping the other to build health. The seiki that comes out of my hands and body penetrates into the patient's body, helping them move toward greater health. There is nothing more wonderful, mysterious, and enthralling to me than seiki. I want everyone to experience it!

The Transmission or Instillation of Seiki

Seiki, the vital life force, is the primordial energy that exists throughout the entire universe. The transmission of this energy into another human being is called *seiki jutsu*, or the art of seiki. When seiki is transmitted to another person, it will stay with that person for their entire

---

[1] In Japan, during the first years of the Showa era in the second half of the 1920s, there existed a popular hygiene method called "Self-Improvement Life Force Therapy," and this book on seiki was one of its main references.

Figure 7.2

lifetime. Through the daily practice of seiki exercise, your health will be optimized and you will nurture seiki to be available for self-healing. And as this seiki matures within you, you will naturally be led to heal others. (See Figure 7.iii of a seiki session.)

On the day that I instill seiki, I clean the house inside and out. I water the flowers in the living room and in the garden. I make every effort to create a comfortable environment. The bedding is carefully prepared for the recipient. I double-check the temperature and humidity of the room as well as the lighting.

I transmit seiki at a specific place and time. The place is a tiny three-mat room in the corner of the second floor of my house, the same place I received it from my aunt. Like the seasonal rhythms of my garden,

I must wait for the right time to give seiki to a patient. I wait until I know when this should take place.

There are specific locations on the earth where the optimal flow of seiki is available at a certain time of day. These places are all over the world. I can intuitively feel these places, and these places are where I place the seiki stool.

Although I think it is possible to transmit seiki to any person, it is best to give it to someone who has been prepared beforehand. This opens them to be more receptive to its flow.

These general conditions should be met when transmitting seiki: (1) occurrence in a place and time where the purest and most concentrated seiki is available; (2) appropriate preparation of the patient's body so that it is readily open to the experience; (3) the attuned preparation of the body and soul of the transmitter; and finally, (4) a mutual trust between the receiver and the person who gives seiki.

When the receiver comes, he or she first receives a massage treatment and is given time to rest. I then drink some lemon juice and have a light lunch. When the time is right, I bring them to the three-mat room where they sit on the special seiki stool.

I begin by giving the receiver a prayer that asks that he or she will be most pleased and happy with the transmission.

While the person is seated on the stool, which is placed exactly on the spot where the seiki line flows, we give treatment to the head, the shoulders, and the lower back, responding to what I call the "callings of the receiver's body." I do this work with my assistant, Takafumi Okajima.

Preparation of the lower part of the back, the sacrum, is crucial. This is where seiki is received, and special treatment is given to it so that the whole body is relaxed.

I then begin feeling the heavy and abundant flow of seiki gathering from every direction. My assistant and I attract and gather seiki to the area where we are working. This is done by drawing upon the accumulated seiki in our own bodies as well as through the commotion of making loud noises, whether it be from shouting or from banging on the wall. My whole body shakes from this concentrated energy.

I then make the seiki warm and heavy, attracting it to the recipient. We brace ourselves for transmission and get ready for the special moment.

When it is time for transmission, I experience no ego consciousness and there is no separation between my mind and body. I feel that I have become absorbed into the body of the recipient. The seiki will soon flow naturally into their body. When this takes place, they will receive exactly the right amount, and the whole operation will be done in the same manner as a perfectly orchestrated dance.

Finally, my hands and those of my assistant are placed upon one another in order to transmit seiki. It comes through our hands.

My hands will feel like they are absorbed into the receiver's body. I experience the flow of seiki into them both mentally and physically. It will enter their body through their head. At the instant of transmission, the receiver and I will become one being. Our bodies and minds will be brought into harmonious unity.

This is when we feel a beautiful rhythm. As the receiver receives the necessary amount of seiki, their head will become free from the hold of our hands.

The transmitter's hands are put onto the receiver's head again, covering the whirl of the hair. At this moment their body will begin rocking back and forth or from side to side. This takes place gradually and naturally.

When the head of the receiver separates from my hands again, their body will continue to rock. The movements will differ from person to person. The movements may be forward and backward, left and right, a circular pattern, or restricted to the shoulders, arms, or other body parts, while some people will appear not to move at all, although they feel movement within. Some will be more active than others, and there are many different kinds of patterned movements. This natural movement is the starting point of well-being through seiki jutsu.

Seiki Exercise

The daily exercise of seiki in your body (see Figure 7.iv) is called seiki taisou. After receiving transmission, this exercise is conducted every day in order to maintain well-being and health. The recipients of seiki tend to have better health throughout the course of their lives. However, it is my belief that it is not possible to master "self-healing seiki therapy" without the assistance of a seiki master like myself. As priming water is necessary for pumping a well, so is the guidance and practice necessary for seiki jutsu. This is what I call the fulfillment of seiki.

To begin your seiki exercise, seat yourself on a seiki stool.

Next, press the inner corner of each eyeball with the middle finger of each hand. This alerts the autonomic nervous system through the optic nerve, saying, in effect, that "seiki taisou is now starting." The rocking motion already mentioned before in the reception of seiki now takes place spontaneously.

Gradually your head becomes relaxed and you feel ready to excrete the tiredness and waste from inside you. This is when you also bring energy into your body.

Seiki taisou gives rhythm to your body similar to the way music conveys inspiration through vibration. There are many ways in which the seiki exercise may be conducted.

At the end of the exercise, your physical movements will gradually slow down and come to a halt. Place your fingertips on your eyeballs again and send the signal that the exercise period is now over.

Seiki Therapy

Seiki therapy is a treatment approach in which a seiki therapist cures a patient using seiki. The aim of the treatment is to help patients regain their self-healing power. We bring to them the seiki energy that they lost and help them move it through their own body. Once you are filled with seiki, it triggers your own inner healing responses.

We first greet the patient and express our desire that they will return to good health. We then take their pulse, lift their eyelids to examine their eyes, and put our hands on their navel. This is how we diagnose their condition and assess the physical state of their nervous system.

In seiki therapy, the patient is an essential and active part of the healing process. He or she heals him- or herself with the help of the therapist. I treat them as their body directs me to. I respond to the "calling of the patient's body."

There is no fixed system or formula for healing in seiki therapy. The therapist's body can create an almost infinite variety of techniques to meet each client's unique needs.

Originally, seiki therapy was meant to prepare for the transmission of seiki. Today it stands as a therapy itself and helps patients in recovering their health.

In seiki therapy, we place special importance on the treatment of the lungs. The lungs carry oxygen to the whole body and are therefore important in curing any kind of disease.

We always aim for treatments that balance the whole body. Seiki therapy is also called a "one-being therapy" because it transcends the dichotomy between patient and therapist. As these photographs demonstrate, this is truly a therapy of the hands.

The healing energy of seiki can pass through steel and all objects. Over the years, I have been able to give patients telepathic treatments as I ride toward their homes. I am now accustomed to having my seiki reach out from my body to contact a patient, no matter how far away they may live.

I met a young woman from the country who had a lump in her breast and believed that she had cancer. Her conviction of the reality of cancer in her body was so strong that she was afraid to go to a doctor and receive a diagnosis. She came to me, saying that she had heard many wonderful things about our clinic. She asked me not to tell her if she had cancer. I simply replied that I believed that I could remove the lump with her cooperation. She was satisfied with this proposal.

There definitely was an object in her breast that might have been cancerous. All I can say is that I knew I could dissolve the object and I proceeded to do so. We treated her two to three times a day, and within two weeks the lump had completely disappeared. She went home and went to a doctor for an examination. No cancer or lump was detected.

Sometimes discovering whether you have cancerous tissue and having an operation is advisable. However, I believe that when the lymph glands aren't optimally functioning, so-called "lumps" tend to form. The body has the power to dispel these objects. When we tune the entire physical system, even cancerous tissue can be rehabilitated and illness dispelled.

In the act of healing, I sometimes experience a oneness with my coworker. For example, I was once called to the home of a woman who suffered from heart spasms. I took my assistant with me. We sat down together on the tatami mat beside the patient. My hand was instantly called to her heart, and it attached itself like a suction cup. Her heartbeat was extremely erratic. At my side, my assistant quietly began to massage the patient's arm.

Something marvelous grew within me because I knew that one of those magic moments was beginning to take place between me and my assistant. I sensed the gradual union of his mind and body with mine. Our breathing began to synchronize. We were both drawing in seiki from the air around the patient, from the atmosphere surrounding the house, and, finally, from the great, swirling spiral that comprises the whole universe.

Our double intake of seiki and its transmission to the patient resulted in what I call "rendezvous" therapy. Here we are like lovers in our complete understanding of one another and in our united action and feeling.

One hour, two hours, three hours went by in total silence. My hand would not leave her heart. Finally I had the patient take a sip of water. Her pulse normalized and she fell into a sound sleep. My assistant and I rose together and quietly left the house.

Balancing body rhythms in daily life is of the utmost importance in maintaining good health. You must rid yourself of the exhaustion that accumulates in you each day. You may have to be socially rude to get the daily rest that you need. Value your rest more than your social life. Healing means to return to yourself and become your true self. We should follow the wisdom of our bodies—it is the source of our healing.

Shakers of
St. Vincent

Figure 8.1

SAINT VINCENT
GOVERNMENT GAZETTE

(EXTRAORDINARY.)

PUBLISHED BY AUTHORITY.

Vol. 45.]   SAINT VINCENT, TUESDAY, 1 OCTOBER, 1912.   [No. 35.

GOVERNMENT NOTICE.

No. 194.

THE undermentioned Ordinance has been assented to by the Acting Governor of the Windward Islands and is published for general information :—

No. 13 of 1912.—An Ordinance to render illegal the practices of "Shakerism" as indulged in in the Colony of Saint Vincent.

By Command,

V. F. DRAYTON,
Chief Clerk.

GOVERNMENT OFFICE,
1st October, 1912.

PRINTED BY THE GOVERNMENT PRINTER AT THE GOVERNMENT PRINTING OFFICE, KINGSTOWN, ST. VINCENT.

Introduction to *Shakers of St. Vincent*
By Bradford Keeney

St. Vincent is one of the Windward Islands in the West Indies, located approximately a hundred ninety miles north of Trinidad and a hundred miles west of Barbados. The island is lush with vegetation and holds a volcano, Mt. Soufrière, whose previous eruptions have caused extensive damage and loss of life. The early slave trade transplanted African spirituality upon its shores, and by the turn of the twentieth century, a religion thrived that was rooted in both African traditions and Protestant Christianity, most notably the Methodist Church. This religion, characterized by intense displays of ecstatic expression, became known as the Shaker religion. The Shakers often call themselves the "converted people" or "Spiritual Baptists."

In 1912, an ordinance was passed "to render illegal the practices of 'Shakerism' as indulged in the colony of St. Vincent." In spite of constant prosecution, the Shakers thrived. The ordinance was not repealed until 1965. Today, the Shakers of St. Vincent comprise a vibrant community of spiritual practitioners. "Prayer houses" or "praise houses" are scattered throughout the island where meetings are regularly held, often lasting four to five hours.

Baptism and mourning are their most important rituals. No one is baptized unless they first have a dream, vision, or spiritual sign. Once baptized, the initiate is eligible for participation in their most sacred ritual, which is called "mourning," "taking a spiritual journey," a "pilgrim journey," or "going to the secret room." There they seek a vision through prayer and fasting, which typically lasts between six and twenty-one days. Instruction and knowledge, ranging from metaphysics to the practice of healing, are passed on to them in these visions. This learning from the spiritual world is sometimes called "going to school." It is the core experience of the Shakers.

This chapter opens up the largely unknown visionary world of the Shakers of St. Vincent. When a Shaker seeks spiritual healing, he or she sets out on a journey that traverses through spiritual death and rebirth.

In this healing odyssey, the seeker surrenders all his or her troubles and suffering from this life to a powerful spiritual process, so that one's troubled soul may be reborn with new meaning and vitality. The journey may direct one toward the healing of physical sickness.

Again, the name of this visionary journey into spiritual healing is called mourning. One's life is symbolically buried and mourned, opening up the possibility of a personal resurrection. What makes the St. Vincent Shakers unique among global mystical cultures is the extent to which its members seek and find visionary experiences. It is not reserved for the few initiates, but available to every member of the community. On this small island in the Caribbean, thousands of people have been spiritually healed and educated through powerful visionary pilgrimages.

In the pages that follow, leaders of the St. Vincent Shakers describe the process of spiritual healing through the ritual of mourning. In these stories, we find people who heal and inform their lives through direct visionary experiences.

Shaker Meeting

"Prayer House" or "Praise House"

These small buildings usually hold fifty to seventy people. (See Figure 8.2 on page 193.) The altar always includes a glass of water with a flower, a candle, a brass hand bell, a Bible, and a saucer. Other items may include sacred objects dreamed of by the leader.

Worshippers Arrive

Each person goes to the center pole, kneels, crosses himself, and prays, usually carrying a candle and a Bible (see Figures 8.3 and 8.5 on page 193.) Women always wear head scarves. Colored ties around the scarves indicate that they have mourned; otherwise, white ties are worn.

Figure 8.2

Figure 8.3

Figure 8.4

Figure 8.5

Figure 8.6

Figure 8.7

Surveying

Water taken from the glass with a flower is sprinkled three times. Then the brass bell is rung three times in each corner of the room, as well as in the doorways, at the center pole, and at the four corners of the altar. (See Figure 8.4 on page 193.)

Greeting

A hymn is sung while everyone walks around the room in a single file, shaking hands with each other. (See Figure 8.6 on page 193.)

Worship

The main service takes place with long chanted prayers, hymns, and preaching. This is when the Holy Ghost spirit typically touches members of the congregation. (See Figure 8.7 above.)

The Shaker Way of Being Touched by the Spirit

In the first phase of being touched by the spirit, the pilgrim's body will be subject to spontaneous jerks, shivering, and trembling. The pilgrim may also let out unexpected shouts, sobs, hisses, or unintelligible sounds. The pilgrim's body begins to feel a bit out of control as the spirit starts to do its work. Body movements and sounds will appear random, not in an obvious rhythm, and unpatterned. This phase may last anywhere from two to sixty minutes.

In the second phase, the pilgrim moves as the spirit adopts him or her. The pilgrim's body typically bends forward from the waist with knees slightly bent, and will be subject to repetitive, rhythmic movements, typically with strong breathing sounds and profuse sweating. The pilgrim may even touch the flame of a candle and not get burned. The spirit has taken control of the pilgrim. It is the deepest stage of ecstatic spiritual experience. Body movements and sounds are now rhythmic, patterned, and often in sync with the group. Strong overbreathing (alternately sucking air and releasing it with a grunting sound) is typically present. This is called 'doption. This phase may last anywhere from five to twenty minutes.

In the last phase, the pilgrim begins to separate from the spirit. During this phase, the pilgrim often sings or hums, and may even gasp, groan, sigh, or shout. They often feel breathless, and will usually exhibit random conduct. This is a time of bewilderment and confusion, when the pilgrim starts to disengage from feeling overtaken by the spirit. It is not as deep an experience as stage two, but may be more or less deep than stage one. This cooling down period tends to last only a few minutes.

Mourning

Going to the low ground of sorrows
— Mother Superior Sandy

The pilgrim dreams of a pointer (a person whose spiritual role is to point a pilgrim toward a spiritual journey). The pilgrim asks that pointer to help him or her mourn.

Mourning begins with a worship service.

Mourners sit at a certain side of the room, often holding a lit candle with the right hand, the left palm facing up. (See Figure 8.9 on page 196.)

Figure 8.8

Figure 8.9

Figure 8.10

A circular ground-drawing of mystic notations and graphic signs is made with chalk on the floor—a map for the spiritual journey.

Several layers of cloth bands with wax markings (see Figure 8.9 on page 196) are tied tightly around the pilgrim's head and eyes by a pointer. The bands are triangles or squares of cotton fabric and a sacred message or symbol is written on them with wax or chalk. Before being tied around the pilgrim's head, the bands are blessed.

Different color bands have special meanings: red may indicate the blood and love of Jesus, white may represent purity, blue healing, yellow spirituality, brown positivity.

The practice is biblically rooted in Ezekiel 4:8: "And behold, I will lay bands upon thee and thou shalt not turn thee from one side to the other."

The secret to mourners is the seal; that is, what is written in wax on the band. It determines where the pilgrim will go in the spiritual world during mourning.

Figure 8.11

Figure 8.12

The pilgrim is spun around three times, and then the mothers press various parts of the body to help sink the spirit in. Then the pilgrim is laid on the ground as for a burial service. A wooden cross is placed in the left hand and a lit white candle in the right hand. Secret words (pass-words) are whispered by the pointer.

Personal praying (see Figure 8.12 above) begins (alternating between kneeling, standing, or lying down—usually on the right side) with a confession to God and a review of all the sins and wrongdoings of one's entire life. Interspersed Bible reading and prayers are given by the pointer. Daily sunrise and sundown prayer services are held in the mourning room with singing and dancing.

After three days, the pilgrim is covered with lavender flowers, scripture is read about Christ rising from the grave, and the pilgrim is physically lifted up from the ground. Singing, praying, and dancing take place in the mourning room with Shaker elders.

The pilgrim tells the pointer about any visionary experiences. This is called "giving a lesson." The pointer gives "proves" to test the pilgrim's progress. Further journeying is encouraged. The pilgrim is washed and redressed with a robe whose color has been dreamed by the pilgrim or the pointer. The pilgrim is led by a processional from the mourning room to the outside and back into the front of the prayer house.

The pilgrim "shouts" his or her visionary news to the congregation.

SOME SPIRITUAL JOBS RECEIVED IN MOURNING

ARCHBISHOP: leader of Shaker churches

BISHOP, PASTOR, TEACHER, SHEPHERD: church elders

CAPTAIN: the person who directs the spirit in a service, bringing forth spiritual ships, getting people on board, and orienting them toward a spiritual journey

DIVER: goes into the spiritual ocean to help lift up someone who is stuck or drowning during a spiritual journey

DOCTOR OR HEALER: administers healing plants, medicines, touch, and prayer (there are different kinds of healers)

HUNTER: works with spirits of the land

INSPECTOR: investigates spiritual matters

MESSENGER: reports messages sent by the Holy Spirit

MOTHER: female leader of a church

NURSE: cares for baptism candidates and takes care of the mourning room

POINTER: a spiritual teacher who "points" souls to the spiritual world, helping them to mourn

PROVER: evaluates truth of another person (a spiritual diagnosis)

SPIRITUAL WATCHMAN: spies on other spiritual groups

WARRIOR: clears spiritual disturbances by defending with the sword

WATCHMAN: a person who protects the church from danger, usually guarding its main entrance

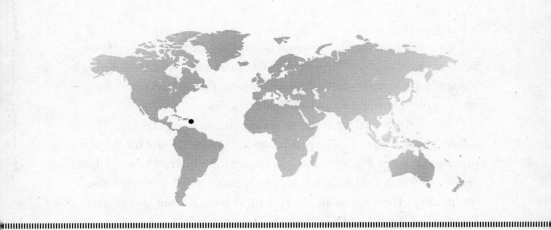

Mother Superior Sandy

I am eighty-one years old and I am delighted to have placed many people on the fasting ground. There you can be taken to many different places in the spiritual world. That's how we learn the sacred ways. When I was a young woman, I was a school teacher, but on September 23, 1945, I took my baptism. That's when I started teaching people about the Holy Spirit.

Baptism is essential. The Bible tells us that it's a must. Look at the third chapter of St. John's Gospel when Jesus talks to Nicodemus (John 3, 1–7):

There was a man of the Pharisees, named Nicodemus, a
    ruler of the Jews:
The same came to Jesus by night, and said unto him, Rabbi,
    we know that thou art a teacher come from God: for no
    man can do these miracles that thou doest, except God
    be with him.
Jesus answered and said unto him, "Verily, verily, I say unto
    thee, Except a man be born again, he cannot see the
    Kingdom of God."
Nicodemus saith unto him, How can a man be born when
    he is old? Can he enter the second time his mother's
    womb, and be born?

Jesus answered, "Verily, verily, I say unto thee, Except
   a man be born of water and of the Spirit, he cannot
   enter into the kingdom of God."
"That which is born of the flesh is flesh; and that
   which is born of the Spirit is spirit."
"Marvel not that I said unto thee, Ye must be
   born again."

Even Jesus left the footprint of Baptism for us. He left home and walked ninety miles to the River Jordan where John was baptizing people (John 1, 29–34):

The next day John seeth Jesus coming unto him, and saith,
   Behold the Lamb of God, which taketh away the sin of
   the world.
This is he of whom I said, After me cometh a man which is
   preferred before me: for he was before me.
And I knew him not: but that he should be manifest to
   Israel, therefore am I come baptizing with water.
And John bare record, saying, I saw the Spirit descending
   from heaven like a dove, and it abode upon him.
And I knew him not: but that he sent me to baptize with
   water, the same said unto me, Upon whom shalt see the
   Spirit descending, and remaining on him, the same is he
   which baptizeth with the Holy Ghost.
And I saw, and bare record that this is the Son of God.

Back in the old days, when I was a little girl, my parents told me that we could not worship God as we like. We had to hide away in the mountains and other places. If they caught us worshipping, they would lock us up.

When I was young, I contracted jaundice and turned yellow. My urine was black, and I was unable to get out of bed. The doctors gave up on me and everyone expected me to die. It was then that I first saw the spiritual world of Jesus. I was shown how I would go on my first mourning. I was told it would last ten days and that I would be given what I needed to help others. I saw all these things while I was on my sickbed.

Then an angel, looking like a woman, came to me and showed me three leaves. She told me what they were and instructed me to tell my mother to brew a tea from them. I called my mother and told her what happened, and she made the tea. I was well in three days. This miracle led me to always trust in the Lord.

The spirit inspires me to write certain things on those bands. Each mourner wears bands that are signed by their teacher, or what we call their pointer. It's like a teacher putting lessons on the blackboard where the children have to solve the problems.

There are saints who help me find out what must be written. I have never told anybody about my saints. Never, never, never. But I will tell you. My saints are Saint Theresa and Saint Michael. Both are wonderful saints.

Not every child sees the world of spirit. It depends on the pureness of your heart. When you go to the Lord, you see things better. If you are blessed, you will see the light. It's a beautiful light. When you start a journey, you find yourself in darkness, but when you pray to the Lord, He may open that light and shine it upon you. When you see that light, hold on to it. I went to that light spiritually. It all takes place by prayer. Remember that Peter walked on the sea but didn't have enough faith. As soon as he took his eyes off Jesus, he began to sink. He said, "Lord help me!" Faith is the most important thing in our lives. You must have faith to go through the many trials and crosses.

The first time I went into the ritual of mourning, or as we used to say, going to the low ground of sorrows, I traveled to a faraway place in a vision. It was as if I was walking into a city. I went into a house where I met a gentleman. He went outside and returned with some kind of a machine. He set it down in front of me. It was made of mahogany and so polished that I could see my face on its surface. It was lovely. He placed it on the floor and I stood in front of it. He then left again and returned with a chair. In my mind I can still see the back of the chair today. In all the places I have traveled in St. Vincent, I've never seen a chair like that. I didn't see it in England, Trinidad, or even in Barbados. In fact, I've never seen anything like it since. The back of the chair was coiled round and round. After he set the chair down, he left again and came back with twelve needles. Each needle had a different colored thread in it. He gave me all these things and then showed me how to work the machine.

In the same journey, he brought me a basin that was as white as milk. He put it in front of me and poured water into it. He then watered a white flower in a glass. Finally, he gave me a leather strap, a bell, and some white chalk. After giving me all of these things, he said, "I am going to make you an evangelist of mine." Being young at the time, I did not understand what was happening to me. I later found out the meaning of the twelve needles and the colored threads. By growing in the spirit I learned what they were. The twelve needles represent the twelve tribes of the House of Israel. And the colored threads are for the material to cover the heads of people who are fasting. The bell calls the sinners to repentance. The basin and the water are used to wash their hands and face and feet. The white flower in the glass represents purity because a person seeking a vision must have a clean heart. The water represents Jesus, the water of life, which will keep you from anger. If the tempter crosses the way when you are seeking a vision and you're about to get angry, take three mouthfuls of the water and it will cool you down and keep you on the straight and narrow.

Sometimes people see telephone lines or power lines on their journeys. Not everyone sees the same thing. If they are lucky, they may see a light. There are all kinds of lights that our Savior gives us. Some of these carry the power along a spiritual electrical wire.

In one spiritual journey, I saw the tree of life. I found myself in a garden where a voice told me that I was standing in front of the tree of life. The Garden of Eden is beautiful. I wanted to stay there because of the many flowers in all the different colors. It's a paradise.

These are the things you can learn in mourning. If you go deep into the spirit you can get the experience of 'doption. It hits you in the belly, tightens you, and pumps your belly up and down. Move when the spirit adopts you. Walk it out. Stomp your feet, swing your arms, and let the sound come out. It will sound like a drum beating inside your chest. 'Doption can show you something. It can bring you a vision or even take you on a spiritual journey. Praise God!

Later in my life, my husband caused me much trouble. I told Jesus: "Father, you have chosen me to do your work. If I am the hindrance, please remove me. If my husband is the hindrance, please remove him because I want a clean, free heart to do your work. There are times when I can't pray with your children because of our screaming fights. Lord grant my request and fulfill my desire." Soon my husband became sick and confessed his sins to me. I freely forgave him from my heart.

It was not an easy road for me. When God took my husband's life, I begged God to take away all my worldly feelings. I meant it from my heart. And so it is. Others told me, "Oh, you can marry again." But I would say, "I have remarried the gentleman right up there."

When things come our way, we must remember that He suffered enough for us. They called Him ill names. They slapped Him and spat in His face. He suffered for us and we have to bear some of it, too. We must rely on Him. As the song says, "Jesus is my deliverer." He unlocked the gate of heaven and let us in because He loved us and He wants us to love Him. It's nice to be with the Lord. It's nice to please Him. He never fails. Never.

Even our friends fail and leave us. But He's the one who never fails. He is with us always. His kingdom shall never be destroyed. He is the one who delivered Daniel from the lion's den. We need only to have faith in God and the same can happen to us. Always believe in Him and He will deliver. He will make good come out of evil. He will deliver you. How do I know this? I know because He delivereth me.

Mother Samuel

I come from Victoria Village. I grew up as an Anglican and I married when I was sixteen. One day when I was coming home with my friends from the post office, I suddenly couldn't speak anymore. I tried to speak but couldn't. I couldn't say anything.

However, inside, I was singing "Rock of Ages." I started to go home, but for some reason I went to my mother's home and fainted on the bed. When I fainted, my spirit traveled to a mother named Mother O'Hara. Then I woke up but fainted again, going again to this lady. When I finally came back, my mother, aunt, and sister were all weeping and said, "You're going to die." I tried to say the name of the lady I had seen in my dream but only a little came out. My mother picked up on it. I ran out of the house and just started running. I ran over a hill and down the next hill. I was going to run until I reached that one place. I heard a voice in spirit say, "Go up this road." I ran straight up that hill and saw a church. I could hear people saying, "Go and call Mother O'Hara, call Mother O'Hara." She was the woman I saw in my dream. And then she came out of the church and said nothing was wrong with me, though my mother was afraid that some evil was with me. She said nothing was wrong and that I was making a promise to God and receiving my calling. It was then that I took my first band and went into the secret room.

Taking a spiritual journey is a real mystery, something very difficult to explain. You must experience it firsthand to understand it. I remember my first journey—although I was praying with my eyes covered with bands, I saw the whole place lit up with light. Then my spirit began traveling to places I hadn't even learned about. And in these places I spoke to people I had never met. I first traveled to Africa and heard the drums. Afterward, I found I could beat the drums in spirit, though normally I couldn't beat them. When I talk with spirit I can beat the drums.

I saw from the future. I saw from the past. There are different places your spirit can travel to. It's like going to a spiritual train station. When I talk about strong spiritual things, I can feel something vibrate. It comes to me as a shivering. If you don't feel this vibration, then the Holy Spirit is not with you. Whenever it comes into you, you're on fire with the power of God. You can't be sitting down and be cold and tell me that you have the Holy Spirit. When you contact Him, you get filled with something that makes you move. Some people block it off.

After I first saw the spiritual light, I began traveling with the spirit. Now I simply lie down and close my eyes, usually around midnight, and the whole place lights up.

I smile and say, "Thank you, Jesus," and I visit Him. Sometimes my head vibrates really fast and my pressure rises.

When you are a spiritual elder, that is, someone deep in the spiritual life, you will see the lines. They look like white telephone lines. They connect you to all the places where you can travel. Sometimes I see a line that is broken: it's not lit up. I then have to go repair it to keep the connection alive.

The spiritual light comes to you in many forms. It can be the white line for traveling, or it can be like a circle over your head. This light is Jesus. He is the most sacred encounter you can have.

Sometimes the lines have light bulbs on them and I'll see a burnt-out light. I have to go to that line and change the light bulb. If you ever see a line of light, you must go toward it. It will take you somewhere.

'Doption is when the spirit gets into your belly. When you feel it making your body tight, you must stand up and stomp the ground. Then let it come out of your mouth. This is a very strong experience. In one journey I took, I came to a fork in the road. A spirit was standing at the middle of the two roads and I asked where 'doption came from. He pointed to the ground and the earth began to shake. He stomped his feet like he was dancing and pointed to the earth. He showed me how the stomping of the feet and the shaking of the earth sent a pumping spiritual energy into the belly. That energy is then pumped up the body, with percussive sounds coming from the mouth. It was so powerful that I went into a top 'doption right there in the journey. When I woke up and came back to myself, my mother was over me. She said, "You were doing a 'doption. What happened?" When I told her that I had asked where 'doption came from, she said, "Don't ever ask that again." I've never asked again. I just accept it.

Sometimes people tell me that I give them an electrical shock when I touch them. This happens when I feel the presence of Jesus. It is not unusual for these things to happen when you touch people with faith.

If you believe in His miracles and you call Him for somebody, He may enter you. When this takes place, you must touch the sick person. This is one of the ways I heal.

When I pray, I have to focus on Jesus; I cannot pray without focusing on Him. When I focus on Him, I start to pray. I have had many dreams about Him. His presence is that of a good friend. When He comes to me, His love pours in me. When I awake with this joy, I say "Oh, God, thank you. Jesus, I am in love with you."

Sometimes I send my children into mourning with a black band. Years ago while I was spiritually traveling, I came to a green pasture. In the middle of it was a little hut with dirt around it. I went into the hut and a voice told me that the color black is not about death, it's about spiritual power. This voice also said that the color red is about love. When you rule in red or have contact with red, you are complete in the sacred blood.

Mother Pompey

I am a pointer who points pilgrims to the place of mourning. When people have a dream or desire to mourn under my hand, we sign and band their heads. Before we band them, we wash them—their hands, their feet, and everything. As the song says, "Wash me, but not my feet alone. My hands, my head, my heart." So while singing this song, we'll wash their feet. Then we sing "My hands and my head and my heart" while we take the water and wash the heart. After we finish washing, we anoint their face, hands, and feet with olive oil before banding them. Then we put the bands around their head. After we finish wrapping the bands, we whisper something secret into their ears. We call those words "the key." No one hears what we say. It's like a secret password. We ask them not to tell anyone. They then use this password while praying. If they sincerely pray with this key, they will travel out into the spirit world. When they come back, they tell me, the pointer, what they experienced. Their vision tells me which spiritual ground they are standing on and how far they are on their journey.

I have put about forty people through mourning. To be a pointer, you have to keep praying. If you want to be a real pointer who points souls, you also have to be clean. That is why I live a clean life. I even fast with the pilgrims and sleep with them, which sends me a little farther along my spiritual journey.

When a pilgrim tells me their vision, we say that he or she is bringing a lesson. If they bring a lesson not directly connected to spiritual wisdom, I will tell them, "No, don't tell me that." Some will sit down and cry. Because I keep close with God, I know when a pilgrim has been given a true lesson.

I have personally mourned ten times. I fasted fourteen days the first time I mourned. After that, my mournings usually lasted seven days. After the mournings, I share my experiences with the congregation. Everyone who comes out of mourning gives a testimony and tells others what they have seen. This is when we "shout" what we have learned.

In one mourning, I traveled to a river and took a bath in it. After I bathed, a gentleman came and took me to a pool. There he asked me if I knew the meaning of the place. I said I didn't. He said, "Have you ever heard about being washed in the River of Jordan, then rinsed in the pool of Shiloh, and rested on the mighty wall in Zion?" Then he went on to explain. When I told this vision to the congregation, the church caught on fire.

Pointer Warren

In the world of the spirit, there are lines and ropes. The lines usually go horizontally like power lines. They carry the spiritual electricity and you can use them to make a phone call to God. They can look like lines of light. There are also ropes of light hanging from the sky. If you go near one of them they can take you anywhere. These are powerful things to see. Only those on a high spiritual path see these ropes. When you see one, concentrate on it and go toward it. Reach for it and don't let go. It will take you somewhere.

'Doption is another special gift from God. When the spirit adopts you, you must move and let it come out. It will bring up a special sound that sometimes sounds like a drum. If you are deep in 'doption, it can give you a vision and even take you on a spiritual journey. 'Doption is communication from the Holy Spirit. When it pulls on you, it can give a spiritual sight. When it's on you, you can prophesy, see into others, and even heal them. God is great. He gives us these gifts. The greatest gift He gives us is the sweet love of Jesus. I love Jesus. He makes me sing all day. I start singing and keep singing until I fall asleep. His joy makes me sing. I have to sing. There is no other way.

People see the light in different ways. Sometimes they see the lines and the ropes. If they go near it, they will be taken on a journey. They can see a lighthouse or a bright sun. Jesus is the light of the world. He shows himself in the Light.

When I travel in the spirit world, I see the lines of light. I go near them and they take me on a journey. Also, there are many schools in the spirit world. They have taught me many things. I am a grateful student.

I remember that in my first mourning I had a vision of gaslights. Then a man came to me and said, "You are a wonderful man." He then put those lights on my head. It was wonderful. I love Jesus. I am holding on.

When we humble ourselves as a child to God, we can go all the way and be touched by Jesus. Once I received a special blessing in which a cloud poured rain on me. It rained only on me. That was a gift.

Sometimes when I lie down in bed, I feel my head vibrate. It makes me want to sing and makes my body shiver. Sometimes when the Spirit walks inside me, I feel like a cloud. I'm so happy that sometimes I want to fly away. I want to fly. The Spirit is so sweet that It lifts me up off the ground.

Archbishop Pompey

In 1955, I became a Spiritual Baptist and moved up to the next stage of my spiritual life. Today I am the archbishop, the only archbishop in St. Vincent and the Grenadines. From a shepherd to a teacher, from a teacher to a pastor, from a pastor to a bishop, I have now become an archbishop.

We call the room where you receive visions a mourning room, or the sacred room. I prefer to use the term sacred room. Everything done in that room is done in secret. When you pray earnestly in secret, the Father rewards you openly. You go to the spiritual room to pray. When you pray to Him sincerely, He will reveal things to you, sometimes things that will really surprise you. I receive a gift every time I go to the spiritual room.

Every time I go, I get lifted higher into the spirit. When you get the call from the spirit to go into the room, you must. I always go when I get a call to go back. I've gone there many times. I used to go every year.

One time I received a tremendous gift. On my journey, I saw a bishop in a vision. Then a gentleman came and placed me in the bishop's seat. After that vision, the archbishop departed this life and I was elected to follow him. That's how I became the archbishop.

Back in 1954, some elders came and told me that many people had shed tears for me. That night, I spoke to my Father and asked him to call me. When I didn't hear His voice, I asked Him to send me a guide. He sent me to a man whom I didn't know, in a village unknown to me. In the spirit I saw the man and saw his place. After the dream, I left to go find the man. Along the way, in Kingstown, I met a friend. She asked where I was going and I told her that I was going to a place called Coal Sill. She said she was also going to Coal Sill to visit a man named Brother D. He was the man in my dreams, so I allowed my friend to guide me to him. I was appointed that Sunday night. At that time I came to be a shepherd.

When you see someone in a vision, ask that person many questions. Ask them who they are. When I asked the name of the gentleman in my vision I got the answer. When I asked where Coal Sill was, they showed me. I asked where the church was, and it was shown to me. On my first pilgrim journey, I heard people say that when your sins roll away they go right into the sea. In my journey, I found myself on a mountain picking mangoes. The mangoes were all ripe and they got away from me. I went to find them, but found myself on a truck where I heard this song: "I am delivered, praise the Lord." That was when I found out about my sins.

For some people, their sin is a big stone to roll away. When I imagined mine, it was four ripe mangoes. I also learned that when your sins are gone, you are not to go looking for them. Because your sins have been rolled away.

When you go on a spiritual journey, you may go to a school, a church, or a hospital where you might get an operation. You might also learn that everyone has a number. The Father above also has His numbers. When you're given your number, use it to talk to Him. The numbers are very important. Your number is your own and my number is mine.

His number is a number that we can call any time. This is very important. Sometimes pilgrims get their number when they go into the sacred room. People may get a number in their dreams. Sometimes people sitting in church hear a telephone ringing. When they say, "Hello," they may get a number.

Sometimes a pilgrim will see white lines on a spiritual journey. These can be both spiritual phone lines and power lines. They carry the electricity of God to you, and they can be used to send messages to God like a telephone. When you get your number, you can send a direct message to God when you pray. But don't forget to use that number in your prayers. No one can give you a number except God.

I tell people that there are only two books I read to pilgrims when they take a spiritual journey—the Bible and *The Pilgrim's Progress*. Our journey during mourning is like Christian's journey in *The Pilgrim's Progress*. We experience many trials and tribulations, but we must have faith and move toward the shining light. I have heard many pilgrims during their mourning tell me that they saw the light.

I know that the deeper you go on this journey, the more the light comes to you. I tell them to keep their eyes on the light. When you take your eyes off it, you will be like Apostle Peter when he stopped looking at Jesus while walking on the sea. Peter wanted to walk on water with him, so Jesus said, "Keep your eyes on me." Peter then walked on the sea. When he looked away, he began to sink and said, "Oh, Master." And Jesus told him, "Keep your eyes on me. Do not look down. Looking forward is life eternal. Looking backward is death." You can't look for the things you left behind. There is something good before you. There lie the gifts of spirit. I pray that all of my spiritual children will keep looking forward. I ask this in the precious name of Jesus. Thank you, Jesus. Amen.

KALAHARI BUSHMEN
HEALERS

Introduction to *Kalahari Bushmen Healers*
by Bradford Keeney

Each Bushman medicine person develops his or her own style of dancing, shaking, and healing through vibratory touch. Most Bushmen healers share the same basic experiences in their development: a mentor places their vibratory spirit into his or her body, and that spirit makes the apprentice healer sick; the new healer absorbs some of the stylistic moves and patterns of his or her mentor; all Bushmen healers dance without effort; during the dance, shaking and vibrating take place effortlessly; and almost all Bushmen healers experience luminosity and visions. However, the most powerful experience shared by all Bushmen healers is the deep bond and love of relationships among all people. This ecstatic bliss arises when they throw themselves into the spirit of shaking and dancing, which opens the heart to the whole of life.

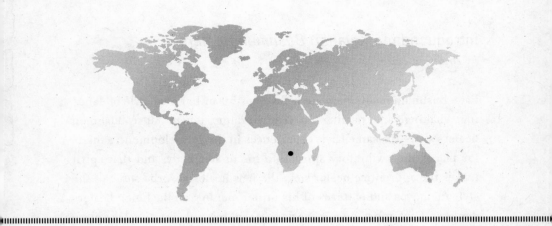

Mabolelo Shikwe

My name is Mabolelo, a name that means "the man who says and knows everything." My grandfather Ciqwe and my father, Sebuabua, were medicine men. They taught their children how to heal others. Grandfather taught my father, my brother, and me. My brother also taught me—he added more knowledge so that my knowledge overflowed. When I was taught, I knew right from the beginning that I had the power in me. But it was only when I became older that I realized that this power was really my grandfather's power. It took time to learn how to use him in our healing ways.

My grandfather's healing song was from his grandfather. In the beginning of the healing dance, the song stays the same, but as the dance progresses, the words change, bringing deeper and more serious meanings. At the start of a dance, the song is flippant. Only later does it become more spiritual as we become more serious about dancing. That is when we sing about the Big God above, the One who made you to be born. The Big God tells me the words to say in the dance. He speaks to me, telling me what to say and how to heal each person.

The God above gives power to my ancestors, and they, in turn, speak to me. The Big God is named Modimo. He sends His power to my grandfathers, and they send it to my father. The ancestors become smaller gods after they die, and they then speak to us in the dance. I talk with my grandfather today because I was taught by him. My father is a lesser god than my grandfather. But as I get older, my grandfather is telling me more about my father. All talk with my ancestors is serious communication.

I went with my grandfather into the bush until I was married. There he taught me. After he died, I became married and raised a family.

The most problematic part of his life was getting water. There is a wild cucumber called *Tsamma* that he used for water, along with other bulbs that he had to dig up.

After the rain falls on the sand, it is gone. The trees catch rain and funnel it toward the stem and into the hollows, and the water collects there. My grandmother went off with ostrich eggs after a rain and sucked the water out of the trees. She would bring it home and give each child their share of rain water. Each child received a few drops of

Figure 9.1

water. When there were many children, the smaller children received the most drops.

After we received water, we would make a little fire and dance, saying thank you to the rain. Those were great moments of my early life. We had a special song asking for rain. When we sang it and the rain fell, we would go out to sip the wells in the sand and suck it from the pipes made out of stems.

We talked to our forefather's spirits, asking them to please help us with rain. Our forefathers would carry our request to God. Yesterday I asked for rain and as you can see today, it is coming.

Learning to heal is a gradual process. As I made progress, I learned to read the inside and outside of people's bodies. After much learning, I could feel people's insides — the flow of their blood as well as the condition of their organs.

My grandfather taught me to put my hands on a man and determine whether the blood was running fast or slow. He then took me to another person to teach me to feel something else. And then I learned to feel other things with other people. He would ask me what I smelled. After a while, I had to go to people on my own to feel and smell them. And then my grandfather would come and smell them to see how well I had done in the test.

I also learned how to go into the bush and feel the power of a plant that could heal. Physical diseases need a hand diagnosis to determine whether a person needs a plant or simply an application of the healing touch. When I touch someone, I don't feel a tingly sensation. I feel their skin in a special way. I throw water on the person and then touch them. Their soul then goes into me and tells me what is wrong. I can also feel their temperature.

I can also make an immediate diagnosis and then heal you by sucking off the illness. If the illness is very bad, I must go and get medicine to help you.

The power is inside me. My grandfather had a very strong spirit inside him. When people were sitting around the fire, he could draw out their illness without touching them. He was that strong. Grandfather sensed a spirit within himself that could heal. It told him how it could be enhanced to help others in even more powerful ways. The spirit is in everyone, although for some it is more developed. My grandfather chose my brother and me to give more spirit to.

Grandfather taught my father's first son — my older brother. I lived with this brother. Both my brother and my grandfather taught me in a special way. They gave me a medicine that made me boil inside. It cooked the spirit into my flesh, and became an integral part of me. They also made incisions into my skin and rubbed medicines on them as a way to enhance my spirit.

The medicine is a drink that I prepare. It consists of *txante*, some cucumber root, and other roots. When I teach someone, I give them the medicine to drink, and then I take them into the bush to show them things. The next day, I give them the medicine again. It is not necessary to take all the ingredients together. The medicine can be taken over several days, or it may be given for a long time. It is a continuous process of learning. I still drink the medicine.

We watch animals, especially the gemsbok, to see what medicines they use. We study their stomach contents and watch what plants they eat. Then we try them ourselves. This is how we learned about some of the medicines of the world. The gemsbok and other wild animals have taught us many things about healing one another. They show us what medicines to use.

It takes me about three years to teach an apprentice about the medicines. I am the one in our community who has taught many of the others.

Tga is the name of our healing trance dance. It started right in the beginning with the oldest of our ancestors. It passed from one generation to the next. It has been unchanged since the very beginning. In this dance, we speak to our ancestors, and we divine and heal.

When we start to warm up, we put our hands on each other. We get close and smell each other to make diagnoses. The big doctor comes around and checks everyone's diagnosis. "No, this is nonsense," he might say. Or, "This man has no problem. Why do you say that he does?" There is a hierarchy of expertise. The big doctor is always in charge.

Figure 9.2

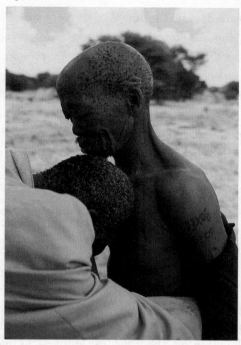

Throughout the ceremony, various people might discuss their diagnoses and treatments, but it is always under my direction. This allows those who want to learn an opportunity to practice. Again, the spirit is in every person, but it is more enhanced in some of us.

For me, the spirit touches my feet first during the dance. It then moves through my whole body all the way up to my head. It fills my entire body. As it comes up my feet, it makes my legs tremble. The trembling shakes my rattles, which are wrapped around my ankles. Other dancers hear this, and it makes their hearts beat faster.

My belly tightens and vibrates as my entire body starts to shake. Shivering occurs gradually—it builds up to a heavy shaking. I'm constantly at a high level of tension because I know I can fall over at any moment, but the people hold me up. However, I can fall over and not get up until the next morning. Now I'm at a stage where I can transfer enough power into someone else so that they, too, fall over.

The old of yesterday and the new of today come together when I move a person's body up and down to give the person enough power to be strong enough for the future. The reason I give my power is so that he or she will be strong enough to handle the challenges of the future.

I worked with someone last night who had the heart of a lion. This person could also turn another person over. The medicine person who gave him this power was as aggressive and strong as a lion. I was concerned that he might become too aggressive and dance in the fire. This was a very strong possession and it might have hurt him. I worked with this person to help him tone down his spirit.

I am in constant communication with my ancestors, even in my sleep. They always tell me what to do during every moment of the dance. My ancestors tell me which roads to take in my life — how to walk right until my death. At that time my spirit will go where my ancestors now live.

When I sleep, I walk in the bush with my ancestors. There we talk with each other. I see my ancestors' faces and they introduce me to my earlier ancestors. I now know my brothers who died before I was born. They continually teach me about healing and how to live my life. They tell me whether I can go back or not. One of these days they will say that I must stay. Then I will meet my death.

While I dance, my spirit stays here, but I also receive spirits from other places and other villages. They may ask me to go there to heal them. When I heal, I touch a person's flesh and my power flows to them. At the same time, the other person's power flows to me, enabling me to understand and diagnose their condition.

When the illness comes into me, I shout and shoot it out. When I do this I also shoot my own illness out. My sickness leaves with their sickness. It is healing for both of us. There is an intermingling of our bad parts and illnesses as they both go out.

Sometimes I lie on the ground and start to shiver. I do this in a restful position to heal myself. When self healing is taking place, my head vibrates at a high frequency.

All body vibrations, whether slow or fast, are essentially the same. These vibrations help you to see the spirits. As a teacher of healing, I help others to channel their shaking and body vibrations to grow and mature with their spirits.

There are moments in the healing dance when I feel like I am standing in a ray of light. In this light, I am able to see inside others. I see everything as if I'm inside you. For instance, I can see the lesions on the liver or disease in the intestines.

The light sometimes seems to be inside other people. That light is given to us to see into others so we can find what is wrong. You can ask a spirit doctor to look into you in this light and take out the bad things. This is how we cure.

When another medicine person shakes with me, we are working together to cure others. If I am not strong enough alone to heal a particular person, I can shake with another healer, and our strengths together will do the job.

Different doctors can shake together to get more power to heal. Sometimes we need four or five people to extract an illness. An illness may look like a needle. If I need to pull a needle from a person's stomach by pulling it out from their neck, another person must push the stomach while I pull it from the neck. Illnesses can look like other things, such as a mouse.

There are times when I will work on my own family, but I cannot do this if I am too tired. It is very important to rest before any healing work.

My wife doesn't know anything about healing so she doesn't help me in my work. No one helps me much now. There used to be another man who helped me doctor others, but no one does now.

Now I am as strong as my grandfather during his time. I know that there are other men who are stronger, but I am not afraid of them. I have all the power I need.

You need a good heart, mentally and physically, to be well. This is also necessary in healing others. The Bushmen of the Kalahari know each other's hearts. We also know the hearts of all the other people in the world. You must open your heart to have a good heart. There can be no jealousy or bad intentions inside you. You must go with an open heart to your neighbor and everyone around you. You must look after everyone. Open your heart and serve one another—this is our way. This is the key to healing.

Rasimane

I did a lot of dancing when I was young. Now I'm old and I still dance, but not like I did as a youngster. I remember the old medicine songs from the past, but unfortunately the new generation does not know them anymore. The old healing songs can only be sung after midnight because that's when the dead people are awake. If they are sung during the day, the dead will want to kill the living. This is because the dead can't sing during the day, and they get upset because they can't join the singing.

I want to explain how I became a medicine man. It began when I started to dream about the dead—our ancestors. They showed me the plants that could be used for medicines. And when the ancestral spirits saw that I was interested in learning from them, they taught me how to be a doctor to others.

When I was forty years old, Naledi, a respected medicine man in our area, told me that the ancestors had come to him to tell him that I was ready to be taught. Naledi said that he was shown the powers given to me by the ancestors. He told me, "Now you must go into the bush and find the medicines you saw in your dreams. Then I will work with you."

Naledi was a very powerful medicine man, and he was also my uncle. When I brought him the medicines I saw in my dreams, he began teaching me how to use them. He made me use the medicines on myself before I could start giving them to others.

Naledi taught me how to detect an illness and quickly expel it from the sick person. He also showed me the healing dance. The most important lesson was when he put his spirit into my body. He did this when we were alone. After the third time, he said I had enough; I was then filled with his spirit.

After each time he gave me his spirit, I became extremely sick. But he always made the sickness go away. It had to happen this way because it is the way with every medicine man. This proves that you are a true medicine man. Otherwise you would doubt that you had really changed. In transferring his spirit, Naledi embraced my whole body and shook me wildly. When he did this, I would also shake. After three different times, I was a fully initiated medicine man.

In the beginning of my training, I would get nauseous whenever my body shook. I would have to vomit and immediately go to sleep. After my initiation, the spirit finally settled into my body, and I no longer became sick when I shook. My ancestors continued to visit me in my dreams, and they still do today. This is how I continue to learn.

In the healing dance, the women's singing helps me to start shaking, which gets me ready to heal others. For me, the amount of dancing I do is determined by the number of sick people who have come to me for treatment. I only dance when someone is sick.

The pain of the sick people makes me shake after it enters my body during the dance. Their sickness meets the spirit inside my body and a fight between them begins; this causes the shaking. The spirit inside occupies my whole body. It does not reside in just one place, such as the stomach, but it is everywhere inside me. When I stomp my feet and dance, the spirit inside is stirred up. It gets ready to encounter the illnesses that come from the sick. When the illnesses come toward me, it not only causes shaking, it also heats up my entire body. The more I sweat, the better the healing. At this moment, the ancestral spirits start to show me things. They show me who is sick and what I must do to help them.

During the dance, I usually see a light that comes from the people around me. This light goes straight up to the sky. I begin to see this light when I start healing during the dance. First I get filled with pain, then the light comes. It takes away all the pain. When there is no light, I feel pain. When the light arrives, the pain disappears.

I feel more pain when the people are not clapping and singing very well. They must be strong for me to be strong and for the light to come. When the light finally comes, it not only takes the pain away, it knocks me out. I fall down and must be brought back to consciousness by others. After the dance, when the light goes away, I feel a little sad. Such is the life of a Bushman medicine man.

I want the rest of the world to know that God will protect and teach all the people of the world, including me. We must accept this truth so that we can have a good life together.

Motaope Saboabue

Motaope means "once again," and Saboabue means "he who speaks again." I live in Zutshwa and am the elder brother to Mabolelo, who lives in the next village. I work with my nose and I will tell you all about my medicine and healing. There is a tribe of people called the Makokou. They believe that they go out into the bush and return as lions. I know medicine like the palms of my hands because I danced with the Makokou Bushmen. I am very happy to tell you what I know because this will make my knowledge travel further into the world. I am now very old, and I wish that my knowledge be told and recognized for the power that it holds.

Most of my knowledge about medicine came from God, but my father and grandfather initiated me as a healer and also taught me many things. They taught me the traditional medicines from plants. However, the quality of divining outside the physical realm came upon me from God. He filled me with special knowledge. When this occurred, I suddenly had the ability to see sickness inside people and heal them. This happened quickly for me and it did not require a long period of training.

Many years ago when I was a boy, I went to the Masetleng Pan. I was very sick, and while I was lying there, I had a dream. I dreamed that I had to go back to my mother, who was also sick, and make small incisions on her skin. I was then shown how to suck out the sickness through her blood. I got up, went to her, and did this. She became well and my sickness also went away.

When I was ten years old, I started shaking. The spirit makes us shake, especially the legs. They start trembling and the shaking expels the bad and removes the illness that is inside you. The shaking, once it starts, stays with you for the rest of your life.

If I get tired during a healing dance, I may lie down and shiver. This makes my heart happy. It makes me get up and dance again. If I am not in a dance and I'm tired, I may still start to shiver. I can then get up and shake out the pain and the fatigue.

The shivering and shaking also have something to do with the illness of the other person. If I am near a sick person, I often shake more. I use my hands to shrug off their ailment. Then the shivering subsides.

My spirit doesn't leave me when I pass out during the dance. I'm never disoriented, and my spirit always stays inside. It's only the biggest spirit that can take you up. It takes me up to a sacred place where I am filled up again with spiritual strength. And then the biggest spirit brings me down.

When it happens, it feels like water rushing into me. It feels like the spirit is throwing water on my feet and face. This is why sometimes I throw water on people when I heal. When the biggest spirit comes to me, I feel like some spiritual water has been brought for me to drink. It slowly goes from the top of my head to the bottom of my feet. It feels hot inside my body.

When I am working on a serious case, my whole body shakes. It feels like I have no bones. When I place my heart against another person's heart, it helps me in transferring my power to them. The more contact we have between our bodies, the easier it is for me to transfer the power.

When I feel that there is nothing wrong with a person, I say, "Don't worry, you are not sick and you don't need any energy." If I put my hands on someone, whether they are sick or not, there is always a flow of power. But if they are not sick, they don't need me to continue giving it to them.

When I dance, I go into a trance and become very tall. I can even fly to another village and dance with the people there. It is only when you sing a lot and get very hot that your spirit can get up and go away.

When you dance and get hot, you will see a rope hanging from the sky. As you stretch and become taller, you can climb this rope. There is only one rope for you—your rope. You wait to find your rope. It is a straight rope that can take you to other places. It is white and thin as a blade of grass. If you dance and see this rope, you don't have to grab or touch it. You just float away with that rope. That line just takes you. You

Figure 9.3

become so light that you simply fly away. You don't know whether your feet are on the ground or not. I feel like the wind when this happens.

You have no control over where you go. You can't say where you want to go. The spirit decides where it will take you. And the spirit brings you back. If the spirit takes you away, it is your spirit that goes away and your body remains on the ground. When you come back, you return to your body. You can never tell anyone else where you went. It is between you and your soul.

Xherema

I am married to Ngwaga Osele and my name, Xherema, means "interpreter for me." Both men and women are healers in the dance. It is better that way. The power of healing comes from our open hearts. We freely open ourselves to others.

I still love my husband because he never changed. He still gives me food and provides for our family. He gave me good children.

We have three children—one son and two daughters. They now live at the village of Xade. They have not learned the medicines, but they all have children.

My husband and I work together in the healing dance. When I touch someone and fall down, it is because there is a lot of pain in that person's life. Their pain goes into my chest. When this happens, my husband comes over to me and touches me so the pain gets released.

I am learning medicine from a medicine man named Kgabeko. He is teaching me to use my hands to heal sick people. I learned to throw bones from another medicine man, but I don't do it anymore. I have also learned to smell illnesses and how to treat them.

I have a message for all the women who want to become a medicine person. Please step forward and do it. Women can be powerful medicine people. It is also very good for both wife and husband to be medicine people. This makes strong medicine.

Ngwaga Osele

My name, Ngwaga Osele, means "the drought for the year." My father and grandfather were powerful medicine men. When they danced, they healed people with their hands. My brother also did this. They shook when they touched people. My brother, father, and grandfather were so powerful that a big snake would show up at the healing dance. They would pick it up and wrap it around their necks.

My father taught me how to feel sickness with my hands. When I was in a ceremony and someone was sick, he would show me how to heal them. From the beginning of my apprenticeship, my father took me into the bush. He found some roots for medicine that he gave me to drink as a tea. After I drank it, I could feel other people's sickness. I only had to drink it once. Ever since that time I have been able to feel sickness in other people.

When you come to me with a problem, I throw the bones to see if you need any medicines. I have a female goat bone, two male goat bones, a hyena bone, a lion bone, a springbok bone, a cow bone and hoof, and an eland hoof.

I can also change into a lion. When I go into the bush, I make this change. Then I come back to the village and people say, "There is a lion!" As a lion, I dance with people in the healing dance. There I say, "My son, don't be shy, I am your father. I'm not really a lion. Let's dance together."

My wife is also a doctor who knows how to dance. But she does not become a lion. When I start to become a lion, I feel pain and start to cry. I have to leave the dance and go into the bush where I make the change. The lion's spirit changes my mind and body. Fur grows out of my skin and claws grow from my hands. This is when I am most powerful.

The energy that is hot within me is called *xhau*. In the dance I get hot in my chest. It is painful in the beginning, but then it becomes very nice. My heart becomes extremely powerful, and I can hug someone and send energy into them from my heart. When I teach someone, I give him my power from my heart. This is the strongest exchange of spiritual powers anyone can have. We feel like one when it takes place. It is joyful and, without a doubt, it is the greatest experience anyone can have.

When the power comes to me and changes me, I see the light coming into my face. The light shows me that there is truth in the dance. It tells me that we are doing the right thing.

When I see the string fall from the sky, I tell it to go away. My job is to stay with the people. When I dance and the ceremony gets very hot and serious, I feel my body fly up into the air. I float up to the height of the people.

My wife is still learning to be a medicine woman. She is learning from the other Bushmen. When we sit together at home, I put my hands on her to give her more powers. She is learning how to use her hands to heal.

When I teach a person to throw the bones, I give them the bones they will need. I first give them my spirit, and then I show them how to throw the bones. After that, the spirit tells you what you need to know.

The power of a medicine man shows in the joy and the openness of his heart. I am free to help all people. I even have healed white men who were sick.

There are two ways to do the healing dance (see Figure 9.ii)—it can be done in the evening until midnight or we can dance through the night. All of our doctors come to the dance. The men and women dance together in our village. It has always been that way.

Other people are not as free or happy as us. They are not as open to share and to help others.

In our healing, we stretch our bodies in every direction. This makes it easier for the spirit to come into us. When we stretch the people who come to use for healing, we do so to concentrate all the internal illnesses into one spot to make it easier for extraction.

The fact that my wife and I are both medicine people brings us closer to one another. When she was a girl, I went to her the very first time I saw her and said, "I want to make a life with you and our children. Let's have a life together and get old together until we die." She said, "I love you, too." At that time we made an agreement to marry each other. Later, when we were older, I asked her, in public, to marry me.

I went to all my relatives and told them that I wanted to marry this girl. They discussed it and said, "Go ahead and marry her." And then the families prepared us for our marriage ceremony. My parents told me to not fight with this woman, to be good to her, and to never separate. Her parents told her, "Hold that man and make him happy." They said, "Don't lose that man, because he is a good man."

In our wedding, the older people sang and danced. Everyone was very happy. Our relatives celebrated and it was a very joyous time for us.

I love my wife with the same love that was there in the beginning. I love her because we make medicine together, and we had children together. I do not want to lose my wife. She makes me happy. That is why I love her.

Komtsa Xau

We have eight medicine men and six medicine women in our village. Our village has around four hundred people.

There are two ways to receive the spirit to heal. The first is if you carry the gemsbok, you will receive power from a drink made from its parts. When the dance begins, you will naturally vibrate and shake. The other way is that a medicine person transfers their power to you by touching and shaking you. My father transferred his power to me this way.

When I dance, the spirit starts to touch the bottom of my spine. This causes my belly to vibrate. I feel the fire that is responsible for my shaking and vibrating. The movement of my feet dancing starts this process. It creates the inner fire that makes me tremble.

Sometimes the vibrating takes place on its own, like when I am lying down to rest. This means that the spirit has arrived. Otherwise, I have to dance for the spirit to come.

When you see the light in a dance, this means that you are in the world of the spirit. You can see sickness and travel anywhere. Your spirit will enable you to do many things. It may give you a string that takes you to other places. Sometimes it takes me to my ancestors and to the Big God. When this happens, others think you have fainted or passed out. The people will try to awaken you.

When I'm in spiritual heaven, I discuss a person's sickness with my ancestors. They will tell me whether I can help that person. They will tell me what to do—whether to get a medicine from the bush or touch them or something else. Sometimes I speak to the Big God and He tells me how to improve my medicines. He has helped me many times.

The Big God has no particular color. He has a different color each time. He is an old man, but not too old. He can change into any form that he wants.

In the dance, the light that comes to me is like a flashlight beam. It is a shaft of light that comes on my body. This light makes you shiver. It causes your body to shake and tremble.

If someone is sick, I start to shake. This shaking of my body shows me that they are sick. I do not necessarily feel hot, I just shake. I then try to pull out their pain. Their pain looks like little bullets. I pull them out and throw them away. Sometimes the pain goes into my hand, travels to my stomach, and then out my mouth. At other times it just comes out into my hand, and then I throw it away. I have to shout in order for their pain to be thrown away. This shout makes you feel good, because you are happy that they are being healed. But more importantly, your body feels very good when you do this. It takes out the sickness and tiredness from you. It is a very good feeling, and it makes me very happy.

For the new doctor who has never felt this before, they will be fearful. The first time when the spirit touches them, they are fearful. The fear makes them think this is a painful experience. When I was a boy, it scared me. But now it feels good.

Every time there is a dance I go into the spirit. It is now automatic for me. It feels completely natural. The spirit comes from the Big God. It comes from my ancestors, through my father, and into me.

Xixae Dxao

I have been a medicine man since I was a little boy. Today the work is a habit for me. It comes very naturally. Although I am physically blind, I am happy to see people who come to visit me. All people are our brothers, and I want you to know that it is possible for others to practice our medicine.

Spirit is different from energy. The spirit comes into your stomach and it makes you shake. Then the spirit takes over your whole body. The word *!num* means spirit. It does not mean energy. It is spirit—the spirit of the Big God, which comes to us directly from our ancestors.

The spirit is in the air. When you dance, it comes down to you. When it gets into you, you can see it as a string of light. The light directs you in the dance. It can take you to another person who needs healing or it can carry you to another village or to the sky. This light is !num. It doesn't have a name other than !num.

The healing songs hold !num, and they help bring it into our bodies. Usually when I try to transmit my spirit into someone else, they get scared. I have transmitted my spirit into the woman who lives next to me. Her name is Nxuka. When you transmit the spirit, you hold the other person very tight. It is like electricity, and it goes right into the other person. Then they start to shake. When they enter the dance, the spirit will come to them. They, too, will see the light and be able to do many things.

With the light, I am able to travel to the Big God. He is huge and He will scare you if you are a weak person. He does not belong to any tribe or culture. He can be all things to all people.

Those who have much spirit also have much sexual energy. The spirit makes you have good sex. There is a connection between spirit and sexuality.

My father could change into a lion. He transferred that spirit into me, and I am able to become a lion. There is a special song that brings this transformation. When I hear it, the spirit comes into me and starts changing me into a lion. I don't do this in the dance anymore because it scares me. However, my father comes to me today as a lion, and as a lion, we travel together in the bush.

I will leave you with a prayer to pass on to others: I ask for the good way for all people. I pray that the Big God will tell all people in the world about the Bushman's spiritual power. And I pray that everyone will be awakened to God.

ROPES TO GOD
EXPERIENCING THE BUSHMAN SPIRITUAL UNIVERSE

Introduction to *Ropes to God*
by Bradford Keeney

Over the years, one anthropologist after another has faced the brutal heat and blinding sun of the Kalahari Desert to find their way to one of the oldest living cultures on earth. The Bushmen have been puzzled by these strangers in their land. They have watched cameras take aim and have heard tape recorders catch their sounds. The gifts given to them have been happily received, although they have unwittingly contributed to altering a way of life. Why hunt when an interview will fetch you a shirt or a box of food?

Anthropologists know the significance of the healing dance and have recorded partial descriptions of what happens to the healers during its practice. In addition, various researchers have tried to dance with them. The elder Bushmen teachers I have known throughout the Kalahari—including some interviewed by other anthropologists and psychologists—repeatedly acknowledge that although they have been open to telling others about their spiritual universe, interactions with researchers left both men and women Bushmen doctors doubting whether outsiders understood their dance and healing way.

Raw spiritual experience is most highly valued by the Bushmen. This experience is born from and expressed by the movement of their bodies, not from the ruminations of reflective discourse. From the Bushmen doctors' perspective, none of their sacred knowledge has been lost. It is encoded in the orally preserved songs and muscle memories of kinesthetic movements and postures. Its expression is sparked by a presumed natural/magical power that moves through their bodies into ecstatic choreographies of healing that are inseparable from intimate touch.

I submit this work with an appreciation of the fact that each Bushman doctor has his or her own way of accounting for the spiritual world. Their descriptions and theories change and are often inconsistent. I do find tremendous consistency in my own experience of dancing and talking with the Bushmen from diverse communities and language groups with respect to what takes place within the body. What vary and breed inconsistencies are the Bushmen's metaphors and explanations of their physical experiences. This variation not only occurs among different Bushmen doctors, but within the ongoing accounts of each doctor. Most important to remember is that a consistent and logic-tight articulation and explanation of experiences in language is not accorded a high value in Bushman culture. What is taken more seriously is what is felt—the body dialogue, the interaction of movement that is triggered and orchestrated by what the Bushmen regard as spiritual power.

Perhaps an analogy can make the point clearer: jazz musicians are less interested in talking about how, what, and why they play, but prefer to simply play the music. As Louis Armstrong once replied to an interviewer who asked him to define and explain jazz, "If you have to ask, you'll never know."

My Bushmen teachers and friends are happy that others will hear the inside story of what they experience when they dance themselves into seeing the Big God. In the spirit of the dance, I invite you to open yourself to the knowings and longings of the heart. Step toward imagining an ecstatic impact that dissolves the boundaries that separate us and transforms our understanding of our immediate relations and natural world. The Bushman healing dance, according to the elders who taught me, is the earliest way of praying, the oldest way of communicating with the Big God, the original form of spiritual expression.

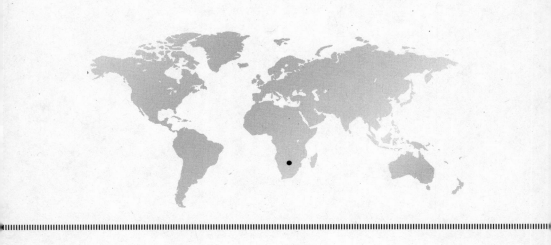

The Bushman Spiritual Universe

as told by Bo, a Bushman doctor

N/om: *The Big Power from the Big God*

Little has changed about our dance and what we know about the Big God. What I know is the same as what my father and grandfather, as well as their ancestors, knew long ago. We sing the same songs, dance the same dance, and see the same God as we did since the beginning of man. This is how it was for the first Bushmen. Since we were the first people, the Big God felt the closest to us. He gave us the gifts we are going to tell you about. It was his way of giving us his love.

In the beginning, people and animals were not separated. All living creatures could communicate with one another. When we think about the first people, we often imagine them as having animal heads or feet on human bodies. This shows that the first people were one with all the animals. When a strong doctor gets the big power, what we call *n/om tcxai* or *djxani tcxai*, he or she can see those ancestors and sometimes feel united with them. The dance, called n/om tcxai, keeps us connected to the beginning of our culture. It keeps us in direct touch with the earliest Bushmen ancestors.

We dance for many reasons. We dance because it is fun. We also dance because it makes us feel better about each other. It fills our hearts with happiness and takes away any bad feelings we might have for another person. Dancing keeps us healthy. In the hands of a Bushman doctor, our sickness may be taken away and our life revitalized. In the dance, special experiences can happen for the doctor. He or she may even see the Big God. This is why the dance is our greatest treasure and mystery.

There is a power that comes from the Big God. It starts with his love for all things. His love is so strong that it can knock you out. This power is in all of life, but it can be concentrated and given to a human being. God can give such concentrated power directly to a human being and make him or her a doctor and, in turn, a strong doctor who has the power can serve as an intermediary and give it to someone else. When a person gets this power directly from the Big God, without the assistance of another human being, it is extremely powerful. These are the most powerful doctors. When you receive it this way, it may throw you to the ground as if you were struck by lightning. In addition, you may see a big light and be shown how you will help others.

In whatever way the Big God touches you, it is assured that you will feel a power or electricity come into your body. It will feel tight and often hot in your belly and cause you to tremble, shake, and jerk. This is the way it is. It has always been this way. The power is so strong that it usually makes you shout or scream a special sound. It can overcome you.

Most Bushmen are scared of the big power that comes from the Big God. When they feel it twitch their body or make them dizzy, they often try to run away from it. That's why you see the young men running all over the place when they get touched by the power in a dance. And some of the women and men run when they think a highly charged medicine man wants to transfer his power. They are scared and somewhat resistant and unwilling to let it overtake them.

It is possible to learn how to be comfortable with this power and allow your body to feel natural with it. This is what characterizes a strong doctor, sometimes called *n/om kxao* ("owner of supernatural power" or "owner of medicine"). After years of dancing and allowing the power to come into the body, such a person becomes more skilled in handling it.

Figure 10.1

Above: this painting shows a doctor lying on top of another person, suggesting the transfer of n/om. Below: the Kalahari Bushmen still follow this practice today.

I received the power directly from the Big God when I was a young man. I felt a heat in my belly and at the bottom of my back that slowly came up my spine and right out of the top of my head. When I looked up, I saw a white light. Inside this light I saw the ancestors and the Big God. They taught me things about healing and the spiritual universe. It took place with no words. It was communicated more by feelings and direct knowing. My body trembled and I was so overcome with emotion that

I wept. Ever since that nightlong experience took place, I always have been able to feel the power inside of me and to use it to touch others.

One of the old men in the Kalahari saw the light of the Big God when he was a child. It happened when his mother was very ill. When he looked into the light, he saw a medicinal plant that he should give to his mother. When he did this, she became well, and he was proclaimed a good healer by the community.

It is rare to be directly touched by the Big God. Usually a strong doctor puts the power into you. They place their hands on your belly and rub the sides of your abdomen as they put power into your insides. This usually happens in the dance, but it can happen at any time. If you become the student of a medicine person (a g!ug_aba), they will touch you, or snap their fingers, or point at you with the purpose of putting the power in you. They may hug and shake you and even lie down on you to pass it into your body. When you first get this power, more often than not, it immediately makes you sick. You feel an extreme tightness in your belly, and you soon feel nauseous and sick. It usually makes you unable to do anything. It makes you wonder if all of your life energy has been removed. Some people think that they are going to die when this happens. It can be a very frightening and traumatic experience.

Years ago, an old strong doctor touched me to pass on his power. After receiving his touch, I laid on the ground all day feeling close to death while the community prepared for an evening dance. As darkness fell and the fire grew strong, the old doctor came over and helped me walk to the dance. When he put his hands on my belly and sides, the pain was taken away. I instantly felt well and exuberant. My body seemed lighter, and without any hesitation I started dancing. The old doctor picked me up and draped me over his back, dancing me around the circle. My arms wrapped around his belly as the dance progressed and he turned toward the fire. When he squatted to place his hands on the women to heal them, my arms and hands were on top of his. I was inseparable from my teacher. Without notice, he slipped out from under me, and I found myself doing the same things that he did—dancing and touching the people. This is one of the ways doctoring is taught.

Nails and Arrows

> *God comes through the animals and plants, and through their songs the arrows are made for us.*
>
> —*Young Bushman from Namibia, January 2001*

I want to explain in more detail what is happening in this experience. What the teacher puts into the student are referred to as nails and arrows, called *!aihn!o·masi* and *tehi*, respectively. These nails and arrows can be of different sizes, and they hold power. One way of thinking about an arrow and a nail is as a condensation of the Big God's power. The power has been squeezed into a narrow object that can be stuck inside another person. The nails come directly from the song of the Big God. This song is called *!Gwa*. The arrows come from the songs of the animals. The arrows and nails go into your belly and abdomen, a place we call *g!u*.

Sometimes my friends say that the arrows are put into the liver. Others say that they also go into the spleen or intestines. When an arrow is inside of you, it will get hot when it is awakened. When it heats up, you feel it as a tightness in your belly. As it gets hotter and hotter, it starts melting and moving up the body. The hotter it gets, the higher it climbs up your body, finally turning into a steam that can leave the top of the head. When that steam comes out, it immediately starts to cool down and fall to the ground. There it becomes an arrow all over again and comes into the bottom of your feet and up again, repeating the process over and over. This is what our doctors do when they dance. They heat up the arrows, bring them up their bodies, turn them into steam, release it from the top of their head, cool it down to become arrows again, and then recycle the whole process from the bottom of their feet to the top of their heads.

Singing and clapping in a dance heats up the nails and arrows. Or when you dance in a certain way, they get heated up. If you think about the times the Big God has touched your life, the arrows get hot. Or if you think of how your special relatives who previously passed on danced and touched you, they heat up. One of the main reasons we dance is to heat the arrows. The things we do to each other in the dance have to do with these arrows.

If your arrows get stolen by evil spirits of the dead, you can get weak and sick. The power or n/om that keeps you alive is in those arrows. On the other hand, if your arrows get dirty, you can get sick. They get dirty either because someone has made them dirty or because they sit still too long in your body. Every Bushman needs to have their arrows heated up and circulated or else they get dirty and make you sick. Heating an arrow cleans it and makes it pure. A new, clean nail looks white whereas a dirty nail is a red or brown color like rust. Medicine people must dance in order to keep their arrows clean. It is very dangerous for a Bushman doctor to stop dancing. A doctor carries a lot of arrows that make him or her vulnerable to sickness if they get dirty. We doctors must dance to keep our arrows clean.

When a person's arrows are dirty, the Bushman doctors can take them out and clean them. Or they can take them out and put new arrows back into you. This is what we mean when we refer to "pulling out the sickness." In our experience, we are actually pulling out the dirty arrows. This is hard work, and it requires the most concentration and effort of any human activity. You can see the intensity of effort on a Bushman doctor's face when he or she is trying to pull out a dirty arrow.

Sometimes a bad medicine person or an evil spirit of the dead shoots a dirty arrow into another person. This, too, can cause sickness and it requires being pulled out. This still happens today, and we have to be on the lookout for this kind of attack from evil-minded practitioners.

The doctor not only helps the sick by pulling out dirty arrows, he helps other people become stronger by giving them new nails and arrows. This is the main way that we teach others to be healers. We simply place the arrows into a person. As opposed to taking out dirty arrows, which is so intense that it is often painful, it feels good to put an arrow into someone. This happens effortlessly and naturally and is mediated by the good feeling you have for the other person. In summary, our doctors take out nails and arrows as well as put them in. The doctor, however, must be in a very special state of being when this is done.

The doctor's own arrows must be heated and risen so that the doctor is transformed and endowed with special sensitivities. As the hot arrows boil and turn to steam, the doctor's eyes feel like they are changed into "new eyes." This enables us to see the world differently. We see light and are able to perceive the spiritual world. Our hearing, touch, and smell are also transformed in this process. We are able to smell sickness and to sniff a person's body in order to diagnose their condition. In a way, all Bushmen are equal when their nails are cool. But when a particular Bushman's arrows heat up, he or she becomes a special person, the most important person in the community. That's when we are truly a Bushman doctor.

A Bushman doctor must learn to heat the arrows and circulate them in and out of the body. A discipline must be acquired in handling these arrows and nails, otherwise the experience of this inner power would be overwhelming, resulting in chaotic behavior as well as an oversensitive vulnerability to passing out when things get really hot. The dances we show anthropologists and visitors who travel to our communities are almost entirely for show. When the dance looks smooth and entertaining, it is usually not the dance of a doctor. The doctor's dance movements are solely for heating the arrows and moving them up his or her body.

As a doctor, my dance begins when my steps slow down and become more purposeful. When this happens to me, I feel like I am creating a more serious manner of stomping. I bend over because of an intensifying tightness that is centered in my gut and chest. This is how the healing dance starts for doctors. Until this happens, he or she is just dancing for fun. The next and most important part of the dance is when I feel a pumping-like motion in my gut that starts pulling the arrows up to my chest, throat, and head. This is when the power really gets strong. The pumping often feels like a drum inside the body that encourages me to make percussion-like sounds that may be heard only by those who are close to me. My arms automatically extend behind my back—a posture that happens spontaneously, without my making a decision or any effort to be in that position. I bend over and stretch my arms from behind when I feel the pump-like movement pulling my insides.

As the pumping continues, my body bends over even more as the stomach contractions get tighter. Now the arrows start boiling and turning to steam. As the steam is pumped into the head, my eyes start changing. One way to describe this is to say that the front of my eyes drop away and a second set of eyes behind them become opened. These second eyes are like seeing from the back of my eyeballs. With this second sight, I still see even when I close my eyes. This new sight differs from everyday vision. The seeing is so strong that it makes me smell or feel in a heightened way. Or it may be said in the opposite way: I may feel or smell something so strongly that it actually makes me also see it. This is why I can say that I see even when my eyes are closed. This is the doctor's way of seeing.

Lines, Threads, Strings, Chains, and Ropes of Light

If the power inside me is strong enough, I will see a special light. Bushmen doctors see different kinds of light. It may be a cloud of light in front of them or a light hovering over the entire community of dancers. When you're very strong you will see lines or strings of light that go up to the sky. These lines may be the thickness of a blade of grass or as big as a rope (*tau*) or chain (*ketanga*). We refer to them as lines, threads, strings, chains, cords, and ropes. When they go up to the sky, they are white in color or shiny like silver metal. It takes big power to see the lines that go up and down.

There are other lines that we see. Some of these are located horizontal to the earth at about knee height. They may be colored green or red. These lines are used for traveling to other places in the physical world. For example, I can send my second eyes and ears to travel along one of these lines and go watch a dance at another village. Every place on earth is connected to every other place by these horizontal lines. Furthermore, every person and every living creature has a line coming out of their belly buttons that is connected to the bellies of other people. These are the lines that we send messages on. We can talk to another person over these lines by sending our thoughts into them. It is similar to what you people call a telephone. This, in our spiritual universe, is a very natural thing to accomplish.

Of all the strings of light, the most important ones go to the sky. They usually look like ropes to me. When I see a rope of light, I walk toward it. As soon as I get to it or near it, I start floating up to the sky. Some doctors feel like they are walking up steps to the sky, while many of us just feel like we float up. If you are really strong, you can see the rope as the connected beads of an ostrich shell. This is one of the strongest ways of seeing it. Seen this way, each bead is like a separate step for walking up to the sky. When we go up, there is a place in the sky where the ancestors live. There I see all of my family members who have passed on from this life. They live there with all the Bushmen who have ever lived before. Most important, they live with the Big God and with the family of the Big God. It is a very special village in the sky where they sing and dance. We each see it in different ways, but I see it with many fruit trees and green plants. It is very beautiful, the most beautiful place I have ever seen.

If you are a big doctor, you may go up the rope of light and be taken to the Big God or the wife or son of the Big God. He usually looks at you and then sends you back. Sometimes he may tell you something, or if you are very lucky, he will touch you. Once after a very strong dance, I went up the rope and met my grandfather. He took me to the house where the son of the Big God resides. To my surprise, when I looked closely at him, he was made of light and had many arms and hands. I walked near him and he touched me with every one of those hands. It was more powerful than anything you could imagine. Then my grandfather led me away and said, "Go back, you have your work set before you." My grandfather walked back with me along a path until we came to the rope of light. I approached it and floated back down. This is how it can work.

Only the strongest doctors go up the rope and learn from their ancestors and the Big God. That's one of the ways we learn new songs, dances, and more knowledge about how to heal others. They show us what plants to use for a certain sickness or how to treat a specific person. Both men and women doctors can go up this rope if they are strong enough.

The rope also goes underground. We are able to go underneath the ground and do things down there (khaba: climb down). When we go under the ground, we are usually accompanied by the ancestors from our past. As I mentioned, the oldest Bushman ancestors often have animal heads or hooves for feet. They come from the beginning when there were no real differences between how people and animals experienced the world. When they accompany us in a dance, they help us do healing work on the people who are sick in the community.

We believe that the red and green horizontal lines that are above the ground are associated with what you call good and evil. The green lines, related to the life of the green plants that help us sustain life, are good. They will take you along the good path. The red lines, associated with the ability of the fire to burn you, are related to evil. It will take you along a bad path.

The Bushman Doctor's Journey

When a doctor heats up his nails and arrows and starts to travel along the lines, the other doctors make sure that he or she is traveling along a good line. We help each other in this way, protecting ourselves from harm and danger.

The women have their own dance for healing, but this drawing in the sand shows how it works for the men. The big circle represents the fire that the women sit around. Around it is the furrow caused by the men's dancing. When we dance around the women and start to feel the power get into us, it usually begins with a tingly feeling in the legs. The legs start to twitch and feel jumpy, which starts you dancing. Soon your thigh muscles start to tremble, and the dance really gets inside your body. The power may also get into your buttocks and cause them to lift your legs in an automatic way. This happens to most of the men dancers. But for the doctors, the power of the dance continues to influence us by triggering an intense tightness of the belly muscles that bends us over. Then the pumping starts, causing the arrows to get hot, as I previously described. Our arms move forward and backward in sync with the pulling rhythm, and eventually our arms are tightly pulled behind us with outstretched fingers. When the pumping causes the arrows to go up the body, we feel the fire pulling us toward it. That's when we go inside the circle of women and get near the fire. The fire actually pulls us toward it, sometimes prompting us to place our hands in it, or our

Figure 10.2

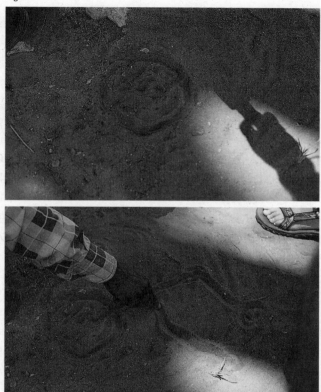

Figure 10.3

Drawings of how the spiritual universe looks to a male doctor who is in the men's healing dance.

bare feet, or our face. Some of the old powerful doctors can stand on their heads in the fire. That's how powerful they are.

When you go toward the fire, the other doctors help you, watching that you don't get burned. This initiates the most intense phase of the dance for a doctor. The fire heats up my insides, helping turn the arrows into boiling steam and opening my second eyes. Here I find myself facing a fire that is associated with evil. Here the bad spirits of the dead want to trick me and bring me in and burn me. That's when I must look away from them and look to another direction. Sometimes I shout at them. They are short with big heads and wear leaves over their bodies. Young, inexperienced doctors spend more time fighting these bad spirits than stronger doctors. Some doctors may never get past this station, doing nothing more than fighting the malevolent ones.

The stronger doctor, however, moves on to see the rope of light going straight up to the sky. The rope goes through the top of my head. It is responsible for pulling my belly up and down, causing the pumping action that pulls up the arrows. When the arrows turn to steam, and the steam is ready to come out of my head, the top of my head starts feeling very tingly. It usually makes me scratch my head or pat it with my hands. My head also feels like it is expanding, and it seems like a hole is opening at the top of my head. In addition, my body may feel like it is being stretched up like a thin line. When we dance the giraffe dance, I feel my neck getting long like that of the giraffe. All of these experiences help me go up the thread of light. All I have to do is move toward the line or just think of moving toward it, and I am carried up to the place of the ancestors.

The oldest Bushmen ancestors have heads of animals, usually that of the eland. While I'm up in the sky village, I may learn from the old ones or from the Big God. When it's time to come down the rope of light, it means that the people are waiting for me to help them. I come down, but I don't come down alone. I bring the entire village in the sky down with me. This village, which holds all the people who have ever lived before us, is brought down and superimposed over the ground where the dance is being held. This is a very special moment. When this takes place, the whole community enters into a spiritual time and space where the past and present are brought together as a singular moment. It is a timeless place of eternity.

My trip down the rope of light doesn't have to stop at this point. The ancestors I bring down can continue taking me down the rope, going underneath the earth. At this time, I must sincerely ask for the help of those ancestors I was closest to when they were alive. For me, it was my grandfather and brother. I don't argue with them or plead endlessly, but simply show them that I am serious and sincere. They must see a serious look in my eyes and hear a strong voice when I sing to them. They also want to see me dancing in the doctor's way. If a doctor is sincere enough, they will always help. Again, you don't argue with them. You show them your sincerity and ask for their help. That is all there is to it. When their help is engaged, they travel with you back to the fire where evil resides. There you must get back any arrows that were stolen from the people by the evil spirits. You usually go into the evil place disguised as the wind or as another animal, such as a lion or a bat. The familial ancestors help you make this transition. In this disguise, you sweep into the evil camp and grab the arrows from the enemy spirits of the dead and return them to the person whose sickness has been caused by their loss.

The sketch both marks different spiritual locations that the doctor visits and points to something else. Each place, called a station and indicated by a circle, is also a moment when your belly tightens with greater strength and causes the nails and arrows to move up. At the first station, you feel the tightness at a time when you must resist the temptation to get burned by the fire and resist getting angry and fighting your enemies, both from the past and present. The malevolent spirits reside at the first station. After that episode, you tighten even more and get more power, enabling you to see the thread of light. This happens as your second eyes open and carry you to the place in the sky. This is where the benevolent ancestors live. They only want to help us. The subsequent station requires another tightening and a consequent surge of power that carries you back to earth and sometimes underground where, with the help of the ancestors, you are able to pull out dirty arrows and rescue stolen ones. The map has nothing to do with showing where your feet walk during the dance. It indicates the different stages of transformation of the doctor and the experiences associated with each stage. It is a way of showing how the escalating process of pumping the hot vaporous arrows up the body is associated with a choreography of healing.

When a doctor brings down all the ancestors, the people know it. They can see the change in the doctor and feel the presence of the original ones. The women's singing becomes the strongest during this time. Everyone knows that the moment is sacred, linking them to their entire past. For that moment, the dance is eternal. The ancestors of the past are dancing with them, and any Bushman dance ceremonies from the future presumably are also present. In this eternal space of healing, the doctor can feel everything at once. What he sees is happening very quickly, sometimes so fast that things look like a whirling blur. He doesn't necessarily go through different stages of experience, for it is possible to go to the sky, bring it down, and heal the people all at once. Here time does not chop up the difference between now and then. Everything feels like it is happening at the same time.

A doctor doing this kind of intense work almost always gets filled with so much power that he or she can't walk straight or carry on a conversation. When this happens to me, I can't utter a single word or sentence no matter how much I may want to do so. When I open my mouth to speak, wild noises come out.

During this time of heightened arousal and power, I feel dizzy and out of control, teetering in my forward motion and ready to fall over at any moment. This is when the other doctors come help me. They allow me to fall safely and then cool me down by rubbing my sides. Some of the women may come with their tortoise shell that holds the medicine powder that helps with cooling. If the arrows aren't cooled down, my body feels like it will completely disappear. In the most powerful moments, I feel like a cloud of energy. When this takes place, there is no body that I can feel. I am simply a cloud or a wind. That's when I can really see things and travel with the greatest of ease!

Where the Spiritual Nails and Arrows Come From

I want to tell you where the arrows and nails come from and what they truly are. It all starts with the understanding that the Big God loves us very much. He sends his love to us in a variety of ways. The major way is for him to first deliver his caring love to the animals, which long ago were inseparable from us. He gives them his love in the form of a special song (*texaitzi*). That is why we have a giraffe song, eland song, elephant song, gemsbok song, and so forth. These are the gifts God gave to the animals. The animals, in turn, give these songs to our doctors when they are in a special state with second eyes and ears. The doctors may receive them in a dream or during a dance. When a doctor gets a song, he or she starts singing it. If this happens during the evening, the people wake up from their sleep, one by one, and go to the doctor's hut. There they listen and learn the song. Everyone then starts dancing with great happiness and gratitude.

These songs, the Big God's way of containing and sending his love, can be literally compacted or squeezed by a medicine person by the way his or her body tightens it. As the body tightens the song, the song becomes more concentrated and dense. With great effort, it becomes a hard nail or arrow. Understood this way, an arrow is basically a condensed song that carries the Big God's love. When placed inside the body of another person, it lies waiting to be heated. When fully heated and boiled, it enables the doctor to return to the time and place where humans and animals belonged together. The arrow takes us back to God. The strongest experience in the dance takes place when you turn into one of these animals or ancestors. It is even possible to feel like you have dissolved into the Big God. This is one of our greatest secrets.

Transformations of the Bushman Doctor

Let me tell you how I became a lion. It was a good dance several years ago and I was feeling the arrows get very hot. When my arrows started to move up my body, I felt the pull of the fire. I went toward it and danced while staring at it. When my second eyes came out, I saw the fire become very large. The whole gathering looked like they were sitting in the fire. The fire then went back to its normal size, but as I continued staring at it, I saw a lion (*n!hai*) in it. I trembled when I looked at it. Then the lion opened its mouth and swallowed me. The next thing I remember seeing was the lion spitting out another lion. That other lion was me. I felt the energy of the lion and roared with great authority. The power scared the people. They knew what had happened. They could see that I had turned into a lion.

Once you turn into a lion, you always have the lion inside of you. Just thinking about the time that you turned into a lion brings back its power. You do not have to see the lion in the fire again. It does not have to swallow you again and remake you into a lion. The transformation has to take place only once and then you have that power for life. You may also see and become other animals. We doctors can become many animals—eland, kudu, gemsbok, giraffe, birds, and many other creatures. These transformations bring us a special power.

We may also see our ancestors from the past. Some doctors are very special. They can see their grandfather in the fire, merge with him, and take on his power. In a way, they become their ancestor. One of the most special things that can happen to you is when the Big God or his family faces you in the fire and you step into him, taking on his presence. This is very rare and powerful. I know several doctors who have experienced this.

When we get the big power, it often makes us feel like crying. Our hearts overflow with love and caring for one another. This is a time when no one can have a bad feeling for anyone else. It is one of the ways the dance heals our community. If, during the course of everyday life, people start feeling irritable with each other, they can call a dance to make everything better. The good feelings from the dance take away all the irritations and disagreements that come into daily life. In this way, the dance renews our relationships and caring for one another.

Doctors like to get together and talk about these things. We talk mostly about the ropes and chains of light. These phenomena are what interest us most. We believe that an ancestor constitutes each step of that line, thread, string, rope, or chain. When we go up to the village in the sky, we are walking on the backs of all the ancestors who have lived before us. Seen in this way, the chain links all Bushmen from the past and takes us to the beginning where the Big God resides. During everyday life, this chain is collapsed into a single point that rests inside our hearts. When we dance and heat up our arrows and nails, our hearts get very hot and burst forth a great love. This, in turn, awakens the chain to unravel and shoot itself straight to the sky. All Bushmen doctors hold this link to the Big God in their hearts, ready to be sent to the sky where our ancestors wait to dance with us.

We believe the line comes from our heart and out of our mouths. It carries the sounds stirred by the heated arrows. The line also goes out of the top of our heads. When we get heated up, that line pulls our tightened bodies up and down. This tightening causes what you see when a doctor dances. A line, which is silver, also goes out of our bellies and connects us to others. We use this line to send a message to someone else. When I dance and want to communicate with someone, I send that thought out of my belly along a line that carries it to the other person. When my nails get hot, for example, I may want to dance with a particular woman. I send her the message and she immediately comes toward me and dances.

The lines also connect us to the animals. We can find an animal through these lines of connection and learn where it is located. This helps us when we want to hunt for meat.

The very old ancestors, the ones who were alive in the beginning of time, have faces and feet that look like that of the animals. The Big God made those people. In the beginning, God made people with animal heads. Animals and men were the same. They didn't need to hunt because their power was so strong that it kept their bellies full. The threads and chains of light gave them all that they needed to be alive.

Then there was an argument between God and Evil. That's when the animals and the people became separate. This started because some people had giraffe heads and others had eland heads and feet. They became jealous over one woman. This started the first argument and that's when evil came in. God stopped the argument by separating the animals from people.

Communication along these lines works in a simple but very powerful way. You cannot send a thought to another person without first being filled with heightened emotion. In other words, your nails must be boiling and your heart fully awakened. In this state you mix your thought, message, or directive with your intensified feeling and make the thought a pure feeling. It is concentrated in your belly, where the intensity of your feeling escalates to a point where it can no longer be held. Then it is released along the line coming out of your belly and directed to another person's belly. They immediately respond when you communicate in this way. It may seem like we send our thoughts, but we are actually sending our feelings. Not weak, arbitrary feelings, but intense, almost overwhelming feelings. More accurately, we take a thought, message, or request and throw it into a feeling, attach it to a feeling, mix it with a feeling, or change it into a feeling. Then we send the feeling. The feeling is the carrier. The thought is the message.

Another secret we Bushman doctors have concerns the power that takes place when men and women dance together. Two of the most powerful things that can happen to us in a dance are to be pulled toward the fire and to dance with a person of the opposite sex. A woman doctor has a way of dancing with you that makes your body get tighter and stronger. This tightening can overcome you quite easily. You must concentrate to keep from falling down when you dance with such a woman.

When a man and a woman doctor dance while holding each other's hands, they can exchange their nails and arrows. This exchange is exhilarating and often makes the male doctor fall to the ground. The women doctors have a lot of power. Although they sometimes tell anthropologists that they are not doctors and pretend to let the men believe they are weaker, I know that some of our women have very strong power. They are the ones who want to dance all night and every night. The men complain, saying, "We're too tired to dance all night." But the women doctors always want to go on. They love the dance and are always eager to call forth its healing power.

When we have a strong dance, the doctors often fall to the ground and require the help of the others to revive them. This goes on throughout the night. The strongest doctors are our teachers. When I was learning, the old doctors would have me fall over their backs while they danced me around the fire. I could feel the rhythms of their steps and the tightness of their bodies. More important, I could feel their bellies and chests pumping the nails up their bodies. This helped me start the pumping motion in my own body. With their hands, the teachers put nails into my sides and belly. This made me feel tight and hot.

Now, I am a teacher. I carry (*llae*) the others on my back and place my hands on their bellies. I give the arrows and nails to others. This process makes me feel very happy. It is the best feeling you can have.

It is possible to heat your arrows without a dance. The strong doctors can treat someone without a dance. They usually sing a song and heat their arrows up until they are ready to help someone. But dancing is better. Then it is the strongest because we can more easily help each other.

After a good dance, I go to my home and fall asleep. The power is so strong in me that I may travel during my dreams. That may be the time when I see the ropes of light and go up to the sky. Dreams (*cunkuri*) that take place after a strong dance often bring good teaching. We doctors look forward to the dreams that come after a dance. The dance makes you ready to have big dreams of the ancestors and the Big God.

We believe that the dance is for everyone. We are not the only ones who can dance and see the ropes to the Big God. We do not understand why the people who come to study us do not have these experiences. We want them to know God. They cannot understand us unless they know how we experience the Big God. It is the most important part of our lives. The ropes and chains to the Big God make our lives worth living. We live to dance. It is our prayer and our tracks to the longed-for relatives who have gone on.

BLESSINGS FROM THE HEALERS

There is a prophecy in most of the world's traditional cultures that tells of a time when the healers were to start sharing their secret knowledge with the world in order to heal it. Each of the healers who shared their culture and stories with Ringing Rocks Foundation was pleased to have the opportunity to be a part of fulfilling this prophecy. They each expressed a large measure of gratitude for the chance to help avert the disaster that they see coming. That you are reading this work says that you are part of the solution as well. For your part in being the change, please accept these blessings from the healers.

From Walking Thunder:

In Beauty before me I walk,
In Beauty behind me I walk,
In Beauty below me I walk,
In Beauty above me I walk,
In Beauty all around me I walk,
It is finished in beauty,
It is finished in beauty,
It is finished in beauty,
It is finished in beauty.
The mountains, I become part of it.
The herbs, the evergreen,
I become part of it.
The morning mists, the clouds,
The gathering waters,
I become part of it.
The dew drops, the pollen,
I become part of it.

From Otavia Alves Pimentel Barbosa:

With the help of the spirit priest, my brother, and all the other spirit guides, I ask that your life be blessed. Through the forgiveness and love of Jesus I pray that you find happiness and light. I want you to know the joy and love that I have held in my hands and in my heart. God bless you.

From João Fernandes de Carvalho:

Jesus, here I express my gratitude
            for everything that was given to me and my family,
and for the mercy that I could divide it with many needy people.
            When I was young, I always wondered
whether God would find me worthy of a happy future.
            Then the time passed all too quickly
                and without financial resources.
            But with divine help
                and the assistance of my friends,
        my life was able to take place. Today I can see
            all the fruits of a healthy spiritual plantation
            and these give us life and happiness.
Good-bye, good-bye, my friends. Jesus, bless all of you.

From Gary Holy Bull:

I have lived a turbulent life and have made many mistakes. But I never forget that the wind of change waits to move each of us toward walking the sacred path. On this path, each day begins with a sunrise that brings us all together under the same light of the Creator. I pray that you will live in good relationship with all of God's Creation.

Get ready, they're coming.
Get ready, they are here.

Mitak'oyas'in (All my relations)

From the Guarani:

Every day I have to grab my rattle and pray, "Great God, you must protect me. My true father and true mother, please help me." You, too, must pray for help. Spiritual gifts always come with an evil that challenges you. Always ask the gods for help.

From Vusamazulu Credo Mutwa:

In the name of the light, in the name of the dweller of the doorway, in the name of the commander of the seas and the skies, in the name of the empress of the stars, in the name of the one mother, let me give my blessings to all of you. May the light accompany you as you walk across the plains of this world. May the truth be the star that shines not only above but deep within the kernels of your souls. May peace, the most fragrant of flowers, attend you no matter where you go. May food never be lacking in your village. May water never be lacking in your streams and rivers. May love never be lacking in your hearts and in the hearts of your children. May your beds always be fruitful and friendly. May love always be with you to the end of your days. May war be away from the borders of your countries. May anger be away from the mountains of your lives. May you be protected, shielded, cherished until you see the beginning of the new.

From the Balians:

Om, Swastiastu.
Based on religious teaching, as light in the darkness
Give priority to good deeds, it being the smooth way.
Knowledge as a means of learning difficult teaching
Surely it will be attainable, that holy light within oneself.
What is actually called light, constantly without bound in the heart?
The six enemies will not tempt us due to our calm heart
Because our goal is quite certain: to come to the supreme truth.
Is there any clear picture about the meaning of light in the heart?
At last, the wish is that you gain happiness.
Om, Shanti, Shanti, Shanti, Om.

From Ikuko Osumi, Sensei

I have given you a glimpse of seiki, the vital life force. You should not live without it. It brings true fulfillment to your life. It is like the tide of the sea that approaches to satisfy and quench the thirst of seashore sand.

Thanks to seiki we can maintain our health and embrace each other peacefully, respectfully, and forgivingly. It brings about a generous frame of mind.

This generous mind asks that we nurture and prosper with seiki, benefiting ourselves and the universe at the same time. The door to seiki is open to everyone who wishes to enter.

From Cgunta !elae, an elder Bushman healer of the Kalahari:

When I get close to the Big God, I feel his heart. It makes me want to be good to all people. When I am touching someone with power, I feel my heart touching my father, my grandfather, and all of their ancestors, all the way to God. In that moment, I am able to see and feel everyone who has ever lived. That's when I feel every person's heart. Every Bushman who has ever lived is one step or link that makes up the chain that goes all the way to the Big God. God is on top of this chain. All of God's family and every person who ever lived are the points of this chain. When I'm not dancing, the whole chain collapses to a small point and sleeps in my heart. When we dance, the ancestors wake up and the chain shoots up toward the sky. In this way, God and the ancestors live in my heart. When they awaken, they form the chain that reaches to the sky.

God sleeps in our hearts when we are not dancing. When we dance, he wakes up. When we get angry, or jealous, or irritated with someone, all we can do is wake up God. God then chases the trouble away. To wake him up, we must dance. Whenever I feel bad or have bad feelings, I must dance to wake up God. If we never prayed, sang, or danced, we'd be in trouble. Evil would take over. In addition to the Big God, there is a smaller god who plays tricks with people. The small god is called a jackal. He kills people and also steals arrows from them. He can be evil. The bad spirits of the dead are part of the small god. That's why they can change color at any time. What you call Satan is also similar to the small god that acts like a jackal.

You must learn to wake up God. This is the most important thing we have to teach. We believe that many people have forgotten this truth. We want to remind them to wake up God. We hold the truth of God while the rest of the world is in trouble. We wish that everyone would start dancing and wake up God. We pray for the other people of the world. We hope that they start dancing with us.

From Nancy Connor:

Being raised Roman Catholic, I recited the Lord's Prayer in church along with everyone else, but it really didn't hold much meaning for me. When I was much older, I learned about the Gnostic roots of Christianity and discovered for myself the lost scrolls of the Nag Hamadi and other ancient libraries. I stumbled across the truth that there were many variations of the early gospels and prayers. I discovered that due to codification of the gospels and prayers by ecumenical councils, much of the ancient wisdom of Christianity had been lost or suppressed. Added to that, the monks and priests who translated the documents from the original Aramaic to Greek, then to Latin, and later through several forms of English, each put their own bias into the translations. Since Aramaic words, like English words, can have several meanings, anyone who translates a phrase can select the meaning that they feel is most appropriate.

In Christ's time, most followers of Judaism used a form of morning "body prayer"—walking while chanting a prayer and meditating on its meaning for the coming day. During the meditation, each word in the prayer would be carefully considered in order to determine the correct meaning that would be useful for them to keep in mind. In our time, we have lost this practice, which seems a shame, since it gives so much life to prayer instead of it being a rote recitation.

Among the Nag Hamadi scrolls, a copy of the Lord's Prayer was found. New translations—made directly from the Aramaic to modern English without all of the intervening languages—have yielded surprisingly different interpretations of the Lord's Prayer from the one I learned in my youth. One of these translations has deeply touched my heart; and despite the fact that I am no longer a practicing Catholic, I still use this version of the Lord's Prayer often. I pass it along to you as my blessing.

O cosmic birther of all radiance and vibration!
Soften the ground of our being and create a space within us
where your Presence can abide.
Fill us with your creativity so that we may be empowered
to bear the fruit of your mission.
Let each of our actions bear fruit in accordance with
our desire.
Endow us with the wisdom to produce and share what
each being needs to grow and flourish.
Untie the tangled threads of destiny that bind us, as we
release others from the entanglement of past mistakes.
Do not let us be seduced by that which would divert us
from our true purpose, but illuminate the opportunities of
the present moment.
For you are the ground and the fruitful vision, the birth-
power and fulfillment, as all is gathered and made whole
once again.

REFERENCES

Douglas-Klotz, Neil. *Original Prayer: Teachings and Meditations on the Aramaic Words of Jesus*. Boulder: Sounds True, 2000.

Keeney, Bradford. *Balians: Traditional Healers of Bali*. Philadelphia: Ringing Rocks Press, 2004.

———. *Gary Holy Bull: Lakota Yuwipi Man*. Philadelphia, Ringing Rocks Press, 1999.

———. *Guarani Shamans of the Forest*. Philadelphia: Ringing Rocks Press, 2000.

———. *Hands of Faith: Healers of Brazil*. Philadelphia: Ringing Rocks Press, 2003.

———. *Ikuko Osumi, Sensei; Japanese Master of Seiki Jutsu*. Philadelphia: Ringing Rocks Press, 1999.

———. *Kalahari Bushman Healers*. Philadelphia: Ringing Rocks Press, 1999.

———. *Ropes to God: Experiencing the Bushman Spiritual Universe*. Philadelphia: Ringing Rocks Press, 2003.

———. *Shakers of St. Vincent*. Philadelphia: Ringing Rocks Press, 2002.

———. *Vusamazulu Credo Mutwa: Zulu High Sanusi*. Philadelphia: Ringing Rocks Press, 2001.

———. *Walking Thunder: Diné Medicine Woman*. Philadelphia: Ringing Rocks Press, 2001.

Ropes to God

Bleek, Dorothea F. *More Rock Paintings in South Africa*. London: Methuen & Co., 1940

Pager, Harald. *Stone Age Myth and Magic*. Graz, Austria: Akademische Druck-u. Verlangsanstalt, 1975.

Gary Holy Bull

Densmore, Frances. "Teton Sioux Music." Washington, D.C.: *Smithsonian Institution, Bureau of American Ethnology Bulletin 61*, 1918.

Keeney, Bradford. *Shaking Out the Spirits*. New York: Station Hill Press, 1994.

Mails, Thomas E. *Fools Crow*. New York: Avon Books, 1979.

———. *Fools Crow: Wisdom and Power*. Tulsa: Council Oak, 1991.

ART CREDITS

INDEX

Note: Locators in boldface type indicate figures.

ABOUT THE EDITOR

Nancy Connor holds a Bachelor of Science degree in Mathematics and Computer Science and worked in the computer field for eleven years. During this time she founded, and later ran, a successful software company in Massachusetts. She left the company just prior to its public offering in November 1993.

In December 1995, she established Ringing Rocks Foundation, whose mission is to explore, document, and preserve alternative cultures and healing practices. It has co-sponsored programs with universities and museums around the world to preserve indigenous cultural artifacts. Ms. Connor is a certified Reiki practitioner (I and II) and has participated in ceremonies with healers from Japan, New Mexico, Bali, St. Vincent, Botswana, Namibia, and South Africa. For more information on Ringing Rocks Foundation, visit www.ringingrocks.org.

In December of 2004, Ms. Connor opened a retail business, S.A.G.E. Crafts, which sells arts and crafts supplies to artists in Sedona, and offers arts and crafts classes to beginning and experienced creative spirits. She believes that expressing oneself through art or craft can be healing. She enjoys teaching classes at SAGE (Shaman Angel Goddess Enterprises) to those who are interested in expanding their creative abilities because she feels that opening up a new door to creativity is healing for both the teacher and student. Ms. Connor's goal at the store is to provide those who walk through the door with inspiration so that anyone can learn to express themselves, whether they are a potential or experienced artist.

She teaches classes in many different types of art and craft mediums so that anyone can find the medium that will allow them a way express their feelings and creativity. For more information on S.A.G.E. Crafts, visit www.sage-crafts.com.

ABOUT THE ETHNOGRAPHER

Bradford Keeney, Ph. D., has been called "an all-American shaman, the Marco Polo of psychology, and an anthropologist of the spirit" by the editors of *Utne Reader*. Elders of indigenous traditions throughout the world have embraced Keeney as an elder and spokesperson for their ways of ecstatic shamanism. Following an academic career as a systems theorist and psychotherapist, he spent over a decade traveling the globe; living with spiritual teachers, shamans, healers, and medicine people who trusted him to share their words with others — modern cultures in need of Elder wisdom.

The result of Keeney's work is one of the broadest and most intense field studies of healing and shamanism practices. His autobiography, *Bushman Shaman*, tells how he became a n/om-kxao (shaman) with the Kalahari Bushmen. Keeney presently conducts his clinical work at the Center for Children and Families, Monroe, Louisiana. He also serves as Professor of Transformative Studies, California Institute of Integral Studies, San Francisco; Honorary Senior Research Fellow, Rock Art Research Institute, University of Witwatersrand, Johannesburg, South Africa, and founding director of the Bushman (San) N/om-Kxaosi Ethnographic Project, Institute for Religion and Health, Texas Medical Center, Houston.